RUSSIA

MUSCOVITE ARCHITECTURE.

"Tent" style. Church at Ostrovo, near Moscow. Mid 16th century.

RUSSIA
A SOCIAL HISTORY
By D. S. MIRSKY

EDITED BY
PROFESSOR C. G. SELIGMAN, F.R.S.

LONDON
THE CRESSET PRESS
11 FITZROY SQ. W.1
1931

Printed in Great Britain by
THE SHENVAL PRESS

FOREWORD

THE volumes of the Cresset Historical Series necessarily present considerable variety in outlook and content. Russian history begins in the ninth century A.D., and pre-history and archæology, except in a few limited areas, are vague and speculative. In Japan authentic history begins early in our era and we know something of what lies behind the legendary history, which dates conventionally to 660 B.C. In China the incised bones of the Shang-Yin dynasty bear witness to a ritually advanced civilisation towards the middle of the second millennium B.C., and, though it may be true that we have no bronzes certainly antedating the beginning of the first millennium, it is certain that our earliest specimens are very far from the beginning of the art and that we cannot even surmise the appearance of a primitive Chinese bronze. Centuries earlier there are the "painted-pot" burials of Kansu and Honan, the burials of a people whose remains scarcely differentiate them from the Chinese of the present day but of a culture that with the exception of one or two points of contact was totally different from anything we call Chinese. Again, in the Levant, history extends over a long period, lengthened by an archæology continually becoming better known and integrated with surrounding areas. The Siberian volume on the other hand will deal for the most part with peoples of the Tundra and Steppe, rude and barbaric hunters and fishers, whose wealth consists of herds of half-wild reindeer.

Thus while some of the series will contain much that is strictly of anthropological and archæological interest, *Russia*, the first volume to come from the press, is mainly historical in the ordinary but best sense of the word. *Russia* is indeed likely to be of special value at the present time; it should serve to remove many commonly held but mistaken beliefs about the greatest of the Slav nations, while Appendix II presents a mass of ethnic, linguistic, and cultural information hitherto inaccessible to English-speaking readers.   C. G. SELIGMAN.

PREFACE

THE present book—as the present series in general—is not intended as a substitute for the usual type of historical manuals. It is not a chronicle of events, but an attempt to represent in its broadest outlines, the changes undergone by a society as a whole. The book was completed more than a year ago, in the spring of 1929, and this gives me to-day the possibility of seeing it with a certain amount of detachment. I am fully conscious of grave defects in it, the most serious of which is the absence of a single point of view. This serious shortcoming is due to the fact that in the course, and under the direct action, of my work, my own historical conception underwent an adjustment, which, at first imperceptible to myself, only crystallized after it was completed. If I were now to rewrite it, it would be more strictly consonant with the conception of historical materialism, and economic facts would have been more consistently emphasized as the one and only protophenomenon of all historical reality. But this would have necessitated a complete recasting of the mould and, possibly, in such a way as would have made it no longer suitable for the series of which it is to form a part. So I have to leave the book as I originally wrote it, and console myself by the thought that however unsatisfactory, it may at least be of use as offering on many aspects of Russian history points of view that will be new to the English reader.

The book ends with the fall of the Monarchy. The transformation of Tsarist Russia into a Union of Soviet Republics is a revolution of so enormous importance that of all landmarks in the history of mankind it may most safely be taken as a real turning point. To treat the twelve years that have since elapsed on a scale with the earlier period, would have meant either adding perhaps as many pages as have been devoted to the same number of preceding centuries, or limiting myself to a few superficial generalizations.

An explanation is also due on the limits of the subject in—geographical and ethnical—space as well as in time. As the geographical aspect of Russian history has been particularly emphasized, all peoples and countries absorbed by the Russian Empire have been drawn into the scope of the book. But I must make it clearly understood that it is primarily the history only of the Russian, that is to say Great Russian or Muscovite people, and other peoples have been dealt with only in so far as they belong to the historical milieu in which the Russian people moved. This refers also to its two nearest relatives, the Ukrainian and White Russian peoples, the treatment of whose history is emphatically not on the same scale as that of the Russians. To write a general history of the nations of Northern Eurasia—or Eastern Europe and Northern Asia—not from the point of view of one of them, but as a section of the history of mankind, is a task that is overdue and ought to tempt the historian, but it has not been attempted by the present writer.

The bibliographical footnotes in the text are by no means exhaustive and even far from systematic. They were merely intended to give authority for controversial statements, or to indicate works of ampler introduction. As for general works on Russian history, every student must read the *Lectures on Russian History* of V. O. Klyuchevsky (English translation in four volumes), which though conspicuously lacking in a constructive point of view are unsurpassed for wealth of concrete matter, especially in the late Medieval and Muscovite periods; and the works of the patriarch of Marxist historiography, Professor M. N. Pokrovsky, whose general scheme of Russian history is the most adequate hitherto proposed and has rendered obsolete all others. The only one of his books available in English is his four-volume *Russian History* (International Publishers, New York, in progress), an early work which though in parts superseded, is invaluable, apart from other considerations, as containing the only good account of the Petersburg period. A more detailed catalogue of events and legislative measures (as far, only, as 1774) will be found in the monumental work of S. M. Soloviev (29 volumes, 1851-79). English readers will find a more condensed chronicle of the outer facts in Sir Bernard Pares's *History of Russia* (Knopf).

I am deeply indebted to the Editor of the series whose attentive and critical reading of the manuscripts has preserved me from more irresponsible statements and loose phrases than I like to think of. I am also much indebted to Dr. Ellis Minns who (apart from his part of responsibility in causing me to write this book) gave me most valuable advice in the sections on Art.

I further owe my thanks to Professor N. S. Trubetzkoy, of Vienna, and Professor P. N. Savitsky, of Prague, from my conversation and correspondence with whom I have drawn a great wealth of valuable knowledge. The ethnological and linguistic passages in particular owe much to the former; and the geographical and archæological to the latter. I must however plainly state that their general views are *toto coelo* removed from mine, and that consequently they bear no responsibility whatever for the use I have made of the information I have drawn from them.

I have also to thank Mr. David Roden Buxton for allowing me to make use of four photographs taken by him on a recent walking tour in the U.S.S.R.

August 1930.

CONTENTS

xiii

CONTENTS

CONTENTS

XV

LIST OF ILLUSTRATIONS

LIST OF MAPS

Chapter I

INTRODUCTORY

1. THE GEOGRAPHICAL BACKGROUND.

2. RUSSIA BEFORE THE RUSSIANS.

3. THE SLAVS.

I. THE GEOGRAPHICAL BACKGROUND.

THE background of Russian history is the great Eurasian plain, bounded on the north by the Arctic Sea; on the east by the plateaus of Eastern Siberia, the Altai, Tarbagatai and Tien-Shan mountains; on the south by the piedmont regions of Turkestan, the Caspian, the Caucasus, the Crimean mountains and the Black Sea; on the west by the Carpathians, the Baltic, and the granites of the Finno-Scandinavian massive. Between the Black Sea and the Carpathians, and between these and the Baltic, the plain extends westward without interruption, but these narrow extensions are as different from its main expanse as the North Sea is from the Atlantic.

Most of the great plain is a rolling country, that does not rise above 600 feet. The only real uplands are the Urals. Extending over 18 degrees of latitude in an almost due north-to-south direction they look very conspicuous on the map. But their real importance as a barrier is insignificant; for the greater part of their length they form a single narrow and worn-down chain with a mean altitude of about 2,000 feet. In the middle section (between 56° and 59° north) the elevation is even less, and before the days of highroads easy portages connected the headwaters of Cisuralian rivers with those of Siberia. Neither do the Urals form a meteorological barrier, their only climatic effect being slightly to deflect to the south, by their moderate elevation, the latitudinal belts of climate and vegetation. Since the 19th century the Urals have been officially regarded as the boundary between "European" and "Asiatic" Russia. But the essential unity of the great plain should not be obscured by this conventional wording.

The principal feature of the great plain is the regular succession from north to south of its climatic and vegetation belts.* Their strictly latitudinal character is particularly well marked east of the longitude of Nizhni Novgorod (50° E.). West of that line the influ-

*See article by Professor B. Keller on *Distribution of Vegetation in the Plains of European Russia*, in the *Journal of Ecology*, August, 1927.

ence of the Atlantic is more distinctly felt so that the summer temperature increases and the humidity decreases in a south-eastern direction, and the latitudinal belts are deflected to the south-west.

Apart from the treeless tundra that lies to the north of the Arctic circle and has little importance in the human geography of the country, the other belts of natural vegetation may be broadly classified as woodland and steppe, each of which can be further subdivided into secondary belts.

At one end of the scale is the formation styled by Russian geographers "desert" or "arid steppe." North of 45° N. it is not an absolute desert, but a poor grassland that can support a pastoral population of one or two to the square mile. It receives less than ten inches of rain and the mean temperature of the hottest month is 77° and more. The rainfall is insufficient for agriculture, and the lay of the land makes irrigation (without power-stations) impossible. The arid steppe does not extend to the western limits of the great plain. Its farthest western extension is marked by the low but steep escarpment of the Ergeni, which runs almost due south of Stalingrad (Tsaritsyn) along 44° 30′ E. and divides the agricultural from the non-agricultural steppe. East of Stalingrad the northern limit of the arid steppe follows the Volga to about latitude 50° N. along which it runs to the foothills of the Altai.

The next belt, going north, has a rainfall of from ten to twenty inches and a mean July temperature ranging from 67° to 77°. It is for the most part covered by a thick layer of loess, the upper stratum of which has been turned, by the decay of grasses under semi-arid conditions, into the famous *chernozem* ("black earth"), one of the most fertile soils of temperate latitudes. It is richest and thickest near the northern limit of this belt. Desertwards it grows thinner and lighter ("chocolate" and "chestnut" soils), remaining, however, very fertile, so that the southern limit of agriculture is not so much conditioned by the deterioration of the soil, as by insufficient rainfall. Great annual oscillations in the rainfall make much of the black-earth belt subject to recurrent famines, the latest and most disastrous of which was that of 1921. Irrigation, here again, is out of the question; for the rivers rise from sources lying below the loess layer and flow in deeply eroded valleys. The black-earth steppe is treeless, except for gallery woods along the river courses.

4

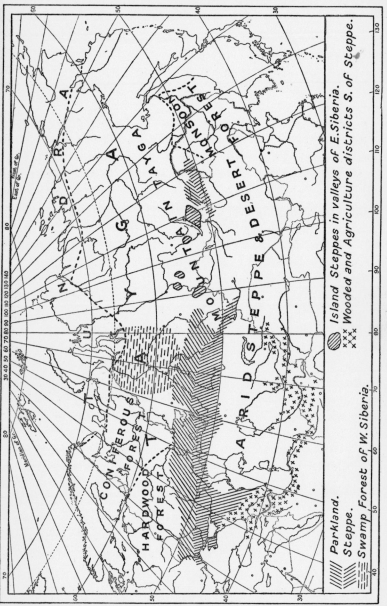

Fig. 1. *Vegetation Belts.*

5

Its northern limit passes south of Kishinev (47° N.), Poltava (49° 30′ N.) and Kharkov (50° N.); reaches the Volga near Saratov (51° 30′ N.); follows that river to near Samara (53° N.); then deflected for a short space by the South Urals continues east between 54° and 54° 30′ N.

North of this line lies a belt of parkland (the "forest-steppe" of Russian geographers and ecologists) where patches of open black-earth steppe alternate with islands of hardwood forest. In natural conditions, before the advent of man, or when man was forced to leave it untouched (as he was in the 16th century when much of it was a no-man's land between the settled agricultural forest and the grazing grounds of the nomads), the forest was in a state of steady advance at the expense of the steppe. For the climatic conditions (a July temperature not exceeding 70° with a rainfall not below 17 inches) are suited for forest-growth throughout the belt, but the forest has not yet had the time to occupy all the ground it can. The country was reafforested in post-glacial times from the north, and all the forests of the parkland belt grow on "degraded black-earth," that is to say, on a soil that was originally formed in semi-arid steppe conditions but has been transformed in recent times by the more humid environment. These facts dispose, at any rate as far as Cisuralian Russia is concerned, of the theory so readily accepted in England and America of the desiccation of northern and central Eurasia. For the greater part of its length the parkland belt is narrow, not more than two degrees of latitude. But south of Moscow it widens considerably and this country, known to-day as the "Central *Chernozem* District," plays a particularly important part in Russian history. Farther east, within the great bend of the middle Volga the parkland belt is still wider, but here the proportion of forest to steppe is so high as to change the general nature of the country. This densely wooded section is the cradle of one of the oldest agricultural civilisations in the whole plain.

The line dividing the partly wooded parkland from the woodland proper starts at the foot of the Carpathians, about 49° N., passes south of Kiev (50° N.), north of Orel (52° 30′) and near Kazan (55° 30′ N.). Deflected by the Urals to about 53° N. it reaches its northernmost point immediately east of them, near Irbit (57° 45′), whence it gradually descends to near Novosibirsk (Novonikolayevsk) on the Ob (55° N.). North of this line the mean temperature of July is nowhere above 66° and the rainfall (though it diminishes towards the north-east as well as towards the south-east) is everywhere heavy enough to create conditions of excessive rather than deficient humidity.

The forest is subdivided by climatic boundaries, less obviously marked, but no less important than those of the steppe. As the dividing lines depend to a large extent on the temperature and length of the winter, and as those are strongly influenced by distance from the Atlantic, the dividing lines inside the forest belt are not everywhere parallel to those farther south, and assume sometimes a marked south-eastern direction. This is particularly true of the northern limit of deciduous trees; a line drawn from Leningrad (60°) to Kazan, where it intersects at a sharp angle the northern limit of the parkland belt, may be taken as marking a limit, north of which the oak, the maple, the ash, the lime and the apple-tree are either absent or very rare. The boundary is not of very great importance from the standpoint of human geography for it hardly affects agricultural conditions. But the landscape of the hardwood forest is very different from the forest farther north where the monotony of fir and larch is only broken by the whiteness of the birch. The Siberian term of *tayga* is usually applied to the purely coniferous forest. The triangle of deciduous woodland that advances like a wedge driven from a western base into northern Eurasia is the only part of the Russian plain presenting a type of landscape that can be described as European. It is not without its significance that Russian history begins inside this triangle and that 11th century Russia was almost conterminous with it.

An economically more important boundary is offered by the northern limit of agriculture—not the absolute northernmost limit of the possible cultivation of cereals (which lies partly beyond the Arctic circle), but the limit beyond which the culture of rye and oats cannot support a population of however limited needs, and economic life is dominated by non-agricultural pursuits. Much of north Russia and most of north-western Siberia is swamp, and would be agriculturally useless even in lower latitudes, but under adequate conditions of drainage the limit of agriculture is marked by a line running from about 61° N. on Lake Ladoga, to north of

Ustyug (62° N.), then north of Tobolsk (59°) and to Yeniseysk (58° 30'). Conditioned as it is by the length of the winter on the one hand and by the temperature of the summer months on the other, the line shows no very marked deviation from a purely latitudinal direction.

Three types of economy have from the earliest recorded times divided, and still divide, between them the population of these belts. Each of the peoples of the great plain is closely associated with one of these types, and all the human groups inhabiting it may be classified under one of the three headings: hunters,* pastoralists and agriculturists. The tundra and the northern forest are the home of the former. The arid and the black-earth steppe gave rise to the pastoral civilisation of the nomads. The western wedge of deciduous and agricultural forest, together with the more densely wooded parts of the parkland, were the cradle of the agricultural communities. In terms of human geography the recent history of Russia may very largely be described as the advance of the agricultural wedge against both hunters and nomads. Until the agricultural wedge was driven in between them the latter two were, east of the Kama, immediate neighbours. Their cultural area extends to the east far beyond the boundaries of the great plain.

A more or less homogeneous cultural area of Arctic hunters reached from Lapland to the Pacific, ever since the beginning of known history, the country east of the Yenisei presenting, except for a more varied relief, conditions of life similar to those of northern Russia and north-west Siberia. The area of pastoral civilisation reaches east to the foot of the great wall of China. The high steppes of Dzungaria and Mongolia are similar except for their altitude to those between the Volga and the Irtysh; the poorly wooded mountains that traverse them are no barriers for nomads, who ever since they mastered the horse were free to move from China to the Danube. The essential unity and great cohesion of this world of pastoral and equestrian civilisation is one of the major facts in the history of the Old World and in the background of Russian history. The hunters on the contrary were always dispersed and without

---

*The reindeer-rearers of the tundra may be regarded, in a broad classification, as a specialised branch of the hunters.

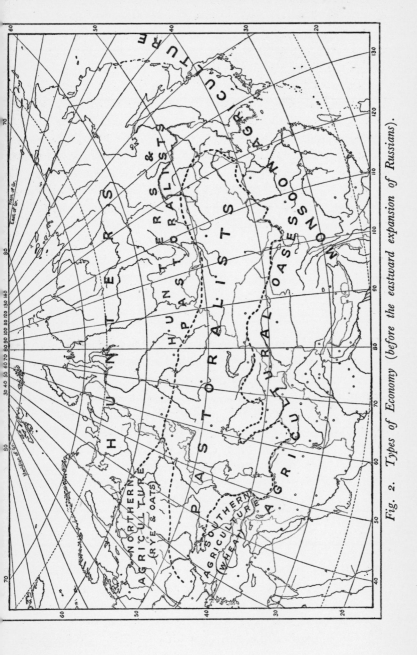

Fig. 2. *Types of Economy (before the eastward expansion of Russians).*

9

cohesion, and played no active part in history. Culturally, they were for the most part under the influence of the nomads.

The agricultural area of the Russian plain is, as we have seen, an eastward extension of the agricultural forest of Europe. The type of agriculture is the same, based on the plough, the horse and the cow, with rye and oats as the staple crops, and flax as the most important industrial plant. Still the difference between Europe and even the agricultural part of Russia is great—a difference of climate and position. East of a belt running from the Gulf of Finland to the mouth of the Danube snow covers the ground and the rivers are frozen over for four months and more; the difference between the mean temperature of January and July is greater than 45° Fahr.; the beech, the yew and the ivy are absent. The continental climate corresponds to a continental position. Of the rivers, none fall into an open sea, and the greatest of them, the Volga, discharges its waters into the landlocked lake known as the Caspian Sea. No barrier separates the agricultural wedge either from the steppe or from the Arctic forest, and this more than counterbalances what similarities of vegetation the hardwood forest of Russia may have with Europe.

The Baltic is the only sea on which the Russian agricultural woodland actually borders, but nothing makes the essential continental character of Russia so clear as its relation to the Baltic. The innermost bay of the Gulf of Finland, and that at the cost of prolonged efforts, is the only part of the coast to have become culturally and ethnically Russian. All the other Baltic coastlands from Finland to Latvia have always had their back to the continent and their face to the sea, for the Baltic has always been a Mediterranean that united rather than divided the inhabitants of its opposite shores. Though included at one time in the Russian Empire, the "Baltic provinces" never became Russian, and to-day they are again outside the cultural and political unity that has replaced the Empire. In spite of this secular opposition between coastland and interior the Baltic lands have been, especially in modern times, an important zone of contact between Russia and Europe.

The Baltic puts Russia into direct touch with the more progressive and active maritime regions of northern Europe. The gap between the Baltic and the Carpathians offers a wider front of ontact, but gives immediate access only to the backward districts ast of Germany, the very backwoods of Europe. Here the transi- on from west to east has always been most gradual and a definite oundary most difficult to trace. The Carpathians themselves are ntirely European and un-Russian in their physiography, and 10ugh the Russian power extended for a long time—and Russian peech still extends—to their summits (and even beyond) they annot be regarded as a boundary, but must be included in Eur- pe. Even their north-eastern foreland is European rather than .ussian; the presence of the beech and the yew are a botanical ymbol of their western character, while its political expression is o-day the land of Eastern Galicia with its Ukrainian people and .ustrian civilisation. But the secular struggle between Russia and 'oland for a " natural frontier" is the unmistakable counterpart 1 history of the vagueness of the boundary between Russia and ,urope.

Farther south the agricultural woodland is bounded by the teppe. Along the Danube the steppe penetrates into central :urope where the Hungarian plain was long a natural advanced amp of the nomads. South of the steppe, in the Crimea and :aucasus, as well as farther east in Turkestan, the ground rises, nd with it the rainfall; the country is once more wooded, and has rom the earliest times been occupied by agriculturists. But separ- ted by the steppe from the Russian woodland, these southern iedmont and mountain regions offer a different type of agricul- ural civilisation, more closely related to the civilisation of the Vlediterranean and of western Asia. It was through these lands hat the steppe came in touch with the oldest civilisations of the)ld World. The Crimea in particular, half steppe and half Medi- erranean garden, played an important part in these early con- acts. But the woodland farther north was long screened by the teppe from the sight of civilised nations. When it emerged into the ight of history this was due to the great rivers which, rising in the orest, traverse the steppe and throw themselves into seas (we may .ccord the Caspian that name) bordering on lands of ancient ivilisation. The rivers were always the allies and instruments of he sedentary peoples and the enemies of the nomad. His real do- nain is east of the Volga, where the steppe is practically riverless.

11

The Yaik (Ural river) is no serious obstacle and from the Yaik it is possible to ride to the Chinese Wall without crossing a single stream. But the Volga, the Don, and the Dniepr were serious barriers for the nomad, and convenient ways of penetration for the boatmen of the forest. The steppe reaches of these rivers have a life and a history quite apart from that of the surrounding plains with which they came into real contact only when South Russian wheat became an exportable commodity. Only the Dniepr is barred in its passage through the granite belt of the Black Sea steppe by difficult navigable rapids, a defile that gave the nomads a hold on the Dniepr which they never had on the Volga.

The importance of the great rivers to the forest belt cannot be over-estimated. Nowhere, except perhaps in North America, do flowing waters form such a complete and convenient network of ways. The level character of the land makes their incline insignificant, and allows their headwaters to approach so near to each other that in early times boats could be easily carried over the intervening portages, while later on the building of canals met with no serious difficulties.

A particularly remarkable junction of this system of routes occurs in the country north-east of Smolensk (and W.N.W. of Moscow). Hence the Dniepr flows into the Black Sea, receiving on the way tributaries that put it in touch with the Vistula and the Niemen; the Duna into the Gulf of Riga; the Lovat and the Msta into Lake Ilmen, which feeds the Volkhov and thus the Neva; and the Volga to the east.

The Volga is not only the longest river of the Cisuralian plain; it is the most important and most centrally situated. Between its upper course and its southern tributary, the Oka, lies the central Russian Mesopotamia which is the best connected and most central part of the hardwood wedge. The westward connections of the Upper Volga are assured by the portages leading into the Dniepr, Duna and Neva basins. Its northern affluents approach within easy distance of the Sukhona, one of the headwaters of the Dvina. The Dvina, whose other affluents put it in touch with the Neva and Kama basins, falls into the White Sea, and is thus the only route connecting the agricultural forest with a sea which, though icebound for more than half the year, has freer access to the open cean than either the Baltic or the Black Sea. When warmer seas have been obstructed by hostile powers (as they were in Muscovite times) the Dvina and White Sea route remained the only channel connecting Russia with the West.

After receiving the Oka and issuing into the steppe, the Volga is joined by the Kama which carries more water than the main stream and drains all the western slope of the Urals. Portages that may be termed difficult only in comparison with the easy portages of the plain, connect the eastern affluents of the Kama with the Tura which sends its waters to the Irtysh and Ob, so that a scarcely interrupted waterway gives access to the whole of Siberia; for the Ob is separated from the Yenisei by one of the easiest of easy portages.

Below the confluent of the Kama the Volga traverses the steppe at its greatest breadth and falls into the Caspian, beyond which lies Persia. One more easy portage leads from the western bend of the lower Volga to the eastern angle of the lower Don, thus affording the north-east direct communication with the Black Sea. The Don itself (the only one of the great Russian rivers that rises on the outer fringe of the forest and drains none but parkland and steppe country) extends its headwaters to those of the southern affluents of the Oka, thus completing the wheel of rivers that diverges from the Mesopotamia of Central Russia.

2. RUSSIA BEFORE THE RUSSIANS.*

No finds assignable to the lower Palæolithic have been made i
any part of Russia. Upper Palæolithic stations, revealing a cultur
related to the Aurignacian, Solutrean, and Magdalenian phases i
western and central Europe, with, however, some features c
notable originality, have been discovered all along the souther.
fringe of the forest and in the parkland belt from the Dniepr to th
Don and Oka†. One of them was on the site of Kiev, which i
thus one of the oldest human dwelling-places in the country.

In the Neolithic and Bronze ages the finds become more numer
ous and their distribution very characteristic. All the norther
forest was occupied by a backward, but highly specialised, "Arc
tic" civilisation of hunters who preserved Palæolithic technique
into the Bronze age, and were remarkably skilled in the artisti
handling of animal forms.

The steppe, up to the dawn of the early historic age (c.700 B.C.
was occupied by a people whose main characteristic was the prac
tice of a peculiar funeral rite. After removing the flesh from th
bones of their dead they painted them in red ochre; hence thei
designation as the "ochre-grave" or "painted-skeleton" people
They do not seem to have domesticated the horse, but only hunted
it. Their culture was rather poor and featureless but it was related
to a more highly developed culture (dated variously from c.2500
to c.1000 B.C.) that flourished in the piedmont region of th
northern Caucasus, and has yielded metal work of considerabl
artistic value, and of obvious Mesopotamian affinities. This northern Caucasian culture is also related to the bronze culture of the
Upper Volga and Oka (Fatianovo culture)—an indication of the
early importance of the Don and Volga waterways.

*On the Archæology of Russia see esp. the works of the Finnish Archæo-
logist Tallgren; *Südrussland im Altertum*, by Max Ebert, Bonn & Leipzig 1921;
and the relevant articles in *Reallexikon der Vorgeschichte*, edited by the same,
Berlin, 1924 *et seq.*

†See survey of Palæolithic finds by Efimenko in *Chelovek*, *I*, Leningrad, 1928
(in Russian).

The most interesting point of the Fatianovo culture is its piderlike connections with other parts of the Cisuralian plain. Besides the northern Caucasus and the Steppe, it has affinities with the northern forest and with the Baltic. With the former it hares its style of animal carving, from the latter it imported amber and borrowed its type of weapons. It can thus be regarded, in the entral role it played, as the prehistoric prototype of the later Muscovy. But its remains are few and sparse, and it seems to have been short-lived.

The west of the Cisuralian plain stood in closer contact with Europe. The Baltic coast had a common culture with North Germany and Scandinavia, and what is now Poland was inseparable rom central Germany. In the south-west, between the Dniepr nd the Carpathians, in the forest fringe and in the parkland, there flourished in the 3rd millennium B.C. an agricultural civilisation which has been given the name of Tripolye (Trypillya, a town near Kiev). It extended west as far as Transylvania, and, at one time at east, as far south as Thessaly. Its principal characteristic is its painted pottery, which is related in style to the neolithic culture of he Danube, so that German archæologists find it possible to regard it as merely a local form of that great agricultural civilisation. But s the pottery is painted, and as painted pottery was unknown in central Europe at that time, Tripolye has also to be associated in ome way with other painted-pottery civilisations beyond the teppe, as those of China and Transcaspia.

Some time about 2000 B.C. the Tripolye agriculturists appear to ave been rather suddenly overwhelmed and exterminated by the chre-grave nomads. Towards the end of the second millennium .C. a new sedentary civilisation with clear Western affinities nakes its appearance in the steppe between the Dniepr and the Danube, extending into the Crimea. Its bearers have been tentatively identified with the Cimmerians of Greek history who were usted from the South Russian steppe by the Scythians about 00 B.C. and whose consequent invasion of Asia Minor remained a rrible recollection for the Ionian Greeks. The Scythians followed hem into Hither Asia, and left there a lasting impression on the ews and Assyrians, but ended by settling in the South Russian eppe.

The Scythians* were the first mounted nomads, masters of th·
horse and possessors of iron weapons, in the history of the Eurasia·
steppe. They are also the first nation of the steppe our knowledg·
of whom is derived from literary sources. They are thus a doubl·
important landmark, marking the end of the prehistoric perio·
proper. They spoke an Iranian tongue, but their civilisation was ·
a different type from that of the Persians. It was a nomad civilisa·
tion whose cultural area reached from Hungary and south Russi·
to the upper Yenisei and to the Chinese border. Our principa·
thread in tracing the extension of this "Scytho-Siberian culture" ·
a characteristic style ("Scythian Animal style") which reveals a·
extraordinary genius in the handling of animal forms in a way a·
once highly conventional and strikingly lifelike. The style ha·
obvious affinities with the animal carvings of the Arctic Stone ag·
These ornaments are found in great quantities in the tumuli i·
which the Scythians buried their chiefs, together with numerou·
skeletons of horses and male and female attendants of the de·
ceased which were immolated at the master's funeral. These burial·
are as typical of Scytho-Siberian culture as the "animal style."·
How great was the cultural unity of the Scytho-Siberian worl·
may be gauged by comparing Herodotus' account of the Scythian·
of the Black Sea steppe with early Chinese descriptions of th·
Hiung-nu of Inner Mongolia; scarcely a detail is different. Th·
Scythians spoke an Iranian dialect, the Hiung-nu were probabl·
Mongols or Turks. We have here a typical case of what should b·
constantly borne in mind by the student of the history of civilisa·
tion: linguistic affinities are not identical with cultural grouping·
and language is no certain indication of cultural relationship.

The Scythians appear to have been the most powerful and ac·
vanced nation of this cultural group. Their political centres wer·
in northern Crimea, in the steppe between the Lower Dniep·
and the Sea of Azov and in the plains of the Kuban. Not long aft·
the Scythian invasion the Greeks began to found colonies on th·
north coast of the Black Sea†. Olbia at the mouth of the Boh (Bu·
and Chersonnesus near the present site of Sevastopol were th·

*See *Iranians and Greeks in South Russia* by Rostovtzeff, Oxford, 1922; a·
Scythian Art, by Borovka, Benn, 1928.

†See *Scythians and Greeks*, by Minns, Cambridge, 1913.

ıost important. The barbarian (pre-Scythian) kingdom of Cim-
ıerian Bosporus on both sides of the Straits of Kerch also received
ireek immigrants and developed a mixed, but strongly Hellen-
ed polity. In the 5th and 4th centuries B.C. it was a great
ommercial centre and the chief exporter of grain to Athens. All
ıese places became centres of Greek influence on the Scythians,
'ho eagerly bought Attic goods, especially Attic pottery and metal-
'ork. Their animal style became modified by Greek artisans;
cythian slaves served as policemen in Athens, and Attic writers of
ıe 4th century made of the Scythian the first noble savage in
uropean literature.

In the 3rd century B.C. the Sarmatians crossed the Volga and
ıe Don and drove the remains of the Scythians into the Crimea
nd Dobruja. The Sarmatians were a group of nations of Iranian
ıeech and Scytho-Siberian civilisation, but their culture was
oorer and less markedly aristocratic. Certain archæological indica-
ons make it probable that they were the descendants of the ochre-
rave people. They dominated the Black Sea steppe for about
ıur centuries, during which the Greek colonies declined, while
ıe Kingdom of Bosporus became increasingly associated with
[ellenistic Asia. In the 1st century A.D. the Romans extended
ıeir power to all the north coast of the Black Sea. The Sarmatians
ere less open to Roman than the Scythians had been to Greek
ultural influence, but the conquest of Dacia by Trajan provided
.oman commerce with an advanced base whence it radiated
ver the south-western part of the woodland; numerous finds of
.oman coins have been made throughout Galicia and in West
Jkraina.

The consolidation of Roman power diverted the Germanic
ations from the west, where their advance was held up by the long
ıpregnable *limes* to the east. In the end of the second century the
ioths descended from the Vistula to the Black Sea, and spread
ıeir power from the Danube to the Don. In their new environ-
ıent these Central Europeans came under the cultural influence
f their neighbours, the Sarmatian nation of the Alani, who con-
nued to occupy the Ciscaucasian steppe and with whom later
ıe Goths partly amalgamated. This mixed Germano-Sarmatian
vilisation played an important part in the formation of medieval

17   C

Europe to which it bequeathed its military methods (armoured horsemen) and its style of ornamentation: for the so-called Merovingian style is a development of Scytho-Siberian forms modified by various contacts in the steppes that neighboured the kingdom of Bosporus. That kingdom in the Roman period was a great melting pot where cultural currents of Scytho-Siberian, Roman and Oriental origin were fused. A Jewish community was an important ingredient in the mixture.

In the second half of the 4th century, the coming of the Huns who drove the Goths before them, introduced a new ethnical element. The exact affinities of the Huns are unknown, nor are we certain as to whether they may be identified with the Hiung-nu of Chinese sources. They appear, however, to have been of Mongoloid race and probably spoke a Turkic or a Mongolian tongue. Their civilisation was of the same nomadic type as that of the Scythians, but of another variety. They still practised the Scytho-Siberian art forms, which however, soon disappear from the steppes to survive only in Germano-Sarmatian Europe.

In the 5th century the Huns, welded by Attila into a powerful empire, occupied the Hungarian plain and menaced the very existence of Roman civilisation. The Hunnish Empire brought into motion and absorbed, among other European elements, the Slavs who make their first appearance in history as subjects of the Huns.

The Empire hardly survived its founder, and in dissolving left the east of Europe and south Russia in a state of chaos and fermentation. The Slavs invaded the Balkan peninsula, while another section of them under the name of Antes or Antae occupied the steppe north of the Danube and of the Black Sea. But soon new nomadic peoples, the Avars and the Bulgars, came from beyond the Don, and the Antes faded away into obscurity. The Avars (who seem to have been Mongols) restored a nomadic empire in Pannonia ; the Bulgars, whose speech was Turkic, divided into two groups, one of which crossed the Danube and became the point of crystallisation for a part of the Balkan Slavs, while the other founded a kingdom on the middle Volga.

At the same time beyond the lower Volga and extending eastward as far as the Tien-Shan mountains, there grew up the Empire of the western Turks, which, though short-lived, is an important

andmark in the history of the steppe. It gave national consciousness to the great Turkish race, and foreshadowed on a small
scale the Mongol Empire: the *pax Turcica* gave a powerful stimu-
us to commerce and breathed new life into the great caravan
routes from the Black Sea to China. In the third quarter of the
7th century the Turkish Empire fell, destroyed by the Arabs and
he Chinese. But its cultural work was continued by the Chazars,
who about 650 established themselves on the lower Volga and
ower Don—at the junction of all the most important trade routes
of the steppe—and developed a civilisation curiously mixed of
urban and nomadic elements. Their power was at its height in the
ater 8th and early 9th century, when their authority extended
rom the Caucasus to the Dniepr and to the Urals, and many peoples
of the forest paid them tribute. Itil, the Chazar capital (near
Astrakhan), was a crucible where various cultural elements were
mixed, and where Arabs, Christians and Jews (the descendants of
hose of the Bosporus) formed independent communities with
autonomous jurisdiction. The Chazar kings (Kagans) and aristocracy finished by adopting the Jewish faith.

At the same time the Eastern Empire was consolidating its
power north and east of the Black Sea, and Chersonnesus now
became an important centre of Byzantine civilisation.

The woodland farther north continued prehistoric till the 9th
century. Herodotus, it is true, gives many names, some of which
belong undoubtedly to real, not mythical, peoples, but his notions
of the hinterland of Scythia were so hazy that it is impossible to
ocate these peoples with any degree of certainty, still less to iden-
tify them with historical nations. Archæology is more helpful. We
ind Scythian influence powerful and Arctic affinities present in an
agricultural civilisation that flourished in the lower Kama in the
7th-3rd century B.C. ("Ananyino culture") and was continued
without any abrupt break into the "Piany-bor culture" of the
early centuries A.D. Immediately north-east of these districts, in
he middle Urals, old mines have been found most probably assignable to about the same period, while the region of the western
affluents of the Kama seem to have been great exporters of precious
urs to Sassanian Persia. Silver plate was imported in payment for
hem, and the country between Kama and Vyatka has yielded

more Sassanian silver than all the rest of the world together
Farther west, the central Russian Mesopotamia harboured another agricultural civilisation with less clearly marked affinities
than Ananyino, while the Baltic coastlands continued their intimate connection with Sweden and Germany.

Gradually history begins to reach into the darkness of the forest.
Ptolemaeus (2nd century) and Jordanes (8th century) give lists of
nations that are much more recognisable than those mentioned by
Herodotus. Combining them with later Greek, Latin, Arabic and
Russian sources, and with archæological, ethnological and linguistic evidence we may make ourselves a fairly clear picture of the
peoples of the Cisuralian forest towards the beginning of the 9th
century.

The northern *tayga* was occupied by a sparse population of
hunters of Finno-Ugrian stock. Part of them formed the Permian
nation who probably acquired the Sassanian plate just mentioned, and whose descendants are the Komi (Zyryans and
Permyaks) of to-day. The same linguistic stock extended west to
Finland and Estonia. These western Finns stood on a higher cultural stage. They had learned agriculture from their Baltic neighbours and were being drawn into the common net of north-
European civilisation, though they long preserved certain primitive features (notably the cult of the bear). Finno-Ugrian peoples
of still a different branch, known to the Russian chronicler as
Ves, Merya (probably identic with the Mari) and Muroma occupied the central Mesopotamia and the valleys of the upper Volga
affluents. They were acquainted with agriculture, but do not seem
to have been numerous.

On the middle Volga and in the parkland inside the big bend a
more advanced agricultural civilisation was already fully developed by the 9th century. Certain features* make it probable that
it was not an extension of the European agricultural province but
was related to the north-Caucasian region. The oldest ethnical
component of the middle Volga culture was Finno-Ugrian, whose
modern representatives are the Mordva, the Mari (Cheremis) and
the Votyak. But in the 8th and 9th centuries the eastern Bulgars

---

*Especially the cultivation of spelt, which is extensively practised only on
the Middle Volga and south of the steppe in the Crimea and Caucasus.

were already the dominating force. They spoke a Turkic dialect (from which the modern Chuvash is descended) closely allied to that of the Chazars, but rather divergent from the main Turkic stock.* Neither the Bulgars nor the Chazars formed part of the west Turkish Empire and the Turks proper did not regard them as kinsmen. The Bulgars must have established themselves in the middle Volga and lower Kama some time about 700, and their cultural influence on their Finno-Ugrian neighbours and subjects was enormous. The agricultural vocabulary of the region is mainly Bulgar. The primitive Finno-Ugrian religion of the Mord-va, Mari and Votyak disappeared without leaving a trace, and was replaced by the monotheistic and aniconic religion of the Bulgars. All the east of Cisuralia now formed one cultural area that stretched from the Vyatka and Vetluga to the Caucasian pied-mont and from the Crimea to the south Urals. Its two centres were Itil and the Great City of the Bulgars, near the mouth of the Kama; its main artery the Volga, with the lower Don as its second commercial mouth. The rise of this eastern economic and cultural system preceded by more than a century the formation of corresponding Western system that gravitated to the Dniepr, and which developed into the kingdom of Russia. Chazar and Bulgar influences were active in the formation of Russia and not least in the domain of agricultural civilisation. Thus, buckwheat, one of the staples of Russian diet, was introduced from the Orient through the intermediary of the Chazars.

The western half of the woodland shows no sign of awakening till the mid 9th century. The Baltic fringe (the modern Latvia, the Niemen basin and Prussia east of the Vistula) was inhabited by numerous nations of Lithuanians, a people racially related to the other Baltic coastlanders and speaking a language that presents, in many ways, a linguistic type hardly different from common Indo-European. They seem to have inhabited their country for count-less ages and to have had a full share in the development of the prehistoric cultures of the Baltic. Their cultural influence on the Baltic Finns had been great, but they had taken no part in the great movements of the Völkerwanderung and were by now an archaic people, with a civilisation that was typical of earlier ages.

* Chuvash presents also certain similarities with the Caucasian languages.

The interior of the western woodland south-west of the Lithu
anians, south-east of the Finno-Ugrians of the central Mesopo
tamia and north of the steppe was inhabited by the eastern Slav
who were destined to form the main ethnical substratum of the
Russian nation.

THE Slavonic branch of the Indo-European linguistic family is closely related to the Lithuanian or Baltic branch. The two branches have so much in common that they are sometimes spoken of as one Slavo-Baltic group. The similarity of vocabulary (as distinct from phonetics and grammatical form) is particularly great and appears to indicate a corresponding similarity in prehistoric culture. Of the other Indo-European languages the Iranian group is nearest to the Slavonic. The two branches must have been immediate neighbours at the end of the period of Indo-European unity; while later the Slavs borrowed a certain number of Scythian or Sarmatian words. At a later period again they borrowed numerous words from the Gothic, which form a suggestive cultural layer, including as they do numerous terms referring to agriculture, to building and other crafts, and to political organisation. A special group is formed by words taken by the Goths themselves from the Greeks and Romans. All these words obviously go back to the late Roman period (2nd-4th centuries), while the few and doubtful words of Turkic origin would be relics of subjection to the Huns and Avars.

The sum of linguistic, toponymic and archæological evidence, together with the oldest historical mentions of the Slavs (who first appear as "Venedi" in Ptolemaeus's list of northern nations), has made it certain that the home of the Slavs before their first migrations (i.e. before the Hunnish invasion) was the country lying between the middle course of the Vistula and the upper Dniepr. Southward it did not reach as far as the Carpathians or the parkland belt, whilst northward it is unlikely to have extended into either the Niemen or Duna basins. The Slavs were first brought into movement by the Huns, and after the collapse of Attila's empire they spread with extraordinary rapidity over the Balkan

---

*See *Slovanské Starozitnosti* (Prague, 1904 *et scq*) and *Manuel de l'Antiquité Slave* (Paris 1922) by Niederle; and *Introduction to the History of the Russian Language* by Shakhmatov, Petrograd 1916 (in Russian).

peninsula, the eastern Alps and the Elbe basin, while the Slavonic nation of the Antae occupied the Black Sea steppe. The Antae disappear from history, pushed aside by the invading Avars, but the Carpathians and all the parkland between them and the Dniepr remained Slavonic. At some period between the 5th and

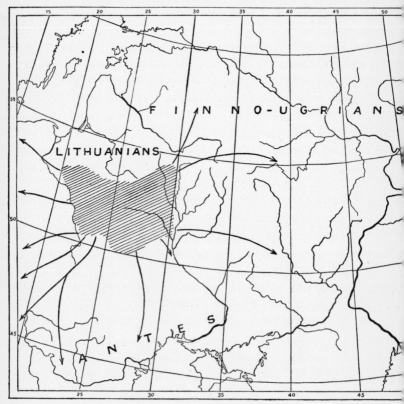

Fig. 3. *Original home of the Slavs (early centuries A.D.) and direction of the first migrations (5th-8th centuries).*

9th centuries other groups of Slavs began to expand eastwards into the Don, Oka and upper Volga basins, and northwards into those of the Duna and of the Neva.

The common cultural inheritance of the Slavs was so poor that it can hardly be said to have survived their expansion. For as they expanded the Slavs came in contact with, and under the influence of, much higher civilizations, and what they borrowed from these different civilisations very soon entirely obliterated what each section had in common with other branches of the Slavonic race. The Czechs and Poles and other north-western Slavs were latinised by contact with their German neighbours, and entered the family of western nations; the southern Slavs, together with the Greeks, Albanians and Vlakhs (Roumanians), contributed to form the characteristic cultural province of "the Balkans," and were partly byzantinised, partly latinised by neighbourhood with the Venetians and Austrians; the eastern Slavs were "Russianised," that is to say, transformed into a more or less autonomous cultural unit by a variety of external and internal forces. By the 9th century, the process of differentiation had already gone far, and is well illustrated by archæology. While the prehistoric Slavs have left us absolutely no archæological trace and their original home is archæologically the emptiest district of the Old World, discoveries that can be assigned to the centuries after their expansion reveal several distinct areas, each one more closely related to its earlier civilised neighbours than to other Slavonic lands.

There was only one element of unity that was somewhat more stable: till about the 11th century the Slavonic language remained substantially one and mutually intelligible to all Slavs. This had important cultural results, for it allowed the "Church-Slavonic" language of the Macedonian Slavs to be accepted as a literary and liturgic language by the Russians. The linguistic unity of the Slavs survives to a certain extent to the present, for in spite of considerable changes undergone by the individual languages (chiefly in the 12th-14th centuries) there still remains much in common between them, at least in phonetics and grammar, and in the oldest layers of the vocabulary. But the cultural vocabulary of the individual languages is entirely divergent, for it has been produced by such different influences, that though the Slavs may still pretend to a certain linguistic unity, this is purely formal and in no way cultural.

The common prehistoric culture of the Slavs may on the whole be described as an impoverished reflection of the civilisation of their Germanic neighbours. They were agriculturists of the common Central European type, but hunting and collecting were for them more lucrative pursuits than tillage. Of their social organisation we know very little, nor can we say for certain what kind of units the "nations" were. Procopius speaks of their "democracy," and other writers employ similar expressions. It would appear that chiefs played a smaller part than in Germanic society, nor do the Slavs seem to have had any kind of aristocracy. Russian historians have disputed the question whether the Slavonic polity was based on the patriarchal clan or on the village community. The former may have existed, but has left no traces (for Yugoslav institutions of this type are of "Balkanic" not of Slavonic origin), and its existence can be postulated only on theoretical grounds. Some kind of territorial organisation of neighbours must have existed and may be the direct ancestor of the old Russian territorial community of the 14th-15th centuries (not to be confused, of course, with the village commune of the serfdom period).

The Slavs had religious beliefs, but no organised religion. A number of gods worshipped by various Slavonic peoples are mentioned by medieval writers, but criticism has made it practically certain that none of them can be assigned to the period of Slavonic unity, when their religion as far as we can see was a somewhat primitive nature-animism.* Survivals of Slavonic unity are found in the rituals of the annual vegetation cycle, but even here two of the most important feasts bear the suggestive Roman names of *Kolenda* (Calendae) and *Rusalii* (Rosalia). Altogether, in speaking of historical times, it is impossible to use any such term as Slavonic civilisation.

The eastern Slavs emerge into the light of history in the second half of the 9th century. Their distribution over the territory that was to become Russia at that time can be fairly well outlined, mainly owing to the information given by the Russian Chronicle. The northernmost of the East Slavonic nations were the Slovene, who occupied the basin of Lake Ilmen, and had Novgorod ("Newtown") for their urban centre. The upper basins of the Dniepr and Duna and the country east of Lake Peipus were occupied by the Krivichi, whose chief towns were Smolensk, Polotsk and Pskov. In the old forest home of the Slavs lived the Dregovichi, Derevlyane and Radimichi; in the parkland and forest fringe east of the

*See *Die Religion der Ostslaven*, by Mansikka, being No. 43 of *FF Communications*, Helsinki 1922.

Dniepr, the Severa; and in the upper Don and Oka basins the Vyatichi. In the country round Kiev on the border of forest and parkland lived the Polyane. In the south-west as far as the Carpathians we find mentioned the Duleby, the Volynyanë, the Luchanë and the Khorvaty—names some of which may be synonyms, and others mere glosses. South of these nations, and as far as the Black Sea, Podolia, Bessarabia and Moldavia were occupied by the Ulichi and the Tivertsy, presumably descendants of the Antae. At the opposite end of the East Slavonic territory there were Slavs in the upper Volga basin, but we do not know to what nation they belonged; dialectology points towards early colonisation from the north-west (i.e. from Novgorod), but the Finno-Ugrian aborigines of the country had not yet been eliminated by the newcomers.

In how far all these "nations" presented an ethnical unity before the rise of the Russian power is highly controversial matter. The linguistic unity of all the Slavs was very great and lasted well into Russian times; the East Slavonic dialects present certain additional features in common that separate them from the other Slavs. But other lines might be drawn showing similarities between the dialects of south Russia with, e.g. those of the Slovaks. Ethnologically also certain characteristic features of the Great Russians show affinities with the Lithuanians and Finno-Ugrians, and are not found among the Ukrainians. The thesis of Great Russian historians has always been that the eastern Slavs formed a pre-established unity from the beginning of time. The thesis of the Ukrainian historians is that the eastern Slavs had two centres of gravity—one in the north and one in the south, and that the southern group was originally not much more closely related to the northern than it was to other groups in the Balkans or in Central Europe. The sum of evidence seems to be increasingly favourable to a view that is closer to the Ukrainian than to the Great Russian thesis.*

*On the racial type of the Slavs and Russians, see Appendix I.

Chapter II

THE KIEV PERIOD
(IXth—XIIIth Centuries)

1. " THE BEGINNING OF RUSSIA."

2. THE KINGDOM OF RUSSIA.

3. RUSSIAN SOCIETY IN THE ELEVENTH AND TWELFTH CENTURIES.

4. THE RUSSIAN TERRITORY.

5. THE DISSOLUTION OF RUSSIAN UNITY.

6. THE CHURCH AND CIVILISATION; RUSSIA AND HER NEIGHBOURS.

I. "THE BEGINNING OF RUSSIA."

IN the western half of the Cisuralian forest history begins with the appearance of the Norsemen, and the creation by them of new trade-routes. Archæological evidence shows the whole north-west of Russia covered, in the 9th and 10th centuries, by a dense net of Scandinavian occupation. Its centres were Novgorod, at the meeting of the Volga and Dniepr routes to the Baltic, and Smolensk, at the junction of the Duna, Volkhov and Dniepr waterways. At Novgorod, and other places of the East Slavonic north, they founded independent kingdoms. In the Bulgar east they never became anything more than tolerated merchants or river pirates.

Towards the middle of the 9th century they founded a kingdom at Kiev, which occupied on the Dniepr a position exactly parallel to that of the Great City of the Bulgars on the Volga—at the point where the river, after receiving its last forest-fed affluents, issues from the forest into the open parkland. Before the coming of the Norsemen, Kiev was a dependency of the Chazars to whom it paid tribute, and a commercial centre of a sort, though by no means comparable to the Great City of the Bulgars.

From the first, the kingdom of Kiev bore the name of "Russian."* The problem arises whether the name was originally that of a Scandinavian people who took a leading part in the Norse invasion of Russia, or the name of a territory round Kiev. The first view is that of the Russian Chronicler, a Kievian monk writing about 1100; his opinion has little value, as it is obviously based on no real tradition but is his own learned conjecture. There are, however, more serious arguments in favour of the "Scandinavian theory"; the Finnish name for Sweden is *Ruotsi;* the Arab historians

---

*The Old Russian *Rusĭ* is a collective noun (" The Russians ") ; the singular is *Rusinŭ;* the territorial designation *Rusĭskaya Zemlya* (" Russand "). The Greek names for " Russians " and " Russia " are οἱ Ῥῶς and Ῥωδδια the Arabic *Rûs.* Latin fluctuated between forms with *o* and *u,* until it settled on *Rutheni* and *Russia.* Norse has no corresponding form. Its name for Russia, attested from the 11th century, is *Gardariki,* derived from *ard,* or *Holmgard,* the Norse name of Novgorod.

31

distinguish between the *Rús* and the Slavs and seem to apply the
former name to the Norsemen; Constantine Porphyrogenitus
writing about 960 gives the "Russian" and the "Slavonic" names
of the Rapids of the Dniepr; the latter are good Russian, as we
would call it; the "Russian" names are partly unintelligible,

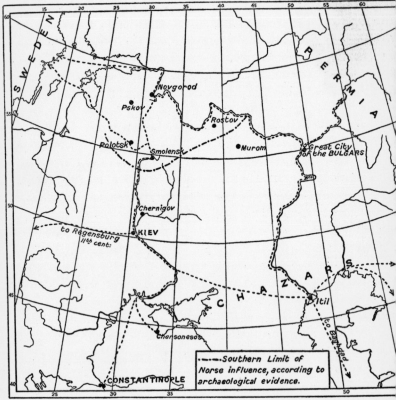

Fig. 4. Trade Routes, 10th century.

partly explicable from the Norse. On the other hand, the old
Russian name for the Norsemen is *Varyagŭ* (from *Varengŭ*—Norse
Varingr), and at least as early as the later 10th century these are
clearly distinguished from the *Rusĭ*. The problem is further complicated by the existence of ʿΡῶς in the Crimea in the very beginning of the 9th century. In presence of all these facts it is impossible
to solve the question. The only certainty is that at least in the
later 10th century, *Rusĭ* and *Rusĭskyĭ* were names applied in

32

Russia only to Kiev and its district and that they spread to the rest of what became Russia only as a sign of its conquest by the kings of Kiev.

The question of the origin of the name "Rusi" should not be confused with the question of the part played by the Norsemen in the formation of the Russian kingdom. There can be no doubt that the kingdom of Kiev, like the kingdoms of Novgorod and Polotsk, was founded by Norsemen and that the commercial awakening of the country was due to them. All the earliest kings of Kiev bear Norse names, and the names of their "companions" and of the "Russian" merchants enumerated in the Russo-Greek treaties of 915 and 945 are all Norse. The Norsemen were thus undoubtedly the founders of the Russian dynasty and the kernel of the commercial and military aristocracy whose interest that dynasty represented. But very early a native element penetrated it. The first king of Kiev to bear a Slavonic name, Svyatoslav, was born about 940, and Constantine Porphyrogenitus, writing some twenty years later, though he speaks of the "Russian" language as distinct from Slavonic, uses Slavonic terms to denote "Russian" administrative methods.

On the other hand, the Norsemen were only a first stimulus to the general awakening of the country. The enormous number of archæological finds from the 9th and 10th centuries, which stand in such marked contrast to the preceding centuries, cannot all be put to their credit. This is especially true of the hoards of Arabic coins that are numerous in the central Russian Mesopotamia, while south of Smolensk the style of the finds is generally free from Scandinavian affinities. It is significant too, that the Norsemen have left no trace in place-names and that those of the commercial centres that grew up in the 9th and 10th centuries, are all Slavonic.* Nor was Norse cultural influence deep or lasting. Very few Norse words were introduced into the language, and soon after 1000, all traces of Norse influence disappear entirely.

Though the civilisation of the Norsemen was much higher and more characteristic than that of the Slavs, the absence of any deep Scandinavian impress on early Russia is natural. Finding themselves in new surroundings, the Scandinavians did not stick

*Except perhaps Izborsk (near Pskov), which has been explained as Ísborg.

D

21937

to their home tradition. They easily adapted themselves to the heterogeneous influences that commerce was rapidly introducing into Russia. The funeral of a rich *Rŭs* merchant (obviously a Norseman), witnessed by the Arab traveller, Ibn Fudlan, on the Volga about 920 is strikingly similar to the rites practised by numerous steppe-peoples from the Scythians onwards. As in Normandy and in Sicily, the Norsemen brought with them great appetites and much energy, but no stable tradition. They were a powerful stimulus, a potent crystallising and a still more potent dissolving force. The social and economic revolution of which they were the most apparent, if not the principal agents, produced a civilisation with no roots in pre-Russian Slavdom, but with no roots in Norse tradition either. It may be regarded as a beginning.

2. THE KINGDOM* OF RUSSIA.

THE Russians of Kiev first appear in history about 860, when they made their first spectacular but ineffective attack on Constantinople. Some twenty years later (in 882, according to the Russian chronicler), Oleg, the Norse king of Novgorod, ousted the Norse king of Kiev, and brought under one domination the two ends of the great western waterway.† He remained in Kiev and on his death was succeeded by his kinsman Igor, according to the chronicler, son of King Ryurik of Novgorod, founder of the dynasty of the Kings of Russia.

The kings of Russia were merchant and pirate kings. Originally their only function was to organise the predatory exploitation of the east Slavonic hinterland by the armed merchants of Kiev and of the other cities associated with it. Even the judiciary functions of the king appear to date from a relatively later period; the oldest version of the Russian Law (*Rusĭskaya Pravĭda*), which goes back in substance to the early 10th century, makes no mention of the king or his officers. But in the course of the 10th century the royal powers grew rapidly. Oleg appears as a *primus inter pares* among the armed merchants who signed the treaty with the Greeks in 915. But in the second half of the century the dividing line between the king and the "boyars"‡, the descendants of the armed merchants of earlier times, was already unbridgeable. The king had taken full advantage of his special facilities for exploiting the country and had accumulated wealth that placed him high above his former peers.

*I use the term "king" rather than the usual "prince" to render the old Russian *kunyazĭ* (mod. Russ. *knyaz'*) not so much because it is derived from the Gothic word that corresponds to the English *king*, as because it is invariably rendered into medieval Latin by *rex*.

†The historicity of Oleg's connection with Novgorod has been called into question (cf. Parkhomenko, *At the headwaters of Russian History*, Leningrad 1927 in Russian)). But to reject it seems hypercritical, especially in view of the undoubtedly Norse character of all the proper names in the chronicler's story.

‡The word is found only in Old Russian (*boyarinŭ*, plural *boyare*) and in old Bulgarian (*bolyarinŭ*, *bolyare*) and seems to be of Turkic (Bulgar-Chazar?) origin.

The *locus classicus* on the economical methods of the kings of
Russia is a passage of Constantine Porphyrogenitus' work
De Administrando Imperio and refers to the middle of the 10th
century. Each winter the kings set out on an expedition up the
rivers into the hinterland to levy tribute on the Slavonic population. In the more outlying districts the work was done by the
king's lieutenant who might be his son or kinsman, or a member
of his following (*druzhina*). In the spring, caravans of boats carry-
ing the goods gathered on these expeditions assembled on the
Dniepr near Kiev. Private merchants joined them and the great
caravan sailed down the Dniepr into the Black Sea and to Constantinople. Of the goods exported slaves were the most important.
Next came forest-produce, honey, wax, furs, and hides.

The Slavonic population at first offered some resistance. In
the story of Igor we still find primitive kings or chiefs ruling over
the backwood nation of the Derevlyane (N.W. of Kiev). They
were conquered by Igor's successor, and in later times we find no
more mention of non-urban or non-"Russian" kings.* The rival
Varyag kings of the north were also eliminated. The conquest of
East Slavia by the Russians of Kiev was completed by Vladimir
(Volodimer, 980-1015) and Yaroslav (1019-1054), who fixed the
western limits of the Russian nation. Kiev, under these two
rulers, became the effective capital of all the East Slavonic territory, and conditions were created for the adoption of the name of
Russian by all the peoples ruled by the dynasty of Russia.

The conquest of the western woodland of Cisuralia was an
economic necessity for Kiev, but the theatre of their more spectacular exploits lay on the shores of the Black Sea. Oleg and
Igor repeatedly attacked and threatened Constantinople and
extracted advantageous treaties from the Emperor.† The task of
the kings of Russia was greatly simplified by the peaceful power
of the Chazars who formed an effective barrier against the eastern

*Except, perhaps, the Kings of Bolokhovo (see note on page 45).

†The Arabic historians speak of invasions of the *Rūs* into the Caspian
provinces of Persia (first half of 10th century), but we never know whom the
Arabs mean by *Rūs*, and the Russian chronicler has nothing about these
inroads.

nomads.* But Igor's son, Svyatoslav, destroyed the Chazar empire, subdued the Slavonic tribes that paid tribute to it, and even conquered considerable parts of Ciscaucasia. He then turned westward and conquered Bulgaria, where he tried to establish his residence. But he was ultimately defeated by the Greeks and had to withdraw to Kiev. On his way back, at the rapids of the Dniepr he was attacked and killed by the Patzinaks (Russian *Pechenegi*), a Turkish nation† who had taken advantage of the destruction of the Chazar power and invaded the South Russian steppe—a striking piece of "poetic justice." From this time onwards the steppe became once more the grazing ground of warlike nomads, who formed an increasingly effective barrier between Kiev and the sea. The Russian colony of Tmutorakan, at the mouth of the Kuban, remained the only reminder of Svyatoslav's Black Sea empire.

By the time of Vladimir, the Russian ruling class spoke the Slavonic of Kiev (which henceforward we may call Russian), and were in an increasing proportion adopting Slavonic in preference to Scandinavian names. Culturally, however, Russia was neither Slavonic, nor Scandinavian, but a country with no cultural tradition, and subjected to conflicting influences. The conflict of rival cultures is well symbolised in the Russian Chronicle's tale of how Vladimir invited representatives of the great religions to decide which he should adopt. There came Moslems, Jews, Roman Catholics and Orthodox Greeks. Islam was already dominant with the Volga Bulgars. Judaism was the religion of the recently destroyed Chazar empire. The Latins were rapidly advancing from the west, but were just too late. The conversion of Hungary, Poland, and Sweden had not yet been completed, and the first Latin missionaries reached Kiev some fifteen years after Vladimir had decided in favour of the Greeks, and the Russians adopted Eastern Christianity (988).

Everything, in fact, pointed towards Constantinople. Rome and the centres of Islam were known only from hearsay; Constanti-

---

*The only nomads who passed through the South-Russian steppe in the later 9th century were the Magyars, who were culturally very closely allied to the Chazars : borrowings from a language of the Bulgar-Chazar group form a very important layer of the Hungarian vocabulary.

†The name Pecheneg is not however Turkish, but Circassian.

nople was a regularly visited market. All Kiev's economic ties were with Constantinople and the attraction of Byzantine civilisation was unescapable. On the other hand, subjection to the Eastern Church was politically safe, for though the Emperors regarded as their subjects all nations whose clergy received consecration from the Oecumenical Patriarch, Constantinople was too far and too weak to be an effective suzerain of Kiev, and Russia might be confident she would not share the fate that had only recently befallen Bulgaria. So while Russia became a province of Eastern Christendom, her geographical position prevented her from becoming a dependency of the Eastern Empire. The course of events continued to increase the political and geographical distance, and Byzantine civilisation on Russian soil developed into something essentially different from what it was at home.

RUSSIAN society grew out of the commercial and political revolution of the 9th century and had its active centres in Kiev and the other commercial cities. The pre-Russian society which Russian expansion destroyed and dissolved, disappeared only by degrees. The Derevlyane were conquered in the middle of the 10th century and the Vyatichi preserved their paganism till after 1100. But we know little or nothing about these pre-Russian communities, and can only speak of them starting from theoretical preconceptions. As all our information comes from Russian sources and is connected with the coming of Russian power, history begins for each given district only from the moment it becomes Russian. Nor does our more intimate knowledge of later periods reveal any survival of a pre-Russian, Slavonic type of society. Everywhere we find social conditions going back to a Russian origin. Only in some outlying districts, such as the valleys of the Carpathians, can we expect to discover any survivals of a pre-Russian order.

Russian society was, first of all, strikingly and extremely individualistic. There is no trace of any tribal, or clan organisation, or of any social unit larger than the family, and even the family is less prominent than the isolated individual. Everything is regulated by contract ; the common law admits all kinds of contracts, and the individual is free to sell himself into slavery. The starting point of Russian social history is extreme individualism ; the anti-individualistic features that are so characteristic of Russian society in modern times are the result of later developments.

Russian society fell into two main divisions, an active and a passive. The former included the king and his following, and the free population of the cities, the latter, the slaves (*kholopi*) and the rural population. A large part of the rural population were "all-round" (*obel'ny*) slaves or temporarily enslaved debtors on the estates of the king or of the boyars. There were also free peasants, but whether they possessed land and whether they lived in villages or in isolated homesteads we do not know, nor can we guess as to their numbers. The rural population is sometimes mentioned as being enslaved by kings in their internecine feuds, or as being protected from the nomads by kings better-intentioned, but never as taking any kind of action.

The urban demos of tradesmen and artisans had a much more prominent and active part. They were the junior partners of the kings and boyars, not so successful as those in the acquisition of power and wealth, but essentially allied to them. Above all, they were armed. In times of emergency, when the professional soldiers of the king's *druzhina* were not enough, the city militia or "thousand" (*tysyacha*) marched out against the enemy. In the later 11th century the *tysyacha* becomes the *vechë*, the recognised assembly of the citizens of the large towns. Its first appearance in Kiev is in 1068 when Izyaslav, king of Kiev, after being defeated by the Cumans, was deposed by the city militia, on their return from the field of battle. In the 12th century the Vechë becomes a leading force. It disposes of the throne; it takes part in legislation and in treaties with foreigners.

The upper class appears in two aspects as the "men" (*muzhi*) of the king, and as the territorial magnates. With the growth of the royal power the armed merchants could retain their social importance only by becoming merged in the king's *druzhina*. So they either gave up trade on their own, or descended a degree lower and ceased to be members of the military aristocracy. By the 12th century the connection between the aristocracy of the sword and the aristocracy of trade was severed, and the boyar had become a landowner. It was only in Novgorod where the king (as we shall see), was always a stranger, and in Galicia, where farming seems to have been exceptionally lucrative, that the boyars became an independent political force. It was in Galicia that the only case occurred of a boyar attempting to usurp a king's throne. Apart from this isolated incident the royal dynasty of the descendants of St. Vladimir had an absolute monopoly of sovereign power, forming a caste by themselves.

When a king died all his sons were entitled to a part in his inheritance. The eldest son got his father's capital, "the eldest town," with the greater part of the revenue, but no authority over his brothers. These got other towns in the order of their reputed "seniority" which answered to their economic importance and desirability. These possessions were not further transmitted from father to son, but when an elder brother died the next brother moved to the "eldest town" and all the others moved one place higher. But no king was allowed to get a better place than his father ; so if a king died before his father, his son was for ever disqualified from becoming "eldest king." Such an orphaned king (usually after much fighting) obtained some secondary town where he was allowed to remain and to hand it on to his descendants, without being entitled to take any more part in the all-Russian partitions.

In the course of time the number of such kingdoms grew and, on the other hand, ties began to be formed between the elder cities and their kings. Thus, Chernigov became the heritage of its first king, Svyatoslav, while Kiev strove to remain with the descendants of Vladimir Monomakh. All this led to constant conflicts and feuds and the history of Russia after the death of Yaroslav (1054) is an almost uninterrupted record of wars between his descendants.

An important feature of these dynastic relations is that the family—a man and his sons—is very vital and stable. The authority of a king over his sons is unquestioned, and a son is always regarded as the safest of lieutenants, a real *alter ego*. But if a son never rebels against his father, brothers after their father's death never fail to quarrel; while among more distant kinsmen, treaty and contract are the only effective form of relationship.

The kings regarded their dignity and the rights attached to it as a property, not as a trust or office. The clergy tried to instil in them a sense of duty towards church and country, but only exceptional men, like Vladimir Monomakh, seem to have acquired it.

Much of their income was derived from their judicial functions, for old-Russian law knew no other form of punishment but fines and the kings always received at least as large a fine as the victim of the misdeed. In general, Russian law till the 15th century was purely a law of torts. A misdeed was punishable in so far as it led to injury of the person, or property of another, and punishment was compensation. A different view of crime as a public offence to be suppressed and extirpated, was introduced by the Greek clergy, brought up on Roman-Byzantine law. But they had great difficulty in making it understood to the Russians.

The Russian Law (*Pravĭda Rusĭskaya*) in its later, 11th century version, is still the code of a highly individualistic and commercial society, living in an atmosphere saturated with money and credit. Debts, and penalties for bad debts, occupy the greater part of it. Of course it directly reflects only the society of the commercial towns and of the upper classes, but the countryside, too, was steadily transformed by the economic action of the towns and of the ever multiplying residences.

THE pre-Russian Slavonic nations were merged by the Russian kings into a single nation, which by the end of the 12th century had learned to call itself by the name of its conquerors. The great commercial cities became the centres of territorial divisions which stood in no relation to the pre-Russian division into nations. Kiev, the capital, was in the 11th century a prosperous and well-built town, that elicited the admiration of its Latin visitors and seems to have been larger than any contemporary town of Western Christendom. East of the Dniepr were the cities of Pereyaslavl and Chernigov, which with Kiev, formed the focus of Russian life in the 11th and early 12th century. Pereyaslavl was, in the 11th century, the centre of a rich agricultural district immediately bordering on the grazing grounds of the nomads. Chernigov was the outlet of an enormous territory which, besides the basin of the Desna, included those of the upper Oka and upper Don, and extended northwards almost as far as Moscow. Much of it was opened up in the 11th century and even later, and this made Chernigov a constantly growing political and economic centre. But in the 12th century the north-east of its territory ceased to depend on Chernigov and was drawn into the sphere of influence of Suzdal.

Their proximity to the steppe was a constant menace to Kiev and to Pereyaslavl. Only a few dozen miles south of the capital the river Ros marked the fortified frontier of agricultural and sedentary Russia. Outside the district of Kiev we do not know the exact steppeward limit of Russian occupation. It did not, however, extend much beyond the outer fringe of the forest, and the greater part of the parkland was never occupied. Only isolated forts lay farther south, while beyond the steppe the Russian colony of Tmutorakan, with kings of its own, survived till about 1100.

The Patzinaks, who occupied the steppe after the destruction of Chazaria, greatly weakened by the victories of Vladimir, migrated westwards into Roumania about 1040. They were replaced by the less dangerous Oghuz Turks. When twenty years later these were defeated and driven away by their kinsmen the Cumans, they sought shelter behind the Russian *limes*, and formed a sort of

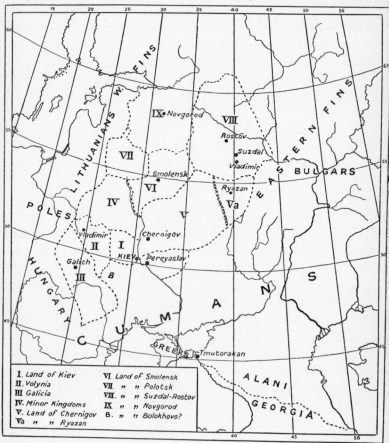

Fig. 5. *Political divisions of the Russian territory. 11th-13th centuries.*

border militia, which in the 12th century played a prominent part in the local politics of Kiev.

The Cumans (Russian *Polovïtsi*, in most eastern languages *Kipchak*), appeared about 1060, inflicted in 1068 a serious defeat on the sons of Yaroslav, and after that, for almost two centuries, remained sole masters of the steppe from the Volga to the Danube. They were divided into a multitude of clans which were ruled by

44

independent khans, but quite able to coalesce in plundering the Russian border. Under the constant pressure of the Cumans the Russian frontier receded towards the fringe of the forest. The city of Pereyaslavl, situated where forest and parkland meet, became, in the 12th century, a mere outpost of Kiev, its territory being abandoned to the nomads. What was more important, the Cumans were now masters of the waterway of the lower Dniepr, cutting off Kiev from the Black Sea and Constantinople, and thus undermining the very basis of its economic life. Only its accumulated importance as the capital preserved it from decline for about a century.

Westward, beyond the immediate sphere of influence of the three cities* lay Volynia and Galicia, rich agricultural countries, the latter extending to the Carpathians and to the Vistula. Their commercial importance too was great, for through them lay the main overland route into Hungary and Germany. They had no one urban centre but a number of thriving towns, of which, in the 12th century, Vladimir and Galich (Halich) were the most important.

The country north of Volynia, the marshy basin of the Pripet and the upper valley of the Niemen, was something of a backwater. The local dynasties played no part in general politics. When, towards 1200, the Lithuanians emerged out of their woods and began their inroads into Russian territory, the petty kingdoms of the Niemen basin could oppose no resistance, and it was largely by their absorption that the Lithuanian power grew into greatness.

The main northern artery was the great waterway connecting Kiev with Novgorod, the metropolis of the north. As long as Norse energy was active, Novgorod remained a constant rival of Kiev. Three times Kiev was conquered by the kings of Novgorod (Oleg in 882, Vladimir in 980, Yaroslav in 1019), each time with the support of Norsemen. After the decline of Scandinavian

---

*South-west of Kiev, in the vicinity of the modern Berdichev lay the and of Bolokhovo, a somewhat mysterious district of which we know very little. It seems to have had a population of "pre-Russian" Slavs governed by their own kings. In the 13th century they were the allies of the Tartars against the kings of Galicia.

interest in Russia its political importance still remained immense and in the 11th and 12th centuries the rulers of Kiev saw to it that Novgorod was in the hands of a reliable lieutenant, usually a son of the king of Kiev. This prevented the city from acquiring a dynasty of its own, and ultimately favoured the development of republican institutions. The rural territory of Novgorod was thinly peopled, and agriculturally very poor. Its prosperity was purely commercial, based on its central situation, between Kiev, the Volga, the Baltic and the fur-bearing north-east.

About half-way between Kiev and Novgorod lay Smolensk, at the junction of routes to the Baltic and to the upper Volga country. In the 12th century it promised to be the successor of Kiev, as the central city of Russia. Polotsk on the Duna, the old metropolis of what is now northern White Russia, was eclipsed by the growth of Smolensk. It early became the possession of a disinherited branch of Vladimir's family, ceased to play any direct part in all-Russian politics and degenerated into a backwater.

The upper basin of the Volga began to receive Slavonic immigrants before the Russian conquest, but even in the 11th century it still contained remnants of its earlier Finno-Ugrian population. The country was commercially important as lying on the road from Novgorod to the lower Volga, but the location of its chief towns shows that this thoroughfare was of less importance than the exploitation of the country itself. For both Rostov, which was created into a bishopric by Vladimir, and Suzdal, which in the 12th century became the political capital and the residence of a king, lie inside the Volga-Oka Mesopotamia, off the main route. Agriculture played as great a part here as in any other part of Russia, and in the 11th and 12th centuries, together with Volynia and Galicia, the land of Suzdal was economically the most progressive district of the whole country.

Throughout the Kiev period, Russian colonisation advanced slowly in a northern and north-eastern direction meeting with little resistance from the sparse Finno-Ugrian population. This was some compensation for loss of territory in the South. There were, however, no migrations on a large scale, only slow penetration into alien land from neighbouring Russian districts, or

ransplantation of the parkland population harassed by the
omad into unoccupied parts of the forest fringe, where the
occupation of the land was still very loose, and there were vast
xpanses of forest waiting to be cleared.

As for the Baltic land situated west of Novgorod, Pskov and
Polotsk, there were only desultory attempts to bring it under
Russian domination. The population here was denser, more
agricultural and more advanced. The Estonians, Livonians and
Letts remained Pagans and outside Russian influence. When,
about 1200, the German knights began their systematic conquest
f the country, they could proceed, unimpeded not only by the
decadent kingdom of Polotsk but even by the powerful Novgorod.

YAROSLAV (1054), was the last king of Kiev to rule over the whole of the country. The last third of the 11th century is filled with uninterrupted feuds. Vladimir Monomakh (died 1125), a king according to the ideal of the élite of the time, succeeded, a the congresses of 1096 and 1100, in establishing a general dynastic peace. As long as he and his son Mstislav (died 1132) were alive their prestige and influence prevented the kings from fighting among themselves, and Russia showed a united front against the Cumans. But with the death of Mstislav the period of peace ended The leading kings of the time were either warriors whose one ambition was to win victories, over whom they did not mind, or acquisitive *Realpolitiker* who took little interest in Kiev and all Russian politics, but were keen on the aggrandizement of their own particular kingdoms. To the former type belonged most of the kings of the houses of Chernigov and Smolensk, to the latter those of Suzdal and Galicia. The latter two powers grew apace Their growth was obviously dangerous to Russian unity, for Galicia was commercially as closely related to Hungary and Poland, Suzdal to Bulgar and the Caucasus, as either was to Kiev. The house of Smolensk alone was, by its geographical position suited to replace Kiev, but most of its members were light-minded or romantic adventurers, and Smolensk missed the part it might have played.

The kings of Galicia laboured under the handicap of having to do with an exceptionally riotous and independent aristocracy. Yaroslav Osmomysl ("the Eight-witted," died 1189) was a powerful ruler with more than usually autocratic habits, but even he had sometimes to confess himself beaten by his boyars. Roman, king of Volynia, who after Yaroslav's childless death became also king of Galicia, went farther than any contemporary in asserting his autocracy. He is the first Russian ruler to whom the chronicler applies the title of Autocrat (i.e., Imperator). But he died leaving a minor and the Galician power once more received a set-back.

The creator of the Suzdal power was Andrew of Bogolyuby 1174), who transferred his capital to the newly-founded town f Vladimir on the Klyazma, where he could rule unhampered y tradition and by the people of the large cities. In 1169 his army ook and sacked Kiev, but Andrew, while assuming the title of Great King, refused to leave Vladimir for the Southern metropolis, which he contemptuously gave to a junior kinsman. These vents mark the definite loss by Kiev of its primacy. Andrew's vork was carried on by his brother Vsevolod (1212), the most owerful king of his time. Besides his own extensive territory of uzdal, he was usually able to control Novgorod, while the kings f Ryazan and Murom entered with him on treaties of vassalage. But after his death his kingdom was split up between his numerous ons, and Russia was as divided as ever.

The 11th and 12th centuries were a period of agricultural proress. But this was merely an extension to new land (mainly to noccupied gaps inside the old territory) of the old semi-nomadic griculture which exploited a plot of ground till it was exhausted, nd then began another.

The growth of agriculture was a force that militated against nity. The Russian unity was based on commerce, and on the redatory exploitation of the hinterland by an organised commercial minority, established in a small number of interdependent rban centres. The commodities exported were the produce of var (slaves), of the chase (furs and hides) and of collecting wild honey and wax). For agricultural produce there was no xternal market, only an internal market on a limited scale Novgorod lived on grain brought from the Suzdal country). The rowth of agricultural production was due to the growth of conumption on the spot, and meant the extension of natural economy. ncrease of consumption was due to the increase of population, specially to the rapid increase of the upper and non-productive lasses—the direct result of the multiplication of kings and royal esidences. This decentralisation, due to the decreasingly commerial character of production, would in itself have been enough to issolve the none too solid empire of Yaroslav into a group of utually independent districts. It was further hastened by the ecline of Kiev, and by the divergent orientation of what com-

merce there was left towards foreign markets. Towards the end of
the Kiev period money became very rare in Russia, and com
merce ceased to be a dominating force, except in Novgorod.

In its first stages the multiplication of kings strengthened th
cities and their *vechë*, for it was obvious that a king who only con
trolled the district of Kiev was easier to cope with than a kin
who controlled all the land from Novgorod to Galicia. But as wit
the decline of commerce the cities declined too, the triumph of th
vechë, except in Novgorod, was short-lived. As Russia became
rural country, the kings became mere rural barons, with th
exception of those few who owned the remaining urban centre
and who could gradually impose their authority on the other.
The process of subjection of minor to major kings started in th
late 12th century and was practised with particular success b
Vsevolod of Suzdal. But these centripetal processes were infinitel
weaker than the tremendous centrifugal forces which reach thei
highwater-mark in the 13th century, when the dissolving actio
of economic factors was accelerated by external events—the rise o
the Lithuanian power and the invasion of the Tartars in 1238-4
The latter date may be taken to mark the moment when Russi
definitely ceases to exist as a political unity, and dissolves into tw
main groups of units, both of them at first very loose—the nortl
east, the future Muscovy and the south-west—White Russia an
Ukraina.

6. THE CHURCH AND CIVILISATION; RUSSIA AND HER NEIGHBOURS.

THE pagan Russians had no vital cultural tradition of their own. Their civilisation was a changing amalgam of Norse, Oriental, Byzantine, and native Slavonic elements. The kings of Kiev began developing an organised pagan cult only on the eve of their conversion to Christianity. Of the gods whose idols are reported to have been erected by Vladimir when still a pagan, some were of local Slavonic origin, but the chief god, Perun, in spite of his Slavonic name, was an obvious avatar of Thor. The only arts of the pagan times we know of are the gold and silver ornaments found in graves. North of a line passing south of Polotsk, Smolensk and Murom, the style of the ornaments is distinctly Norse. Farther south it is a mixture of Byzantine and Chazaro-Oriental elements.

Byzantine influence grew steadily throughout the 10th century. Christianity was introduced into Kiev many years before the conversion of Vladimir. Queen Olga, the widow of Igor and mother of Svyatoslav, travelled to Constantinople to be christened by the Emperor in person. During Vladimir's short enthusiasm for idolatry there were Christians in Kiev who suffered a martyr's death.

When Russia became Christian she *eo ipso* became the inheritor of the Christian beginnings of the Balkan Slavs. The gradual conversion of the Southern Slavs to Orthodox Christianity had begun soon after their settlement in the Balkan peninsula, but only took an organised form in the 9th century. It was powerfully promoted by Sts. Cyril and Methodius, two Greek brothers from Salonika, who composed a Slavonic alphabet* and translated the liturgies and Scriptures into Slavonic. The language used by them was based on a Bulgarian dialect of south Macedonia. The translation was originally intended for Moravians, not for Bulgarians, and was made at the request of a Moravian king. But it was adopted by the Bulgarian and the other Orthodox Slavs

*The alphabet invented by Sts. Cyril and Methodius was the *glagolitsa*, still used by some Roman Catholic Slavs of Dalmatia. The alphabet that now bears the name of St. Cyril, the *Kirilitsa*, is a later adaptation of 10th century Greek uncials to the phonological elements of the *glagolitsa*.

of the Balkans, and in a slightly modified form became the official and literary language of the first Bulgarian Empire. Though based on a definite local dialect, "Church-Slavonic" (as the language is usually called) was not itself a local dialect, but the common cultural language of all those Slavs who, having adhered to the Eastern Church, could use Slavonic to translate the Scripture and liturgies from the Greek. As late as the 11th century the Slavonic languages were sufficiently one for the language of Salonika to sound to all Slavs, not as a foreign tongue, but as a standardised form of their own vernacular. So when Russia adopted Christianity, "Church-Slavonic" was naturally adopted as the language of the Church.

The Russian Church was, of course, a copy of the Greek. Russia was an ecclesiastical province of the Patriarchate of Constantinople. It had at its head a Metropolitan appointed by the Patriarch and almost invariably a Greek. The other Bishops, on the contrary, very soon became the nominees of the local kings and were invariably Russian. The bishoprics were few and their immense territories stood in sharp contrast to the small city bishoprics of the Eastern Empire.

The fact that the Metropolitans were Greeks and their nomination independent of the king's pleasure gave them an authority and an independence which otherwise would not have been theirs and placed them above the turmoil of Russian feuds. From the start the Church became an autonomous society within the secular society, not much affected by, but greatly influencing the latter. The bishops possessed jurisdiction over all the clergy and all persons who had anything to do with the Church, as well as over all such crimes as sorcery, heresy, marriage in forbidden degrees of kinship, that were not crimes in the eye of the Russian law, which recognised no crimes but torts. The bishops, the monasteries and the clergy of the collegiate churches received considerable endowments in land, tithes and other revenues, for the kings and other rich men, anxious for the welfare of their souls were lavish in gifts to the Church. Monasteries were founded by the kings and rich people, but under Vladimir and Yaroslav their importance was insignificant, and the secular clergy of the towns were more prominent than the monks. Only in the middle of the

11th century the hermits Antony and Theodosius founded the great ascetic Pechersky monastery of Kiev, which soon became the spiritual metropolis of the Russian Church, the nursery of Bishops and the chief cultural centre of Russia. Henceforward the Russian Church became even more predominantly monastic than the Greek.

Not all the elements of Byzantine culture were transmitted to Russia, but only those that were connected with and necessary for the working of the Church. The Church brought Canon and Roman Byzantine law (the latter necessary for its secular jurisdiction) and the Roman-Biblical idea of God-ordained monarchy, but it did not bring the classical culture of the Greeks, nor their scientific tradition. Traces of acquaintance with the pre-Christian Greek tradition in Russian writings are quite isolated. The range of secular knowledge that opened itself to the Russians was that of the lower strata of Byzantine society. This was largely due to Slavonic becoming the liturgic and literary language of Russia, which exempted the Russian clerics from learning Greek.

In general, education was rare, and limited to the higher urban clergy and to a few members of the dynasty and of the upper classes. There were no schools. The liberal arts were almost unknown, even though there are isolated translations of grammatical and rhetorical texts, and the works of some ecclesiastical writers betray a knowledge of Greek rhetorical devices, and make clever and imaginative use of them.

But the Byzantine outlook early began to crystallize into stable and characteristic forms, and Russian society began to show an inclination towards traditionalism, in striking contrast to the pagan Russia of the 10th century. The foundations of the ritual and conservative Muscovite mentality were laid by the clergy of Kiev.

The Byzantine Christian outlook had to fight for predominance with the military and essentially pre-Christian outlook of the king's *druzhina*. The conflict of the two mentalities is clearly apparent in the two principal literary productions of early Russia, the Russian Chronicle and the poem of the *Campaign of Igor*.* The

*The best account of the literature of the Kiev period is contained in Professor M. Hrushevskyï's *History of Ukrainian Literature* Vols. 2 and 3, Lvov 1923 in Ukrainian).

oldest chronicle that has come down to us was compiled towards
1100 by a monk of the Pechersky monastery. It embodies many
older and heterogeneous elements, but in its essential part it is
a typical product of the Byzantine and Christian outlook. The
chronicler regards all events as the direct action of Providence,
all unusual phenomena as portents, and all calamities as God's
vengeance for the wickedness of kings or subjects. He has a very
definite view as to the duties of a king, who must be generous and
munificent to the monasteries, not too ambitious or acquisitive,
refrain from fratricidal strife and defend the country against the
heathen nomads of the steppe. The same outlook inspires the
greater part of the later chronicles, but the 12th century chronicle
of Kiev includes parts written in a very different spirit. Thus, in
the account of the reign of Izyaslav II (1146-54) that king is
idealised as a great warrior whose one ambition was military
renown, no matter whether won in battles against the heathen
or against his own brethren. These parts are obviously not by a
monkish hand. The idea of all-Russian patriotism, that was
preached by the clergy, is very prominent also in the *Campaign of
Igor*, but stripped of all explicitly Christian associations, and united
with an intenser martial spirit than even the annals of Izyaslav II.
The poem (which is not in verse, but in complicated rhythmic
prose), commemorates the unsuccessful campaign against the
Cumans of Igor, a secondary king of the house of Chernigov
which took place in 1185. The poem, which was written very
soon after the event, is the masterpiece of old Russian literature, and a great masterpiece apart from all comparisons. The
author alludes to the existence in "old times" of some kind
of oral court poetry, and even quotes passages from an old court
poet, Bayan (who is not mentioned anywhere else). In places he
appears to imitate Bayan's manner, but he is a man of letters, full
of literary culture and a Byzantine tradition transformed by an
intensely personal temperament is the background of the poem.*
It is the only work of its kind to have come down to us, but isolated
fragments of comparable style are found here and there in other

---

*There are also striking, but unexplained similarities with late Anglo
Saxon poetry (esp. *Judith*, and the *Battle of Maldon*). Norse court poetry
which might have been a concievable link, is utterly unlike the Russian poem

SUZDAL ARCHITECTURE.
Church of Pokrov on the Nerl, near Vladimir on the Klyazma.
End of 12th century.

contexts. The poem was still quoted and imitated in the 14th and 15th centuries.

The material arts were even more entirely dominated by Byzantine example than literature. Architecture, painting and mosaics remained for a long time in the hands of Byzantine artists. The churches of Kiev and Chernigov and their frescoes and mosaics stand on a very high level and belong to the most important Byzantine achievements of the period. Outside these cities stone churches were rare and very few have survived. Painting remained in Greek hands till the end of the period, but the architecture of Suzdal and Novgorod begins to show a notable originality after the middle of the 12th century. The churches of Suzdal, Vladimir and Yuriev Polskoy, erected between 1160 and 1240 are among the finest and most perfect creations of old Russian art. They exhibit many foreign affinities. Their style is related to that of the contemporary churches of Georgia and Armenia, while the stone they are built of was quarried in the Urals—significant reflections of the importance of Suzdal's connection with the middle Volga and the land reached by that way. But western affinities are also present (especially with a group of churches in southwest France—the Périgueux group) which have not yet been satisfactorily explained, and in Suzdal German masons were reputed the best of their trade. The churches of Novgorod of the same period are the predecessors of a style that reached its full development in the following century.

———

Most of Russia's neighbours were either heretics or heathens. Except the Eastern Empire the only Orthodox nations with whom she stood in any contact were Georgia, which in spite of its relations with Suzdal was, after all, very far off, and Bulgaria, which during the greater part of the period was suffering a total political and cultural eclipse, and could not compete with Russia for the leadership of Orthodox Slavdom.

At the separation of the churches in 1057 Russia, as a province of the Oecumenical Patriarch, remained with Greece. A religious barrier was thus erected between her and the West. It grew up by degrees. As late as 1100 the Russian Abbot Daniel in his pilgrimage to Jerusalem speaks of the Franks with no shade of religious hostility, but by the end of the 12th century it was complete and impenetrable. When, soon after 1200, the German knights in their conquest of Livonia came in touch with the Russians of Polotsk and Novgorod they met like two alien and hostile worlds.

Relations with the Muhammadan and pagan East were dominated by the religious difference between Christian and miscreant. After the fall of Chazária the Russians had no non-Christian neighbour they could regard with any sense of cultural inferiority. The relations between Suzdal and the Muhammadan Bulgar were alternately commercial and hostile, and there must have been much mutual influence in the sphere of material culture, for the commercial foundations of the two countries were similar. But we see no trace of strictly cultural intercourse. The Cumans were divided from the Russians by economic and social as well as cultural differences. As aggressive nomads they were the natural enemies of the agriculturist, and as pagans they were abominable to the Church. The Church, supported by the urban classes, considered it to be the principal duty of the Russian kings to fight the Cumans, but the less patriotic kings thought differently. They were constantly inviting Cuman armies to join them against their cousins, and intermarried freely with Cumanian dynasties. A sort of international military society began to grow on both sides of the border, wiping out the religious and national differences. We find unmistakable traces of sympathetic acquaintance with Cumanian heroic tradition in the more military parts of the Chronicle. Towards the end of the period, Cumanian Khans begin to be converted to Christianity. We cannot guess how far this *rapprochement* of Russia and Cumans would have gone without the intervention of the Tartars. As it is, the remains of the Cumans were partly absorbed by the invaders, partly fled westward and became merged in the Hungarian nation.

Chapter III

WHITE RUSSIA AND UKRAINA
(XIIIth—XVIIIth Centuries)

1. THE TWO WEST RUSSIAN NATIONS.

2. GALICIAN AND MOLDAVIAN PERIODS IN UKRAINA.

3. THE GRAND DUCHY OF LITHUANIA AND RUSSIA.

4. POLISH RULE IN UKRAINA, AND THE RISE OF THE KOZAKS.

5. UKRAINIAN CIVILISATION.

6. THE WHITE RUSSIANS AFTER THE UNION OF LUBLIN.

7. THE JEWS.

In the 13th century the primitive Russian nation dissolved into a number of more or less loosely connected groups, which began to crystallize round new political centres. The north-eastern groups, by the end of the 15th century, were hammered together to form the Muscovite Empire. The south-western gravitated towards the western centres of Lithuania and Poland and, with the exception of small sections absorbed by Hungary and Moldavia, were ultimately merged in the Kingdom of Poland. By the time Muscovy started her policy of imperial expansion, the West Russians had become sufficiently alien to be incapable of assimilation to the Muscovite Russian type. They had, in fact, become distinct nations. Ethnological and historical facts preventing their fusion into a single West Russian nation, they crystallised round two centres and formed two nations—the Ukrainian and the White Russian.

The mutual relation of the Great Russians (or Muscovites), the Ukrainians and the White Russians is a thorny subject, difficult of satisfactory solution. It has been complicated on the one hand by the current Central and East-European conception of nationality as a permanent, complete and watertight unity; and on the other by political passions and the memories of oppression and injustice. It is further complicated by the absence of any unimpeachable distinctive appellation for each of the three nations The traditional name for all is Russian (*russky*). It was generally used by members of all three nations, from the earliest times till quite recently, when it became too closely associated with Great Russian Imperialism and "russification" to remain acceptable to Ukrainians and White Russians. The alternative names for the North-East Russians are "Muscovite" and "Great Russian"—but the former, in its Ukrainian and Polish form (*moskal*), has received a somewhat derogatory meaning, while the latter is purely artificial and hardly used except by philologists and statisticians. So the Ukrainians (and the Poles, in whose language

59

ruski means West Russian), have solved the question by forming from the Great Russian name of Russia—*Rossiya*, the rather artificial adjective *rossyïs'kyï* (Polish *rosyjski*).

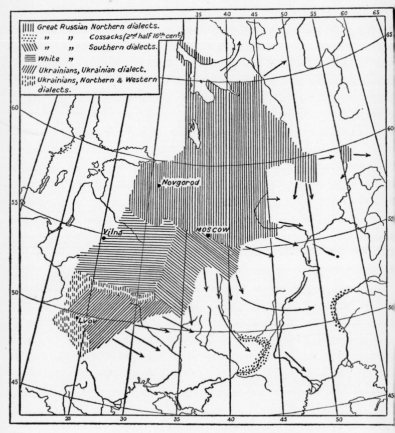

Fig. 6. Russian ethnical groups c. 1550.

"White Russian" is as artificial as "Great Russian," and only came into general usage in the 19th century. As opposed to the other Russian groups, the White Russians (who are essentially the Russians of the Duchy of Lithuania), called themselves and were called Lithuanians, but with the revival of the real Lithuanians as a nation this has become an obvious absurdity.

"Ukrainian" was at first a purely territorial designation, the word Ukraina meaning "frontier land," "march," and being applied to many Russian borderlands. In the 16th century it was used in particular of the parkland belt on both sides of the Dniepr, and as it was here that Ukrainian political consciousness found its fullest expression, the name of Ukraina became associated with national aspirations. But it was only in the 19th century that it was finally chosen by the cultural leaders of the people as a designation for the whole territory and only within the present generation that it has become universally current. The alternative name of "Ruthenian" (Polish *rusin*) was used by the Poles, by the Roman Church and by the Austrian administration, but was never accepted by the people themselves. "Little Russia" and "Little Russian" (*Malorossiya* and *maloross*) were used officially of the autonomous Ukrainian territory in the 17th-18th centuries and passed into official Russian to designate the whole Ukrainian people. The names were, however, resented by the Ukrainians as redolent of Muscovite imperialism and to-day may be used only by militant Great Russian chauvinists who deny the existence of any such thing as an Ukrainian nation.

The official appellations of the three nations are to-day Russian, White Russian (*Belorussky*) and Ukrainian. I will use the latter two without further qualification and for all periods from the 13th century onwards, but I will replace the former by "Great Russian" whenever there can be any ground for misunderstanding.

The distinctness of the Russian nations partly originated in very old, pre-Russian, ethnical differences, but is partly due to historical developments that do not go back earlier than the 12th or 13th century. The relative part played by early and later elements is not the same in the case of each of the three nations. The difference between Great Russian and Ukrainian is very largely of pre-Russian and early-Russian origin. The White Russians are, geographically and ethnologically, a transition between the two other nations; their national distinctness is the produce of medieval historical developments.

Between the nations into which the eastern Slavs of the pre-Russian period were divided, and the Russian nations of to-day, no direct relationship can be established. The most that can be said is that certain differences of dialect appear roughly to coincide with what we may take to have been some of the old international boundaries. From the linguistic point of view all the East Slavonic dialects before the 12th century must unquestionably be regarded as one language. But archæology has shown that Old Russia had two centres of attraction—Novgorod in the north, with its influence reaching as far as Smolensk, and Kiev in the south. The oldest Russian documents present dialectical differences, indicating a dividing line roughly coinciding with the line established by archæology. Of the ethnological characteristics that distinguish the Great Russians from the Ukrainians, some, at least go back to early-Russian or pre-Russian times. Thus the 11th century chronicler speaks of the Russian steam bath, which is unknown to the Ukrainians, as of a Novgorodian custom that seemed ridiculous to a man of Kiev. Other features of material culture that divide the Great Russian from the Ukrainian and relate him to his Finno-Ugrian (and Lithuanian) neighbours may also reflect very old cultural divisions. The Ukrainian ethnical territory such as it formed itself by the 16th-17th centuries does not, however, include all the former area of Kiev's immediate influence. The latter, besides territory which subsequently became Ukrainian, included the south of White Russia (basin of the Pripet, Sozh, Berezina and Niemen), as well as all the basin of the Desna and Seym, and parts of the upper Don and Oka basin, which became Muscovite only about 1500.

The White Russian unit cannot be related in this way to any early Russian or pre-Russian cultural entity. It is a product of political history, and coincides with the boundaries of the Duchy of Lithuania, as finally constituted. The ancestors of the White Russians were the South Russian nation of the Dregovichi, the equally South Russian Radimichi, and the characteristically North Russian Krivichi of Polotsk. The White Russian language has very few phonetical or grammatical features that are not to be found in either Ukrainian or Great Russian, and those it has are recent innovations. Viewed from a purely "linguistic" (i.e., phonetical and morphological) standpoint, White Russian is little more than a group of Great Russian dialects with, towards the south-west, a gradual transition to Ukrainian. But it vocabulary is much more close to Ukrainian, and permeated with Polish influence. It is this combination of features that constitutes its, rather unapparent, originality.

The phonetic system of Ukrainian is, on the contrary, strikingly original and Ukrainian speech is as different from Great Russian as broad Scots is from southern English. But most of these phonetic features are demonstrably innovations and did not come into existence before the 12th-14th centuries. Only a few of them reflect dialectical differences that existed in early Russian times, and these have served to establish the correspondence between the archæological and the linguistic bipartition of early Russia.

The Ukrainians never formed a political unity. Their active national consciousness is due to movements which found only imperfect expression in outward political organisation. Only a section of what we now call the Ukrainian nation played an active role in its formation. We must consequently distinguish between a wider, ethnological, and a narrow, political meaning, of the word "Ukrainian." This difference between an active and central majority and an outer string of passive ethnical minorities is reflected in the distribution of Ukrainian dialects. Ukrainian proper, the "Ukrainian dialect of the Ukrainian language," is spoken in the outer forest fringe and in the parkland from the environs of Lvov (Lemberg) to the eastern limits of Ukraina and in all places colonised by natives of this belt. A line drawn from Kiev to Lvov may be regarded as the central axis of this dialect before its steppeward expansion. It coincides with the political and cultural axis of medieval (13th-16th centuries) Ukraina. A striking feature of the "Ukrainian dialect" is its extraordinary uniformity, so that the speech of Lvov, Kharkov and Krasnodar are (apart from recent differences in their vocabulary) practically identical. Such linguistic uniformity is, of course, explained by recent expansion from a relatively small centre and gives the Ukrainian people a degree of cohesion which might not have been deduced from its chequered and divided history for the last three centuries. But west and north of Ukraina proper, in the Carpathians (from Bukovina to the upper San) and in the interior of the forest zone (from the San to the Desna), dialects are spoken of a divergent type which in some cases are not much more akin to standard Ukrainian than to standard Russian. Most of these districts played no active part in the building of Ukrainian nationality and for the most part have only a dim sense of being Ukrainian, rather than "Russian in general."

2. GALICIAN AND MOLDAVIAN PERIODS IN UKRAINA.

(XIIIth-XIVth Centuries).

At the time of the Tartar invasion the political and economic centre of the future Ukrainian territory was in the politically united lands of Galicia and Volynia. Fertile, and situated on the great commercial route from Central Europe to the Black Sea, Galicia had a denser rural population and a greater number of towns than any other part of the Russian territory. It had to recognise Tartar supremacy, but it stood in close contact with its western neighbours too, especially with Hungary, and at one time Daniel of Galicia hoped to make use of these connections against the Tartars. Innocent IV sent him a king's crown, hoping to induce him to enter the Roman fold. Seeing that no real help was forthcoming, Daniel finished by refusing to pay homage to Rome, but accepted the Pope's gift of the crown, and the style of king (in Russian *korol*) of Galicia and Wlodimiria (i.e. Volynia).

Daniel and his successors were great church-builders, and the "Volynian chronicle" that relates their history is one of the most original and remarkable literary productions of old Russia. But its entries cease about 1293 and the ensuing half century is the darkest period in the history of any part of Russia. By this time Galicia was dangerously isolated from all other Russian centres. Her close connections with the Latin West, as long as they did not lead to cultural amalgamation, were a danger rather than a blessing. This seems to have been realised by the Galician aristocracy, and when, in the middle of the 14th century the growing power of Poland began to extend its hands towards Galicia, they opposed no resistance. The final incorporation of Galicia in Poland (1347) was followed by the very rapid polonisation and romanisation of the boyar families, many of them entering the front ranks of the Polish nobility. But the common people of the towns and country preserved their Orthodox faith and their Russian nationality.

About the time of the Polish annexation of Galicia most of the other Ukrainian lands (including Volynia) became feudatory parts of Lithuania, but their history is exceedingly dark till late into the 15th century, and the whole period would be a blank in the history of Ukrainian civilisation were it not for the Roumanian principality of Moldavia. The rise of the Roumanians coincided with the decline of Galicia. Moldavia absorbed much previously Galician territory with its Russian population. Part of the latter, in the course of centuries, amalgamated with the newcomers while part still retains its Ukrainian speech (north Bukovina and district of Hotin). But the Roumanians themselves expanded in all directions, some of them going north, while others settled in the plain. There was much interpenetration and mutual influence between the two peoples, and the Ukrainian population of the Carpathians carries much Roumanian blood.

The Roumanians were Orthodox and used Church-Slavonic for their cultural language. In the second half of the 14th century and in the early 15th, Moldavia was the chief cultural centre of the Ukrainian lands and almost the only Ukrainian documents of the period come from Moldavia. Through Moldavia direct contact was kept up with Bulgaria and Serbia, which explains the strong south Slavonic influence in Ukraina during the period.*

---

*Here is the place to mention " Hungarian Russia " (Uhorska Rus'). Its origin is somewhat obscure. There is no conclusive evidence that the Russian population of the Hungarian side of the Carpathians was already there before the 12th century, or that the country was ever part of the Russian Kingdom. Subsequent migrations from Galicia are testified to by Hungarian sources. The history of the country is closely linked with that of Hungary. As the dialect is archaic and rather different from Ukrainian proper the people have hardly been reached by Ukrainian consciousness, but remained vaguely Russian. Union with Rome was imposed on them by the Hungarians. To-day the country forms a (nominally autonomous) province of Czechoslovakia.

3. THE GRAND DUCHY OF LITHUANIA AND RUSSIA.*

In the beginning of the 13th century the Lithuanians emerged, rather suddenly, out of their primitive and peaceful savagery. By 1250 their raids reached as far as Novgorod, Moscow and Kiev. At first their energy remained purely destructive. But Duke Mindowh (died 1263) was already a political organiser along lines familiar to the Russians. His Duchy, which lay in the hilly country of the middle Niemen and of its eastern tributaries, comprised Russian as well as Lithuanian territory. Of its three principal towns, Troki alone was purely Lithuanian, Nowhorodok (Nowo-gròdek) was Russian, and Vilna stood on the dividing line between the two races. The state called itself the Grand Duchy of Lithuania and Russia ("Magnus Ducatus Lituaniæ et Russiæ"). Its ruling class consisted of pagan Lithuanians and Orthodox Russians. The dynasty and the Lithuanian aristocracy stuck to their paganism and to their nationality, but the Lithuanian language was never written till after the end of Lithuanian independence. The official language of the Duchy was White Russian, first alone, afterwards concurrently with Latin.

The Lithuanian power spread rapidly and continuously and by the end of the 14th century numerous lands, besides the original duchy, owed homage to the Duke. Except Samogitia, inhabited by Lithuanians, all these new lands were Russian. They included all that is now White Russia (with Smolensk), the Ukrainian lands except Galicia, and all the now Great Russian lands of the Desna, with parts of the upper Oka basin. All these lands retained their autonomy. In some cases the Duke became their direct lord, but in others they retained their old feudal lords—the descendants of Russian kings—or were given as fiefs to members of the Ducal dynasty.

The acme of Lithuanian power was reached in the reign of Vitowt (Witold, 1388-1430). At the time of his accession the power

*See especially *Outline of the History of the Lithuano-Russian State to 1569*, by Lvubavsky, Moscow, 1910 (in Russian).

of the Tartars was suffering an eclipse. All the agricultural neighbours of the steppe from Moscow and Ryazan to Moldavia and Wallachia profited by this to push a steady offensive steppewards.

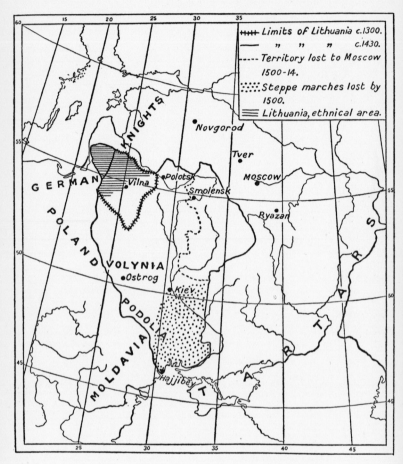

Fig. 7. Duchy of Lithuania, 13th–16th centuries.

Vitowt's Lithuania was by far the strongest of these powers, and its steppe frontier by far the longest. The Lithuanian advance was conducted on a vast scale. Tartar princes of the parkland recognised Lithuanian supremacy. The Crimea was invaded, and Tartars and Karaite Jews brought home and settled at Troki and other places where they still form small but stable communities. The victorious eastward progress of Vitowt was stopped by the defeat of his army by a lieutenant of Tamerlane on the Vorsklo (1399). But the steppe and Black Sea coast between the Dniepr and the Dniestr remained Lithuanian, and even began to show signs of agricultural development. In the early years of the 15th century for the first time since Scythian times, cargoes of grain were shipped from Hajjibey (Odessa), to Constantinople. At the same time Lithuanian expansion continued into Russian territory, and Novgorod and Tver were assisted against Moscow, while in the north-west a victorious resistance was opposed to the *Drang nach Osten* of the German knights of Prussia and Livonia (battle of Grünwald, or Tannenberg, 1411).

The growth of Lithuanian imperialism was complicated by the neighbourhood of Poland. That country had become a great power. Her numerous military gentry were driven by an appetite for expansion that could not be satisfied within the narrow limits of the kingdom. This led to the annexation of Galicia, and produced a constant flow of Polish gentry into the relatively sparsely settled Russian provinces of Lithuania, which seemed their natural prey. With the gentry came the priests. Members of the Lithuanian dynasty and aristocracy, who were just beginning to assume Orthodoxy, were now much more easily converted to Rome. In the meantime the royal house of Poland came to an end and the Polish statesmen conceived the idea of incorporating Lithuania with Poland by marrying Duke Yahaylo (Jagiello) to the heiress of the Polish throne and making him King of Poland (1386). Though Yahaylo was forced to resign the Ducal throne to his cousin Vitowt, the latter had to recognise himself his vassal, and a certain unity resulted. The Polish gentry and the Lithuanian aristocracy obtained equal rights in each other's country, an arrangement obviously advantageous to the more numerous and more pushing Poles. Roman Catholicism was confirmed the State religion of Lithuania. The two countries, had, henceforward, one dynasty, though the reigning sovereign was not always the same.

The clause which excluded all but Roman Catholic nobles from the exercise of political rights was abrogated after a rising of the

Orthodox magnates. Nevertheless, Roman influence grew in organisation and culture, aided by the constant influx of Polish gentry and by the great superiority of the Roman clergy. The Lithuanians proper, from the Ducal dynasty to the peasants, were converted to Romanism. The Russian peasants and townspeople, and the greater part of the Russian aristocracy and their military vassals remained Orthodox. But the Catholics were far more vigorous and retained a paramount influence. The national consciousness of "Lithuania-and-Russia" never became Russian, and inevitably tended to be more and more orientated towards Poland.

Though the Dukes of Lithuania ruled over a vaster territory than any Russian prince since Yaroslav, their power was of a limited nature. The aristocracy, many of them descendants of the early Russian kings or of Lithuanian tribal chiefs, ruled their estates with complete feudal immunity, and met in provincial diets that were independent in all local affairs. The duke's feudal authority over the aristocracy was so loose, that in practice he was master of his own manors only. Beneath the aristocracy there was a numerous class of military retainers and tenants, vassals of the duke or of the magnates. The high clergy, Roman and Orthodox, were limbs of the aristocracy, and like them primarily large landowners; the Romans were active and efficient; the Orthodox supine, worldly and frankly simoniac. The peasants were the feudal subjects of their lords. The subjection gradually turned into serfdom, which, however, was only to reach its fullest development in the 17th and 18th centuries.

Lithuania lay outside the great currents of commerce. Her townspeople, mainly Russian and Orthodox, displayed no particularly progressive or enterprising spirit. Polotsk alone flourished for a time on its trade with Riga and the Baltic. The dukes tried to raise the status of the townspeople and the prosperity of the towns by granting them charters framed after the German model ("Magdeburg Law"), but this did not help matters much. Nor was the development of the urban corporations favoured by another policy of the dukes who, following the examples of the kings of Poland, encouraged the extensive immigration of Jews from Germany. By the end of the Lithuanian period commerce and the crafts were to a very large extent concentrated in Jewish hands.

The cultural history of Lithuania is almost a blank. The Orthodox Church was degenerate and produced neither saints, nor churches, nor literature. The aristocracy looked to Poland for their models. The townspeople were few and feeble, the peasants downtrodden and illiterate. Russian civilisation was stagnant. and Western influence filtered in slowly. Dr. Francis Skorina (fl. 1517-25), of Vilna, who studied at Prague and devoted his life to printing books in Slavonic characters, was an isolated figure. A breath of fresh air came only towards the very end of the period, together with Protestant propaganda. It was to prove the stimulus for a great religious and cultural revival, which, however, had its principal centre not in White Russia but in Ukraina. On the other hand the legislative work of the Lithuanian Diet was of considerable importance. The Code of Laws known as the Lithuanian Statute, elaborated between 1529 and 1588 and based on Old Russian and on German law, is the most remarkable achievement of its kind produced on Russian soil before the 19th century, and by far the most important White Russian document.

The constitution of the Lithuanian state was not suited for an imperialistic policy. After the death of Vitowt the political successes of the dukes ceased. Towards the end of the 15th century the Turks, established on the Danube and in the Crimea, put an end to the Lithuanian domination in the steppe, while a few years later Muscovy won from Lithuania all her eastern dependencies. The incorporation of the Duchy in her more vigorous and progressive Polish neighbour came as the result of another war with Muscovy, begun in 1562 to save Livonia from conquest by the Muscovites.

Poland was then ruled by her numerous and quasi-democratic gentry (*szlachta*), who controlled all affairs through the provincial diets and whose representatives, unadulterated by those of any other estate, formed the national diet. This state of things appealed powerfully to the class of military vassals, who under the Lithuanian constitution had to leave the administration of public affairs to the magnates. Under the pressure of this class the Lithuanian

71

aristocracy consented to a union with Poland, which was finally agreed upon in 1569 (Union of Lublin). Under its terms Poland and Lithuania became one nation, with one king and one Parliament, Lithuania retaining the status of a separate duchy, its separate laws, and (to placate the aristocracy) its privy council and all its high offices of court.

4. POLISH RULE IN UKRAINA, AND THE RISE OF THE KOZAKS.

DURING the Lithuanian period the Ukrainian lands were divided (except for the parts that had become Hungarian or Moldavian) between Lithuania and Poland, the latter holding Galicia, and, after 1437, Podolia. The direct possessions of the duke were fewer here than in the north, and most of the land belonged to the great feudal lords, such as the princes of Ostroh, of Korets, of Vyshnevets, as well as untitled families of native and Polish origin. Polish penetration proceeded faster here than in the northern provinces for there was more to tempt the Polish gentleman in the rich borderland. At the Union of Lublin the pressure of the local Polish and polonised gentry was sufficient to detach the three palatinates of Volynia, Kiev and Bratslav from the duchy and incorporate them in the "Kingdom."

The Lithuanian conquest of the western steppe had not resulted in stable agricultural occupation. By the end of the 15th century the Russian population was thrown back to the fringe of the forest. The annual raids made by the Krim Tartars on the Muscovite and Ukrainian marches were more destructive than the great Mongol invasion. Herds of cattle and thousands of captives were driven away, and Russian slaves filled the markets of all the Mediterranean east.

A counter-advance of the agricultural border began soon after 1550, almost simultaneously on the Muscovite and on the Lithuanian-Polish side. Like the Muscovite, the Ukrainian advance was preceded by freelance pioneers who called themselves Cossacks (Russian *kazak*, Ukrainian *kozak**). The Ukrainian Kozaks settled on the lower Dniepr, where they founded a permanent camp (Sich), below the rapids (hence their name of *Zaporoh*, i.e. "Trans-rapid" Cossacks), a purely military settlement where no women were allowed. Settlements of a more domestic nature were made in river valleys, but on the whole the Zaporoh Kozaks de-

*On the origin, meanings and different forms of this word see footnote on page 133.

rived their livelihood from plundering Turks and Tartars rather than from gardening or fishing. On their light boats they crossed the Black Sea and raided the Anatolian coast, reviving the exploit of the early Russians.

The Zaporoh movement began before the Union of Lublin and among its first leaders were members of the South-Russian aristocracy. But before long it became distinctly democratic and was largely fed by refugees fleeing serfdom and feudal extortions. The Sich recognised the king of Poland as its sovereign, contributing Kozak contingents to all his wars (including the Muscovite war of 1610-19), but enjoyed complete inner autonomy. Its constitution was a military democracy: a camp commander (*koshevyĭ otaman*) was elected by a general assembly of the Kozak and was deposable at will.

The steadier agricultural advance on both sides of the Dniepr reached the southern limits of the parkland by the beginning of the 17th century. The advancing Ukrainian peasants were followed step by step by the authority and protection of the King of Poland, who erected and garrisoned castles along the rivers and employed part of the colonists as a militia of "registered Kozaks." These, being in the king's service, were free from all feudal jurisdiction, but side by side with the royal power there came the feudal nobility, the *pans*, who claimed all the newly occupied land and the services of its occupants. So, unless he became a free Kozak by entering the king's service or by trekking away to the Sich, there was no escape for the pioneering Ukrainian peasant from the social and economic conditions of the place he came from.

At the time of the Union of Lublin, Poland was in the full flush of the Reformation and Renaissance. Large sections of the ruling gentry had been converted by Protestant (Calvinist and Socinian) propaganda, and Catholicism was reduced to the defensive. Though Protestant propaganda encroached on Orthodoxy as well as on Romanism, the Orthodox profited by the religious liberty which the Protestants were able to extract from the government, and the state of religious liberty that prevailed in Poland at the time did much to minimise the opposition of the Orthodox Russians to the Union of Lublin. But the Counter-Reformation was not slow in coming: the Jesuits, led by Peter Skarga, a writer

74

d orator of genius, launched a well-planned and successful
tack against both Protestants and Orthodox. One of their chief
eapons was an appeal to snobbish sentiment. They succeeded in
aking Protestantism unfashionable and Orthodoxy a "serfs'
ith." In about a generation the Protestant gentry had returned
 the Roman fold, and the Russian aristocracy become Polish
d Romish. In 1596 the Jesuits succeeded in cajoling the majority
 the prelates of the Orthodox Church into accepting Roman
premacy as a United Church of the Greek Rite (Union of
est). But the burgesses and lower clergy, and the rural popula-
on refused to hear of union, so that the apostasy of the nobility
d upper clergy drew the line of religious and national cleavage
ong already existing class lines and made Russian and Orthodox
nonymous with plebeian.

An Orthodox movement of self-defence, at first against Protest-
t propaganda, but very soon against Jesuit aggression, was
arted about a generation before the Union of Brest. Its first
aders were great lords, like Constantine, Prince of Ostroh, and
e exiled Muscovite oligarch, Prince Andrew Kurbsky. After
596 the leadership passed to Brotherhoods formed by the bur-
esses of the chief Russian cities, Vilna and Lvov. Schools were
unded by them for the forming of a better educated clergy that
ould be able to meet the Jesuits in argument. The educational
ethods adopted by the first Brotherhood schools were borrowed
om the Greeks. These soon showed themselves to be insufficient,
nd the methods of the Jesuits themselves came to be adopted
 the struggle against them. This development is associated with
e activity of Peter Mohila, a Moldavian nobleman, who became
Orthodox Metropolitan of Kiev (1633-1647) and founded there a
eological academy on the Latin model. But the struggle between
Orthodox and Catholic was primarily a struggle between Ukrain-
n peasants and Polish landlords.

The constitution of the Polish gentry (*szlachta*), the only politi-
ally significant class in the kingdom, was quasi-democratic. Its
embers were considered equal, irrespective of the size of their
ossessions. The middle and lower gentry, who formed the numer-
al majority of the national and provincial diets, were active and
nfluential. But the annexation of the Russian provinces strength-

ened the aristocratic element within the ruling class. The Ukrain
ian lords were much richer than those of Poland proper. The
could maintain whole armies of poor and landless gentry wh
were their soldiers in the field and their voting power in the diet
All the newly occupied territory was formed into feudal estates c
the size of little kingdoms. The Prince of Vyshnevets (Wiśniow
iecki), for instance, owned east of the Dniepr a territory of abou
8,000 square miles with 40,000 tenants, which he ruled from hi
castle of Lubny as a practically independent sovereign. By th
second quarter of the 17th century the great border lords wer
all polonised and Catholic. They exploited their lands ver
largely with the help of Jews, whom they made their steward
and to whom they farmed out their mills and their exclusive righ
to distil and sell strong liquor. The Catholic lord with his Catholi
retinue, Catholic priests and Jewish business agents followed th
Ukrainian peasant wherever he went in search of new land. Ther
remained, however, by the side of the enserfed peasant two socia
groups that retained their freedom, the Kozak, a military farme
in the pay of the king, and a diminishing, but still considerabl
minority of Orthodox gentry, who were either small landowner
or quite landless. The latter regarded with natural jealousy thei
powerful Catholic neighbours, and tended to amalgamate wit
the Kozaks among whom they formed a sort of aristocracy c
birth and influence. The great *pans* viewed with disfavour th
increasing number of Kozaks and imposed on the king the neces
sity of restricting their number, so that all frontier farmers wh
were not included in the strictly limited number of "registered
Kozaks might be restored as serfs to the landlords. It was in thes
conditions that the Ukrainian people or rather its active sectior
the Kozaks, came to national consciousness.

The Kozaks gave their support to the educational work c
the Brotherhoods and of Peter Mohila, but this was only
minor aspect of their activity. In 1592 there broke out the first c
a succession of Kozak rebellions against the *pans*. The rebels in
variably proclaimed their loyalty to the king, but the kin
soon became a mere puppet in the hands of the *szlachta*, an
could not effectively intervene in the struggle. The rebellio
of 1638 ended in a crushing defeat of the Kozaks and in a decad

triumph for the *pans*. They succeeded in reducing the "regis-red Kozaks" to nominal numbers and in curbing the inde-ndence of the Sich. But in 1648 a new rebellion broke out. Its ader was the Orthodox squire Bohdan Khmelnytskyï. After their st successes the Zaporoh Kozaks were joined by the whole mass Ukrainian peasantry and a terrible jacquerie spread over all kraina. Catholics and Jews were massacred in tens of thousands. it Khmelnytskyï was incapable and unwilling to become the artacus of the Ukrainian serfs. His dream was the creation of autonomous Kozak state of substantial yeomen ruled by a tive Orthodox *szlachta*, of which the Kozak commanders would rm the nucleus, and he himself the head. He entered on a policy compromise with Poland and on intrigues with Moldavia, ansylvania and the Khan of Krim, suffered defeats from the les, and was finally forced to beg the protection of Moscow. It as granted and accepted by the Kozak chiefs (1654). Muscovite mies entered Ukraina, and for thirty years the country became e theatre of war between rival factions of the Kozak oligarchy, pported by Poland, Turkey and Muscovy. The Ukrainian asant was forgotten and the misery and devastation was precedented. Ukrainian historical tradition has given this riod the expressive name of *Ruyina* (ruin). The Russo-Polish ar ended in 1667 by the armistice of Andrusovo under the terms which Ukraina east of the Dniepr (the later provinces of Cher-gov and Poltava) and Kiev with its immediate neighbourhood came an autonomous Kozak state, dependent on Moscow, and led by a Hetman (hence its name of Hetmanshchina). The re-aining Ukrainian lands, and all White Russia remained Polish.

During its golden age, which was the reign of the Hetman Ivan azeppa (1688-1708), the Hetmanshchina retained complete tonomy, Muscovite sovereignty only expressing itself in the esence of a few garrisons on the Polish and Crimean frontiers. he country received a military organisation, the division of the ozak force into regiments forming a basis for the territorial vision of the country. The colonels of the regiments and the neral officers, who formed the Hetman's staff, developed into an igarchy which had complete control of affairs and whose ominee the Hetman was. Together with the lower officers, mem-

bers of the regimental staffs, and commanders of territor
squadrons they formed an upper class of "commanders" (st
shina) which, from the outset, showed an irrepressible tenden
to develop into an hereditary gentry. They monopolized m

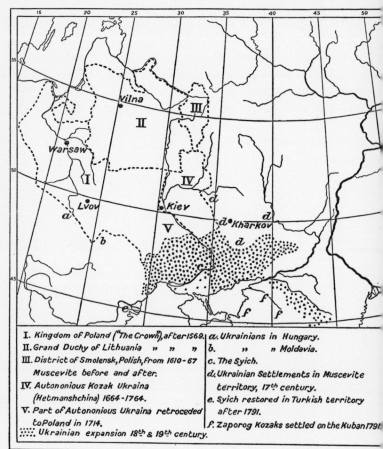

I. Kingdom of Poland ("The Crown"), after 1569. a. Ukrainians in Hungary.
II. Grand Duchy of Lithuania " " " b. " " Moldavia.
III. District of Smolensk, Polish, from 1610-67 c. The Syich.
Muscovite before and after. d. Ukrainian Settlements in Muscovite
IV. Autononious Kozak Ukraina territory, 17th century.
(Hetmanshchina) 1664-1764. e. Syich restored in Turkish territory
V. Part of Autononious Ukraina retroceded after 1791.
to Poland in 1714. f. Zaporog Kozaks settled on the Kuban 1791.
Ukrainian expansion 18th & 19th century.

Fig. 8. West Russian Lands, 16th-18th centuries.

of the land, and gradually reduced their tenants to servitud
Only a minority of the peasants were incorporated in the Koz
force and formed a free yeomanry, subject to the obligation
military service. The number of landless tenants on the estates
the starshina was steadily increased by fugitives from Polan
especially after 1714 when all the parkland south of Kiev w

bandoned by order of Peter the Great to Poland (then his ally)
nd its Ukrainian inhabitants forced to migrate eastwards (an
vent known as the *z-hin*, "the driving-out"). The virtual in-
ependence of the Hetmanshchina was short-lived. In 1708
Iazeppa, whose ambition was to become a completely independ-
nt King, passed over to Charles XII of Sweden, and declared
ar on Muscovy. Supported only by a minority of the *starshina*,
e was easily deposed by Peter, and this began a period of suc-
essive curtailments of Ukrainian autonomy by the Russian power.

The lands left to Poland under the treaty of Andrusovo were
he provinces of Kiev (without the city), Volynia, Podolia, Galicia
nd Kholm. Here the work of polonisation could now proceed
nimpeded. Ukrainian nationality finally became the badge of
ocial inferiority, and by the time of the Partitions (1793-95) only
he peasants, the rural clergy, and a small minority of towns-
eople confessed themselves "Ruthenian."

5. UKRAINIAN CIVILISATION.

BEFORE the great religious and social movements of the Polis period, the Ukrainians were a loose congeries of provincial cor munities with no conscious unity, except a vague sentiment being "Russian," that is to say Greek Orthodox and differe from the Latins. The Kozak period gave them the consciousne of a nation, but only a fraction of it was actually embraced the autonomous Kozak state. This "statelessness" of the Ukrai ian nationality stands in sharp contrast with the intensely imperi character of the Great Russian nation.

The rural commune, as it developed in Great Russia, nev established itself among the Ukrainians, except where there w direct Great Russian influence. The Ukrainian village cor munity (*hromada*) was a looser and freer form of organisatio There was room for more individualism inside it, and its colle tivism was less coercive.

The Ukrainian Church, after the apostasy of the nobility ar upper clergy, likewise assumed more popular and less author tative forms than in Russia. Hence, on the one side, a great intimacy in the Ukrainian's relation to his parish church, tl absence of a hereditary caste of priests, and a closer conta between clergy and people. This also led to a greater depen ence of the Church on the community, and consequently on tl rich. The church, for the Ukrainian, did not become an extern and superior force whose sanction sanctified the nation (as it w. in Muscovite Russia), but a natural function of the nation, an ind vidual attribute, important rather because it was national tha because it was religious. This attitude to the church is akin that of the Balkan nations and essentially different from tl Great Russian.

On the other hand, Ukraina is a much more exclusively rur nation than Great Russia. Urban life may have developed Ukraina earlier, and the percentage of urban population ma be higher than in many parts of Great Russia, but from an ear

80

late the towns were monopolised by non-Ukrainians, Jews, Poles, and from the 18th century onwards, Great Russians. Outside the towns the Ukrainian village is more strictly rural than the Great Russian (especially the North Russian) village. It contains less of that quasi-urban element of traders and workers in home-industries which is characteristic of the forest belt of Great Russia.

Where Ukrainian society developed most freely it formed a sort of pyramid of landowners, evenly ascending from the poorest peasant to the richest squire. Even the townspeople (except the Jews), were primarily freeholders, owners of a house and garden, rather than traders or artisans. The presence of a class of small and middle holders bridging the gap between squire and peasant and forming a continuous social ladder was characteristic of autonomous Kozak Ukraina. In the lands that remained Polish, the Ukrainians were much more of a one-class nation of peasants, for the squires and stewards were all Poles.

Ethnologically the Ukrainian is very different from the Great Russian, in spite of the unquestionable sentiment of close kinship that exists between them, the Ukrainian being more "European," and more "Slavonic." In the Carpathians the ethnological and linguistic transition from Ukrainian to Pole and Slovak is very gradual, the Slovaks in particular having much in common with the Ukrainians. The Ukrainian-Roumanian frontier, too, is by no means clear cut, the population of much of northern Moldavia being obviously Roumanianised Ukrainians.

Polish influence on Ukraina has naturally been very profound, and is reflected in numerous linguistic facts. The Ukrainian vocabulary differs from the Great Russian mainly by its high percentage of words borrowed from the Polish, many of which, especially those relating to arts and crafts, are themselves of German origin. On the other hand, Ukraina was not exempt from Turkic influences. But while in Great Russia Turki loanwords are mainly due to contact with the agricultural Bulgars, to the political ascendancy of the Tartar Empire, and to subsequent trade connections with the Volga and Caspian Sea, Ukrainian borrowings are connected with the pastoral steppe, or with the semi-Mediterranean coastland beyond it.

Ukrainian, as also White Russian, contains more specificall "Slavonic" elements, than does Great Russian. Both Ukrainia and White Russian (like most of the other Slavonic languages have, for instance, preserved the old Slavonic names of the months while Great Russian knows only the Roman names, naturalise by the Church. Ukrainian folklore (especially that of the Car pathians and the forest belt), preserves in its poetry and folk ritual much that can be assigned a pre-Russian origin, while i Great Russian it presents many features in common with th Finno-Ugrians. The early Russian tradition, on the contrary, ha been much better preserved by the Great Russians and left hardl a trace in Ukraina. It was too closely connected with the rulin class (especially with the dynasty), the towns and the clergy, t have survived in a country where the ruling class became renegade the towns were peopled by aliens, and the clergy was for man centuries stagnant and decadent.

The Ukrainian religious tradition is not so much due to th survival of the initial impulses as to later revivals. In the 14th-15th centuries South Slavonic influences are in this respect direct and great. But the decisive factor was the great anti-Roman move ment of Polish times. It was only in the course of this movemen that the Ukrainian Church became a really popular Church and an organic part of Ukrainian life. Before that time the people had remained semi-pagan and little influenced by the clergy, which was exclusively aristocratic and alien to the masses.

Some of the most characteristic types of Ukrainian folklore certainly go back to pre-Polish times—e.g. the numerous folk stories based on apocryphic literature.* The stories in which the Devil is portrayed as having part in the creation of the world, go back to medieval Balkanic sources and must have been im ported in the 14th-15th centuries. They obviously reflect the dual istic theology of the Bulgarian *cathari*, but it is amusing to see how the Satan-Demiourgos of Manichean metaphysics has been trans formed into a comic Ukrainian devil.

But by far the most vital and important part of modern folklore

---

*In Russia the term is used to denote religious writings not directly sanc tioned by the Church, beginning with such New Testament Apocryphas as the Gospel of Nicodemus, etc.

s the product of the Kozak period. Its most interesting section
onsists of elegiac poems (*dumy*) about the Kozaks, their wars,
ınd their misfortunes in Crimean and Turkish captivity. These
legies are still intoned by professional itinerant singers to the
ıccompaniment of a sort of lute (*kobza*, or *lyra*). By their side
Ukrainian folklore possesses a great wealth of lyrical songs of a
very lively and spirited style in which the heroes are the Kozak
ınd his girl. All this Kozak poetry is in rhymed verses, and rhyme
unknown to Old Russian as well as to the older Great Russian
)opular poetry) seems to have been adopted from the West
)efore the spread of literary rhymed verse.

Ukrainian literature begins in Polish times and is entirely an
)utcome of the anti-Roman struggle. It had its centres in the
3rotherhood schools, and after Mohila's time in the Kiev Academy.
.t consists, for the most part, of polemical and scholastic writings.
The language used was a mixture of Church-Slavonic and Polish,
ınterlarded with Latin and Greek words and with a relatively
small proportion of native Ukrainian idiom. A by-product of the
_atinised system of education was the growth of poetry and drama.
The value of this literature was small but it exercised a consider-
ıble influence both on Great Russian literature and on Ukrainian
olklore. The latter result was mainly due to the students of the
Kiev Academy, who were recruited from all classes of society, and
ived a life very reminiscent of the students of medieval Europe.
3etween terms they were apt to turn into itinerant mendicants.
The impecunious and wandering student of theology is as much
ı feature of 17th-18th centuries Ukraina, as of 12th-13th centuries
Curope. The two kinds of literature these *vagantes* made popular
ımong the people were rhymed hymns (*kanty*) and the popular
)uppet play which grew out of the comic interludes of the
cholastic drama or miracle play. The influence of the puppet
)lay left a profound trace on the early stages of modern Ukrain-
an literature, as well as on the early work of Gogol.

Ukrainian folk art is continuously connected with Moldavia
ınd Slovakia, but it has a character of its own definitely different
rom that of its Western neighbours. Very ancient elements, dis-
antly connected (*via* Chazaria ?) with the Orient, are crossed
vith Byzantine, later Turkish and Persian (*via* Crimea), and

recent Western (Renaissance and baroque) influences, producing
on the whole an impression of Oriental rather than European
character. This is particularly true of the beautiful carpet
(*kylymy*) that were made during the Kozak period. Other particularly interesting forms of Ukrainian popular art are embroidered
towels and various kinds of pottery. The latter as well as the curious glazed tiles of the 18th century present more distinctly
European features. In spite of the absence of direct contact between North Russian and Ukrainian embroidery, the geometrical
treatment of the patterns often reveals a similar spirit in both.

In Ukrainian architecture we must distinguish between the
popular and the aristocratic. The former is represented by the
strikingly original wooden churches of the Carpathian valleys
which are territorially contiguous with the only remaining area
of wooden churches in Central Europe in the western Carpathians and Silesia, but quite different in style; and by the old
wooden churches of Ukraina proper. They are characterised by
the juxtaposition of round or octagonal towers, usually five, connecting to form a Greek cross. During the period of Kozak
autonomy this design was transferred to stone. But the Kozak
aristocracy were not satisfied with these relatively simple native
churches, and patronised the more ambitious and splendid style
known as Ukrainian baroque. It goes back to Polish, South German and ultimately Italian models, but developed along original
lines. Its most general characteristic is a wealth of stucco decoration and the boldness with which this is made use of to procure
striking pictorial effects on the outer walls. Its semi-barbaric
splendour is strangely reminiscent of the contemporary churches
of Spanish Mexico.

UKRAINIAN ARCHITECTURE.
Church at Berezna. 18th century.

6. THE WHITE RUSSIANS AFTER THE UNION OF LUBLIN.

THE Union of Lublin and the Roman Catholic offensive that followed, led, as it had done in Ukraina, to the rapid polonisation of the "Lithuano-Russian" aristocracy and upper clergy who had accepted the Union of Brest. The White Russian middle classes joined with the Ukrainians in the movements of national and religious defence. One of the first Brotherhoods founded for the defence of Orthodoxy was that of Vilna. The Sich received White Russian recruits, and one of the most famous leaders of the first Kozak revolts was a White Russian. Another White Russian, Symeon of Polotsk, was the most prominent of the early West Russian scholars that came to Moscow. There was no distinct conscious difference between Ukrainian and White Russian. But White Russia lacked that which contributed most to the growing vitality of Ukraina: free lands to colonise and consequently that class of pioneering peasants and yeomen which was the mainstay of the Ukrainian revival. The circumstance that the country formed the theoretically independent Grand Duchy of Lithuania, while Ukraina was incorporated in Poland proper, contributed to increase the ethnical difference between the two sister-nations, and in the long run the West Russian revival had no positive effect on White Russia.

The Russo-Polish war of 1654-67 was even more disastrous to White Russia than to Ukraina. Under the treaty of Andrusovo Muscovy retained Smolensk which had already been Muscovite from 1514 to 1610. Its district was very easily assimilated to Great Russia—only the gentry receiving some special privileges. The remainder of the White Russian territory remained Polish, and here the Poles were now free to conduct their work of polonisation with increased vigour. The Orthodox burgesses were evicted from the municipalities, and Vilna ceased to be a predominantly Russian city. Polish was everywhere substituted for White Russian as the official language. Even more than in the Ukrainian lands, Russian became synonymous with serf, and the

85

White Russians were turned into what they have ever since remained, a one-class nation of poor peasants. The United Church was imposed on the great majority of the people, but as even "United Greek" retained the stigma of a serf's faith, conversions to Catholicism were numerous, and there is to-day a higher proportion of Roman Catholics among the White Russians than among the Ukrainians.*

The lot of the White Russian peasant was one of more unrelieved gloom than of either the Great Russian or the Ukrainian. His country is less attractive than any other Russian territory situated on the same latitude, for the soil is poor, and much of the land bog. The standard of life has been for centuries, and still is, lower than elsewhere in Russia. Serfdom was aggravated by the squire being of an alien race and faith. It is true that it never verged on slavery as it did in Russia, and the sale of serfs without land was never practised. But while the Great Russian peasant had relatively greater opportunities of gaining money in the towns and in the borderlands, or by selling the produce of his home industry, the White Russian had none. All non-agricultural pursuits were monopolised by Poles or Jews, and all the land belonged to Poles. Vast expanses of forest stood uncleared, the exclusive domain of the squires, and the holdings of the serfs were small.

It is no wonder that the peasant culture that survived under the upper layer of Polish civilisation is poorer and less characteristic than in Ukraina. White Russian folk poetry is monotonous, exclusively lyrical and consistently tuned to the minor key. The ritual of the year-cycle, and the traditional (and expensive) festivities that accompany weddings were the only things to relieve the gloom and monotony of the White Russian's life. Nor did he have the opportunity of developing any artistic handicrafts. The poverty of White Russian popular culture cannot be invoked as any sign of his inherent inferiority, but is the direct outcome o

*The White Russian-speaking Catholics of the country north and west of Vilna are not, however, romanised White Russians but (as the evidence of place-names and certain phonetic features show) Lithuanians who adopted White Russian (saturated with Polonisms) during the Polish domination as a sort of plebeian substitute for their masters' Polish.

an exceptionally unhappy past. Now that the White Russian is free there is no reason to believe that he will not in all respects prove himself the equal of his more fortunate Great Russian and Ukrainian relatives.

7. THE JEWS.*

THE Jews of the Cimmerian Bosporus who transmitted the Jewish faith to the Chazars were not the ancestors of the Russian Jews of to-day. Their descendants survive in the Crimea where they speak the Crimean form of Turki, part of them adhering to the Karaite schism. The early Jewish colonies of Kiev and Vladimir were doubtless of Crimean origin. The descendants of the former may have survived, merged in the later Jewish immigration (the most likely place to look for such a continuity would be the kingdom of Galicia), but we have no evidence to support such a supposition. They certainly did not survive in Vladimir, and Muscovy shut her doors to all Jews most rigorously. The policy of the kings of Poland was different. They began to encourage Jewish immigration as early as the 13th century. The Dukes of Lithuania followed suit, and by the 16th century the two countries had more Jews than any other country in Christendom. They were all German Jews, and spoke the middle German dialect, which has come to be known as Yiddish.

The Jews were invited as part of a general policy that aimed at strengthening the urban element, another aspect of which was to encourage the immigration of German townspeople. The Germans, in the course of time, became polonised and formed the main contingent of the Polish bourgeoisie. The Jews remained segregated in autonomous communities, immune from enserfment and directly subjected to the sovereign. They became the competitors and rivals of the German-Polish bourgeoisie, and this division of the townspeople into German-Polish burgesses and segregated Jews was a main cause of the political insignificance of the middle classes in Poland and Lithuania.

In post-Reformation Poland the Jews definitely became the social allies of the ruling aristocracy. During the opening-up of the Ukrainian parkland, many Jews, countenanced by the leaders

* See *History of the Jews in Russia and Poland*, by Dubnow, English translation, Philadelphia, 1916-20.

88

of the community, became stewards of the nobility, rented their lands and public-houses, thus taking a conspicuous part in the exploitation of the Ukrainian peasantry. This bred intense anti-Jewish feeling among the latter, which assumed horrible forms during Khmelnytskyi's victorious revolt of 1648-1649, when masses of Jews were massacred. Later on the situation was restored and the Jews continued to live segregated and protected by the king and the magnates, monopolising, more or less, most of the urban trades of Poland. Their numbers increased rapidly, resulting in considerable over-population and a low standard of life for the Jewish masses. A practical monopoly of most commercial pursuits, distributed among a great number of very poor traders and middlemen, complete cultural segregation, combined with ubiquitous presence, general poverty against a background of the even greater poverty of the peasants; such were the conditions that favoured the persistence of anti-Jewish feeling among the lower and middle-classes of the Christian population. But at least the Jews were able to preserve unchanged their national civilisation and to develop a curious type of autonomy. Each community elected a *Kahal* who were responsible for the taxes of the members and had complete jurisdiction in all civil and commercial affairs among Jews, which they settled according to rabbinical law. The *Kahals* elected delegates to provincial and general councils, which acted as courts of appeal and had delegates accredited to the king and diet. The rigorous exclusion of inter-marriage with Gentiles further contributed to keep the Jews effectively segregated. They spoke Yiddish and wrote Hebrew, and never learned Polish or Ukrainian except for purely business purposes.

The religious and intellectual life of Polish Jewry was intense, but conservative. The study of the Talmud flourished chiefly for legal purposes, and tended towards extreme logical refinement and casuistic hair-splitting. Lithuania became especially renowned for her learned rabbis, but the dry legalism of the Talmudists could not satisfy all spiritual demands, and by its side the mysticism of the Kabbalah found numerous, often equally learned, adepts. The tragic events of the mid-seventeenth century were followed by a religious revival inspired by the Messianic pretensions of Sabatai-Zevi. His failure to fulfil them was followed by a profound depression among Ukrainian Jewry, and by the "Frankist" movement, which was an appeal to the Jews to abandon their Messianic hopes and become Christians.

The greatest of the mystical movements was Hasidism, initiated by Israel Baal-Shem-Tob or "Besht" (c. 1700-1760), a man of rare religious genius who denounced the futility of Rabbinic learning and taught justification by faith and the duty of man to help God by his good will in the cosmic work of Good. Hasidism easily conquered the more mystically inclined Ukrainian Jewry, but Lithuania, the fortress of rabbinical formalism, sustained a bitter and victorious resistance. Thus, on the eve of the Partitions, the Jews of Poland were split between two essentially hostile creeds, but united by a determination to keep apart from the Gentiles and a complete indifference to modern ideas.

Chapter IV

THE TARTAR PERIOD
(XIIIth—XVth Centuries)

1. "THE TARTAR YOKE."

2. THE RUSSIAN TERRITORY DURING TARTAR DOMINATION.

3. THE REPUBLICAN NORTH.

4. FEUDAL SOCIETY IN THE NIZ.

5. THE CHURCH.

6. THE RISE OF MOSCOW.

7. RUSSIAN CIVILISATION UNDER THE TARTARS; THE BYZANTINE REVIVAL.

I. "THE TARTAR YOKE."

THE Mongol Empire of Jenghizkhan was not in all respects a typical nomad empire. It combined the nomad feudalism based on the idea of individual loyalty to a chief, his kin and clan, with a bureaucratic system derived from the Chinese. The Mongols were not savages. In their wars, it is true, they sometimes practised intimidation by wholesale slaughter and destruction on a larger scale than is usually done by European belligerents. Certain particularly unlucky districts, like Khorassan, never again recovered their pre-Mongol prosperity, and their fate has made a deep impression on the imagination of historians. But the Mongol armies were rigorously disciplined and superior in military science to all their contemporaries. The nations they conquered were given peace and order. A *pax Mongolica* reigned from end to end of the Empire, and allowed merchants to travel unmolested from the mouth of the Don to the gates of Peking.

It was the efficiency of the bureaucratic organisation that assured these economic blessings and held the Empire together. But Mongol family law favoured partitions and these were rendered inevitable by the huge size of the Empire and by the centrifugal attraction of the great conquered civilisations— Chinese and Persian. In the middle of the 13th century it was divided into four part-Empires. The great Khan, who had his residence at Karakorum, in Mongolia, retained Mongolia and China, his descendants being known as the Yuan dynasty. Jagatai took Turkestan, Kashgaria and Dzungaria. Persia fell to Hulagu, the first of the Ilkhans; while the descendants of Juchi ruled over all the country that lay west of the Altai mountains and north of the Caucasus and of lake Balkhash, including the Amu delta (Khwarezm). This part-empire received the name of Kipchak,* or

* The nomenclature of Turkish ethnical division is involved and somewhat confusing. " Kipchak " was the name of one of the original clans that formed the Turkish nation. It was further used to denote several " secondary " ethnical formations that included sections of the original Kipchak clan ; of these the Cumans (Polovîtsi, Kipchak) were the most important. As the country ruled by the

"Golden Orda."† Batû, son of Juchi, who conquered Russia and, in 1242, led the Mongol army into Central Europe, was the first Khan of Kipchak. Their capital was Saray, near the lower Volga, for more than a century a cosmopolis of all the cultures of East and West, as important as Karakorum, and less short-lived.

The division into part-kingdoms did not mean an immediate dissolution of the ideal unity of the empire, but gradually this came to pass. The Yuan became Chinese; the Ilkhans and the Jagatai Khans embraced Islam. Kipchak remained true to the ancestral traditions longer than the rest and did not finally become Muhammadan till the second half of the 14th century. It was the most purely nomadic of the four part-kingdoms and it was only in the second half of the 14th century that it began to show signs of decadence.

North-eastern Russia was conquered by Batû in 1238, and the "Tartar‡ Yoke" lasted, officially, till 1480, and effectively till about 1450. We have seen that the south-west was hardly affected by it. But only the lands incorporated in Lithuania never recognised Tartar supremacy.

The Tartars did not consciously contribute to the disintegration of Russia. They believed in unity and organisation, and never practised the maxim of *divide et impera*. On the contrary they began

descendants of Juchi included the Cuman territory the name Kipchak came to denote all the possessions of that branch. As these are conterminous with the extension of the north-western group of Turkish dialects the latter is also designated by some turcologists (Samoilovich) by the name of Kipchak.

†*Orda* is the Russian form of Turki *ordu*, or *urdu*, which has given English the word *horde*. It does not mean " horde," but a division of an armed force and its headquarters. In modern Turkish it has come to mean " army corps " ; in the Turki of Turkestan " a royal residence." *Urdu*, as a name for Hindustani, is of the same origin, and meant " the language of the camp."

‡Like the Europeans, the Russians called the Mongols Tartars (*tatary*) This is essentially a political appellation and means a "subject of the house of Jenghizkhan." In Western languages the name Tartar is applied to-day to all Central Asiatics, including the Manchu and the Tibetans. In Russian, the " Tartars " of the Golden Orda being all Turki-speaking (though Mongol long remained the official language) the name has become limited to peoples of Turki speech. In particular it is used to-day of the sedentary Turki-speaking people of the Volga (Kazan and Astrakhan), of western Siberia, and of the Crimea, that is to say of the people of the metropolitan districts of the Khanates into which the Kipchak empire dissolved.

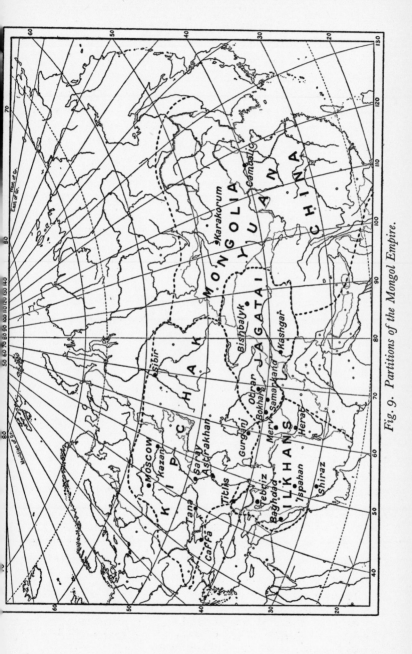

Fig. 9. Partitions of the Mongol Empire.

by giving Yaroslav, Great Prince* of Vladimir, authority over all the other Russian princes, and even added Kiev to his immediate possessions. But the north-eastern principality was no longer capable of becoming a centre for all the lands of old Russia, and Yaroslav never exercised any effective authority in the West. If the Tartars did contribute to the disintegration of Russia it was, on the one hand, by laying waste much of the country along the forest fringe between the Don and the Dniepr and thus loosening the continuity of Russian settlement; but, still more, by failing to bring under their domination the western lands, and allowing them to become the prey of Lithuania and Poland.

The principalities of the parkland, that had been most depopulated by the invasion, became the possession of individual members of the Tartar aristocracy, some of the princes surviving as vassals of the Tartar chiefs. But the main part of north-eastern Russia was placed under the authority of the Great Prince of Vladimir. Yaroslav, realising that this was his only possible course, adopted a policy of complete submission to the Tartars, which was continued by his son and successor, Alexander. The case of the latter is particularly suggestive, for he had only lately made himself a great name by his victories at the head of Novgorodian armies over Latin "crusaders," over the Swedes in 1240 (on the Neva, whence his surname of Nevsky), and over the German Knights in 1242 (on the ice of Lake Peipus, "the Battle of the Ice"). When he died (1263), he was canonised as much for the peace bought by his policy of obedience to the Tartar as for his victories over the Latins.

The first fifty or sixty years of Tartar rule made itself felt to all the population in a multitude of ways. Russians—for the most part artisans, whom the Mongols systematically recruited from all the peoples they conquered, or soldiers pressed into their army—were carried off and dispersed all over the Empire. Even as late as 1330 we find a Russian army unit at Peking in the service of the Yuan Emperor. But the aspect of the "yoke" that affected the masses

*I henceforward substitute " Prince" for " King," in rendering the Russian Knyaz'. It was about this time that Latin authors exchanged Rex for Dux. Honorius III in 1227 addressed a bull Universis Regibus Russiae ; in 1246 Friar John de Plano Carpini speaks of Yaroslav as Dux Russiae. In the same year Innocent IV offered the title of Rex to Daniel of Galicia.

most directly was the tribute. It took, at first, the form of a poll-tax. In order to assess it, censuses of the whole population were taken by Tartar officials who came to Russia with numerous armed followings and, of course, lived on the land. Later, about 1300, the tribute began to be farmed out to Muhammadan capitalists from Bokhara and Samarkand, until in 1330 the Great Prince of Vladimir was made responsible for its collection.

Each prince, as a vassal of the Khan, had to receive a charter of investiture (*yarlyk*) before he could succeed to his father's throne. To obtain it he had to travel to Saray and spend large sums on presents to the Khan, his wives and kinsmen, and all the principal grandees of the Orda. Those princes were successful at the Orda who spent most and toadied best. Those who retained the old military spirit and tried to gain their ends by the sword were severely and cruelly chastised by the Tartars, bringing on their lands all the horrors of invasion, and forfeiting their popularity at home.

H

2. THE RUSSIAN TERRITORY DURING TARTAR DOMINATION.

THE Tartars made a difference between Russia and her Eastern neighbours. The Finno-Ugrian and Turkic country of the middle Volga became an immediate possession of the Orda. The Muhammadan Bulgars were rapidly tartarised and adopted the Kipchak dialect. Kazan, founded by the Tartars to replace the Great City of Bulgars, became an essentially Tartar city. Among the Mordva, Tartar nobles were established as feudal lords, but except in the depopulated parkland no attempt was made to colonise or to tartarise Russia. The Russian population of Saray was sufficiently large by 1261 to warrant the foundation of an episcopal see. But Tartars, mainly of the military class, began to settle in Russia only after the decline of Tartar power made the Prince of Moscow a more profitable suzerain than the decadent Khan.

North-eastern Russia, the future Muscovy, was divided into two essentially dissimilar parts—the country ruled by princes subject to the Tartars in the south and east, and the possessions of the city of Novgorod in the north-west. The latter, in so far as it recognised the authority of the Great Prince of Vladimir, was also, to a certain extent, under Tartar suzerainty, but it was never very effective there.

The possessions of the house of Suzdal were known as the *Niz* ("netherland"), a name that described their position in regard to Novgorod, which held the north-western headwaters of the Volga basin. Its official metropolis was Vladimir, the nominal residence of the Great Prince and after 1300, of the Metropolitan. Suzdal, Rostov, Pereslav and Moscow in the Mesopotamia; Tver, Uglich, Yaroslavl, Kostroma and Nizhni-Novgorod on the Volga; Galich, north of the Volga; and Gorodets (afterwards Kasimov), on the Oka, were the other most important towns and the residences of the several branches of the family.

South of these principalities lay the possessions of various branches of the house of Chernigov, Murom and Ryazan on the middle Oka, and numerous minor principalities in the upper

98

Oka, and upper Don basins. Ryazan alone was an important power, but its importance was diminished by its Princes, who belonged to another branch of the dynasty, having no claim to the paramount throne of Vladimir.

The Tartar invasion had devastated the Russian parkland and thinned the population of the forest fringe, but the Tartar peace that followed it allowed the southern principalities to recover. The decline of the Tartar power after 1359 further favoured Russian expansion. The parkland east of the lower Oka, protected from the steppe by dense forests and inhabited by a branch of the old agricultural nation of the Mordva, was then laid hands on by the Russian princes, and became a field for Russian colonisation. This acquisition proved permanent, but in the south the Tartar invasions of 1382-1408 that followed the Russian victory of Kulikovo threw the Russian population once more back to the forest fringe.

The possessions of Novgorod included primarily the basin of the Gulf of Finland, with the adjoining headwaters of the Upper Volga tributaries. As most of the territory is agriculturally poor Novgorod depended for its corn supply on the agricultural Niz, and this created a permanent link between the rulers of the Niz and the great commercial city, and ultimately brought about its subjection to Moscow. Another link between Novgorod and the Niz was their competing penetration into the basin of the White Sea and of the Arctic Ocean, the "land beyond the Portages" (Zavolochie), as it was called in Novgorod. Novgorod secured control of the north-west with all the seaboard; the Princes, the more agricultural valleys of the Dvina basin with Vologda and Ustyug as their centres. But there was no hard-and-fast territorial division between the rival forces. The independent republic of Vyatka, founded by Novgorodians in the 14th century, was separated from Novgorod by the possessions of the princes. It was a democracy of river pirates who subsisted mainly on the plunder of their Tartar neighbours of Kazan.

For Novgorod (as for the princes of the Niz), the north was a main source of wealth. Novgorod's trade with the west depended on its control of that great treasure house of furs. The Novgorodans had no mercantile fleet and their merchants never travelled

to western markets. Western merchants, from Gothland and from
the Hanse, came to Novgorod where they had a permanent
establishment called St. Peter's Hof. But they were not allowed
to go any farther, so that the Novgorodians retained their control

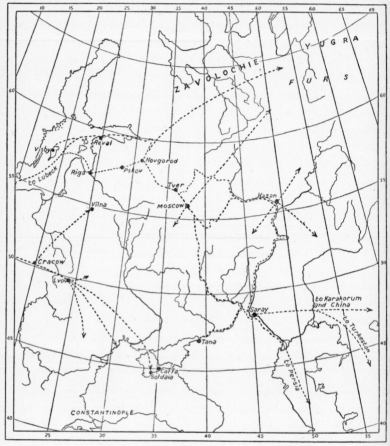

Fig. 10. Trade Routes, 14th century.

of the producing north and the monopoly of German goods in the
Niz.

Novgorod, however, was far from being the commercial metropolis of the whole country. The *pax Tartarica* produced a whole
revolution in the direction of trade-routes. A new route, which,
starting at the mouth of the Don, passed north of the Caspian Sea,
was now added to the old "silk road" from the Mediterranean to

China, *via* Baghdad and Khorassan. The north-eastern corner of the Black Sea and the Sea of Azov became a commercial focus of continental importance. The Genoese succeeded in establishing themselves there under Tartar protection, and their colonies, Soldaia and Caffa in the Crimea, and Tana at the mouth of the Don, became the chief westward outlets of the empire. Eastern Russia was absorbed into their sphere of influence. It was chiefly owing to her advantageous position on the routes leading to Tana and the Crimea that Moscow was able commercially to eclipse her neighbours.* The Volga route to Saray and the Caspian was equally important. This predominantly eastward direction of central Russia's commercial relations was to last for several centuries. It is well reflected in the Russian language, with its innumerable Turki and Persian loan-words denoting every kind ot silk and cotton fabric, metal-work, precious stones, spices and all the other good things that came from the Orient.

But the most unmistakable and characteristic traces of Tartar rule in the Russian language are the borrowings from Turki relating to administration and finance, for one of the principal gifts of the Tartars to Russia was their administrative and financial technique. Such words as *den'gi* ("money"), *tamòzhnya* ("customhouse") and *kazna* ("treasury," ultimately of Persian origin), are lasting monuments of the "Tartar Yoke."

*The leading guild of Muscovite merchants were called *Surozhane*, from Surazh, the Russian name of Soldaia.

CERTAIN important features were common to Novgorod and the principalities of the Niz, for in both survived the essentially individualistic structure of early Russian society with its complete liberty of contract exposing the isolated individual to the free play of economic forces. But the class in whose interest the system worked was, in the Niz, an essentially rural aristocracy of princes who lived dispersed on their estates, and could coalesce only on terms of vassalage; in Novgorod an urban patriciate of boyars which ruled the city as a united corporation, and dominated by its wealth the unruly democracy.

The constitution of Novgorod was a direct development of early Russian political elements, but of the two forces that in the 12th century shared between them the government of the large city-kingdoms, the prince was reduced to the status of a hired captain and honorary magistrate, who could not sit in court unless assisted by a municipal magistrate, could not acquire or allow members of his following to acquire land in the Novgorod dominions, and enjoyed no other revenues than those specified in his electoral contract. He was not a constitutional monarch, but an allied foreign sovereign, who, in return for services rendered, was given certain rights within the city's jurisdiction. It was in the interest of Novgorod to have in him an ally who was also a powerful territorial ruler outside, for one of the essential points of the contract was free trade for Novgorod merchants in the Prince's hereditary dominions. This led to the usage establishing itself of electing the great Prince of Vladimir as Prince of Novgorod, a usage that ultimately contributed to the undoing of the city's independence.

The sovereign power rested with the Vechë, which was an assembly of all the citizens. Its power was unlimited; it elected all the magistrates and could depose them at will. But as it had no form of procedure it could only answer Aye or No to the proposals of the latter. The boyars remained, in practice, alone eligible to the magistracy, and ruled the city, the Vechë being only a riotous but ineffective show. The boyars were not merchants, but capitalists and land-owners who lived on the interest of the money they lent the merchants, and on the revenue of their lands.

The merchants who did the actual trading were organised into guilds. The "ends" and "streets" of the city, minor towns (*prigorod*, "by-towns"), and each rural district formed a corporation of its own. But this did not diminish the essentially individualistic character of Novgorod society, for they were free communities that in no way interfered with the individual and his liberty of contract. The rural districts were mainly divided up into large boyar-owned estates. There was a class of small freeholders, but it was neither socially nor economically important. Slavery and other forms of bondage flourished. The Novgorodian countryside was not a freer land than the Niz.

But in the city and among the boyars there reigned a spirit of liberty, adventure and enterprise that gave Novgorod a romantically "liberal" atmosphere. Young boyars organised gangs of adventurers which went on expeditions into the north, extracting tribute of fur from the Lapps and Samoyeds, or engaged in piracy on the rivers, especially on the Kama and Volga where they were a pest to the Tartars.

The lands in the north were largely owned by absentee boyars, who lived in Novgorod. But some of them settled on the spot, and formed a political community of their own. They early began to resent the rule of the metropolis, and took the first opportunity of offering themselves to Moscow. The separatist leanings of her dependencies were another dark spot in the position of Novgorod, as ominous as the exclusive class character of her constitution.

Pskov, at first a mere "by-town," became independent, and was recognised as "the younger Brother of Novgorod" (Pskov, like Novgorod, is masculine in Russian) in the 14th century. Its social and political constitution were in many respects different from those of Novgorod. There was less anarchy and less social inequality. The Judicial Charter of Pskov is the most elaborately drawn-up legal statute of old Russia. It reveals an essentially bourgeois society of traders and freeholders, almost a democracy. Even the clergy were organised on a constitutional basis.

Foreigners preferred the Pskovites to other Russians, and ascribed to them a higher standard of civilization.

Nevertheless, Pskov was intensely national in political feeling, and a staunch defender of Orthodox Russia against her German neighbours. While Novgorod was the chief enemy of Moscow, Pskov, from the outset, threw herself heart and soul into the conflict for national unity on the side of Moscow. Its intellectuals did much for the cause of unity and Empire, and it was a monk of Pskov who first proclaimed the doctrine that Moscow was the Third Rome. This did not prevent Moscow from putting an end to Pskov's independence when the time came. But the merits of the patriotic town were recognised, and the official Muscovite history of Russia exalts Pskov at great length as the home of the first Russian Christian Queen, St. Olga.

4. FEUDAL SOCIETY IN THE NIZ.

In the Niz the ruling class was a rural aristocracy of princes. As no distinction was made between property and political power (a jurisdiction, a town, a manor, a coat of sables or a golden cup were all private property that could equally well be sold, pawned or bequeathed), a principality was both a state and an estate, and a prince as much a landlord as a sovereign.

Immediately beneath stood the boyars—military servants of the prince and privileged landowners. The two characters were kept distinct, and the boyar's tenure of land was not conditional on continued service. The feudal tie between him and his territorial prince was of the loosest. In European feudal terms his land was an allodial possession rather than a fief. In respect of a boyar's land, as of the boyar himself, the prince was not an owner, not *gosudar*, but *gospodin*—a term that denoted moral, rather than legal authority, and described the relation of father to son, of elder to younger brother, and of one man to another, who had spontaneously agreed to be his "free servant." ("Servant," *sluga*, was an honorific title used only of high-born personages.) A boyar's service was regulated by contract which he was free to denounce at will. The prince, on whose territory his lands were situated, had no right to confiscate them if the "servant" forsook him and "rode off" to serve another prince. The boyars preferred to serve the prince who paid them best. Here, as elsewhere, free competition was the law of feudal Russia.

Below the boyars stood the class of vassals who held land in conditional tenure, or were otherwise remunerated for their services, and by gradual transitions shaded down into unfree servants and slaves. Like the latter they were no longer the "servants" of their *gospodin*, but the "people" (*lyudi*, singular *chelovek*) of their *gosudar'*. Like his lands and his chattels they were his "property," even if they were not actual slaves. Unfree *lyudi* might occupy important places in the administration of a prince's household, and a large proportion of the military gentry of Muscovite times was descended from servile ancestors.

A very large proportion (exactly how large we do not know), of the land belonged to the princes, boyars, bishops or monasteries. Much of it was tilled by unfree labourers for the direct needs of the lord. Another part was occupied by vassals or free tenants. The peasants did not work for the market, but only to keep themselves alive, and to pay their feudal dues. The great majority did not live in villages, but in isolated homesteads, or in groups of two or three houses.

The essentially individualistic character of Russian society was not diminished by the existence of the territorial corporation (*volost'*). It is sometimes regarded as the ancestor of the rural commune, but such a view is quite arbitrary. Not only can no connection be traced between the two, but the institutions are entirely different. The *volost'* was a large territorial unit, extending sometimes over hundreds of square miles. It had rights on unoccupied land and "commons," but all occupied land was in strictly personal possession. Inside the *volost'* the forces of economic individualism had as free play as in Novgorod or Moscow. The land was freely sold, or rented, or given away to monasteries by the individual owners. The *volosti* payed taxes to the territorial princes to whom the land, in theory, belonged, but in other respects they were virtually free communities.

MUSCOVITE ARCHITECTURE.
A Walled Monastery. General view of Troitsa.

5. THE CHURCH.

LIKE all the steppe nomads the Tartars were Shamanists. They believed in a supreme sky God (Tengri), but still more in magic. They were convinced that every religion disposed of powerful supernatural forces, which it was best to keep friendly. But they also had that open-minded interest in other men's beliefs which is natural to the intelligent barbarian. All this made them practise religious tolerance on an almost unprecedented scale. Priests of all faiths were well received at their courts. In all the countries they conquered, the clergy were given extensive privileges and immunities, and told to pray to their Deity for the Khan's welfare. Batû and his descendants extended this policy of toleration to the Orthodox Church of Russia. The Metropolitan was given a *varlyk*, renewed by every new Khan and for every new Metropolitan till the end of the Tartar rule, which made him secular as well as spiritual head of all the clergy. He was subject to none but the Khan. The clergy were exempted from all taxes and from all secular jurisdiction. These immunities made the Metropolitan the most powerful and independent force in the country, especially if one considers that his spiritual authority, derived from the Oecumenical Patriarch, was equally independent of home influences.

For some time after the Tartar invasion the Metropolitan continued to have his official residence in Kiev. But the desolation and political insignificance of the old capital made him look out for another residence. The choice naturally fell on Vladimir, which, in 1300, officially became the Metropolitan see. The King of Galicia, and afterwards the Duke of Lithuania tried to free themselves from their inconvenient subordination to a vassal of the Khan. It was only after 1400 that Vitowt succeeded in obtaining a separate Metropolitan for his duchy, but even before that date the authority of the Metropolitan of Vladimir in the western dioceses was small and his effective sphere of influence was limited to Great Russia.

The Metropolitans did not use their independence to increase their political power. Instead, they chose a secular ally and gave him all the support they could in order that he might realise their ideal of a Christian monarchy. This ally was the house of Moscow. One of the reasons for their choice was that, alone of the larger principalities, Moscow belonged to the Metropolitan diocese, and they could exercise their episcopal functions there. St. Peter, Metropolitan from 1306 to 1326, passed most of his life in that city, and his successors, Theognost and St. Alexis (1353-78) made it their permanent residence. For a long time the Metropolitans were the stronger partners in the alliance. The Prince of Moscow was their protégé, not their master, but a protégé whom they were leading to power.

The times of Theognost and of St. Alexis saw the beginning of the great age of Russian monasticism which lasted for about two centuries. Its characteristic feature was the founding of innumerable hermitages in "the Wilderness," that is in the forest, away from towns and inhabited places. The first and greatest of the great hermits was St. Sergius of Radonezh (died 1392), whose cell, in a wood between Moscow and Pereslav, became the famous Trinity Monastery (Troitsa). Towards the end of his life the saint became the spiritual leader of the nation. After his death the monastery founded by him remained a centre of religious life and culture, and gradually became the greatest landowner in the country.

This evolution is typical of numerous other hermitages founded farther north. A hermit's cell would attract disciples, and grow into a monastery. The monastery would obtain a grant of land to enable the monks to sustain themselves by labour. The hermit's reputation for sanctity would attract people in search of spiritual and bodily cure. At his death it would become a pilgrimage and he would ultimately be canonised. Donations, including grants of land, would flow in ceaselessly from people desirous of saving their souls by the prayers of the brethren, or from persons of property entering as monks. The monastery would become a centre of ecclesiastical influence; the commercial metropolis of the district and the possessor of vast lands, sometimes concentrated around it, sometimes distributed far and wide over Russia. After Troitsa, the greatest of the new monasteries were St. Cyrill's, on the White Lake (Kirillov-Belozersky) and Solovki on an island in the White Sea. The monasteries were a leading force in the colonisation of the north. Where the hermits came in contact with heathen natives they evangelised them, but on the whole the missionary effort lagged behind the ascetic. Only St. Stephen of Permia (a disciple of St. Sergius) stands out as a genuine apostle. The conversion by him of the Zyryans was the greatest missionary achievement in the history of the Russian Church.

By the side of the "wilderness monasteries" others were founded, on the old lines, on initial grants of a prince or other rich man, in, or near, the towns. Some of them acquired as much importance as the great "wilderness" foundations. Whatever their origin and location, the great monasteries became the possessors of vast and well managed estates, the nurseries of prelates, the depositories of the doctrine and the seats of the political influence of the Church.

6. THE RISE OF MOSCOW.

Moscow is first mentioned in 1147 as a manor of the King of Suzdal. A hundred years later it became the residence of a separate prince. Geographical factors favoured its growth, and made it by the middle of the 14th century, the largest city and the economic centre of the Niz. A strong municipal feeling began to grow among the merchant class and attempted to assert itself against the prince, but all the structure of society in the Niz was against municipal development. The prince was much stronger than the merchants, and the Church had no sympathy with democracy. It was during the administration of St. Alexis that the municipal movement was finally suppressed (1375).

The policy of the Princes of Moscow was one of complete obedience to the Tartars; unconditioned friendship with the Metropolitans, who made them their favourites and their candidates for paramount power; and the steady acquisition of everything they could lay hands on. In political ideas they were in no way ahead of their times: the wills of the earlier Princes of Moscow are representative documents of the patrimonial and domestic mentality of the whole class of princes. In buying up from ruined and indebted princes all the lands and jurisdictions that could be got for their money, the owners of Moscow did nothing that had not been done by the other princes, except that it was done on a larger scale. Their territory grew like a snowball, and by the second half of the 14th century reached, discontinuously, from Ustyug, in the north, to Kaluga, in the south, but they still remained princes of the same type as the others, owners of a huge estate rather than the heads of a body-politic. What made them different from the others was their success in securing the permanent possession of the paramount throne of Vladimir. For the Great Principality was different from the others—more abstract and public than any private domain, and to it were attached all ideas of national unity and nation-wide authority.

Ivan Kalita obtained the *yarlyk* for the Great Principality, in

326, and from that time (except for a brief interruption in 1359)
t remained in the hands of his descendants. The importance of
ts acquisition was further enhanced by the right to gather the
Tartar tribute which Ivan succeeded in obtaining from the Khan
about 1330), and which gave the great Prince effective control
ver all Eastern Russia,

The Church did even more than the Tartars to strengthen the
ouse of Moscow. St. Peter, the first Metropolitan to make the
ity his almost permanent residence and to be buried there, was
anonised soon after his death. This gave to Moscow a religious
onsecration that more than counterbalanced any unpopularity
ts princes might have acquired by their unscrupulous policies.
he Metropolitans' policy of unqualified support for Moscow
ulminated under St. Alexis (1353-78), who, during the reign of
he weakminded Ivan II and the minority of Dimitri, was the
ctual head of the Moscow-Vladimir government. His adminis-
ration marks a turning-point in the progress of Moscow towards
nonarchy. It gave the merely economic supremacy of the first
rinces a moral authority. Russia began to see in the Prince of
Moscow not a grasping and greedy upstart, but the moral centre
f the nation and its natural rallying-point.

The collapse of central authority at the Golden Orda after the
eath of Berdibek (1359), and the civil wars that ensued, were
he occasion for Moscow to change her policy of submission to
ne of aggression. This was not done till after the death of St.
Alexis. His spiritual successor, St. Sergius of Radonezh (who,
owever, declined the Metropolitan see), gave his benediction
o the policy of war. Provoked by Dimitri's inroads into Tartar
rritory, the *de facto* Khan Mamay led a great army against
Moscow, but was utterly routed on the plain of Kulikovo field,
ear the sources of the Don. The victorious Russian army included
ontingents from all the princes, who had followed Dimitri as a
ational hegemon. Only his two major rivals, Tver and Ryazan,
efused to join him. But the general trend of opinion is made
rikingly apparent by the fact that it was a clerk of Ryazan who
rote a prose-poem (a rather poor imitation of the *Campaign of
gor*) to commemorate the victory.

The immediate results of Kulikovo were nullified by new

Tartar invasions, the distant echoes of the rise of Tamerlane. Bu
this did not stop the growth of Muscovite power. In 1391 Dimitri'
son, Vasili (1389-1425), annexed the important principality c
Nizhni, with the authorisation of the Tartars, the support of th
clergy, and the help of the Nizhni boyars, who, at the critica
moment, abandoned their prince and "rode off" to Vasili.

Apart from the support of the Church, of the Tartars, anc
after 1380, of organised public opinion, the progress made b
Moscow was mainly due to the Muscovite boyars. Their expe
ience and devotion assured the continuity of her policy an
counterbalanced the mediocrity of her princes.

The constitution of the ruling class that surrounded the Grea
Prince was substantially modified in the first half of the 15th cer
tury by the afflux of numerous princes entering the Muscovit
service. They commended their ancestral lands to the Grea
Prince, receiving them back as his grants, and became his "fre
servants." Besides Great Russian princes there came numerou
immigrants from the Lithuanian sphere of influence. Th
"princelings" gave much new lustre to the Great Princes' cour
and for two or three generations were the most conspicuous pol
tical force in Moscow.

The last serious obstacle on the way towards unity was the cor
flict within the house of Moscow, between the old order of suc
cession, from elder to younger brother, and the new orde
favoured both by the Church and by the patrimonial mentalit
of the princes, from father to son. The greater part of the reig
of Vasili II (1425-1462) was filled by a struggle against his uncl
and cousins. The latter were several times victorious, but Vasi
had the support of the Church and of the Khan, and ended b
having the better of it. The last rebellious cousin was destroyed i
1452; in the same year Novgorod, which had given him refug
was occupied by a Muscovite army and reduced to effective de
pendency.

The Prince of Moscow, hereditary Great Prince of Vladimir
was now the paramount power in Russia, to whom no rivals wer
dangerous. He was prepared to embody the ideal of a God-or
dained national monarch for which he was being prepared by th
Church.

RUSSIAN and foreign writers on Russian civilisation have been in
the habit of denouncing the "Tartar Yoke" as a deteriorating
and impoverishing influence. This view, to say the least, is greatly
exaggerated. In many respects, especially in the political and
economic sphere, the Tartars were greatly superior to the Russians. The devastations of the first invasion were no doubt great,
and the decades that followed it were a time of cultural retrogres-
sion and impoverishment. The 14th century, on the other hand,
was a period of progress and revival, which matured under the
cover of the still stable peace of the Tartars, and only ultimately
resulted in their overthrow.

The contact between Russians and Tartars was limited by the
profound difference in the cultural consciousness of the two peoples.
Russia, at least in her upper classes, was intensely conscious of
her Christian and Orthodox personality. The Church, for all the
friendliness of the Tartars, could not regard them as anything
but "Godless Hagarenes," and outside the administrative and
economic sphere Tartar influence could hardly penetrate. Neither
did the Tartars ever make any attempt to influence the Russians,
though they were, at first, themselves quite open to Russian
Orthodox influences.

The subconscious infiltration of their Russian subjects with
the Tartar spirit is a more delicate and complex subject. The
mainstay of Tartar society—personal loyalty to an individual
chief and his clan—never affected the Russian mind. The spirit
of obedience and self-effacement (or servility as hostile writers
call it), so characteristic of Muscovite Russia may be called
"Oriental," but is certainly alien to the Tartar nomad. In
other cases Russian traits have been ascribed a Tartar origin
merely because the critics disliked them and "Tartar" seemed an
effective term of abuse. The cruelty of the Russian penal law in
Muscovite and early Petersburg times has much closer parallels

in Germany and France than in the Tartar steppe. The seclusion of women in Muscovy was due to Byzantine influence—the Tartar women were never secluded, and those of the upper classes enjoyed the greatest independence. In fact the independence of the Russian upper-class woman, whose freedom to dispose of her property was not affected by marriage, may actually be the fruit of Tartar influence.

If the Tartars were aliens and heathens, the Latins were aliens and heretics. The Niz saw practically nothing of the Latins, and the very existence of Moscow was ignored by the West till the middle of the 15th century. Novgorod and Pskov, on the contrary, were in daily contact with the Germans. But the two worlds were culturally watertight, and the northern republics were as little affected by Latin influence as the Niz. The imperviousness to Latin influence of the two northern cities, which were practically untouched by Tartar influence, shows that the Tartars cannot even be held responsible for the isolation of Russia from Europe.

The only foreigners with whom there was continuous cultural contact were the Greeks and Orthodox Slavs.* A great wave of Greek and south Slavonic influence came over Russia at the end of the 14th century. It was partly connected with the immigration of many Serbian and Bulgarian clerics fleeing the Turk, who had just put an end to the independence of their countries. It added strength to the work of Byzantinising the Russian polity already undertaken by the Russian Church, and its influence on Russian culture was profound and ubiquitous. The height of the wave was reached when Cyprian, a Serb, became Metropolitan of Moscow (1390-1406).

One of the most obvious effects of the changes connected with the name of Cyprian was the reform of the literary language. Church Slavonic in Russia had become greatly vernacularised in the course of the first four centuries of Christianity. Now a new form of Church Slavonic that had been evolved in the Second Bulgarian Empire and used in the so-called Tŭrnovo versions of the sacred books was introduced. It was more rigid and more closely imitative of the syntax and word-order of the originals.

*The Orthodox Georgians and Alans (Ossetes) were fellow-subjects of the Mongol Empire, but were at the time under a cultural eclipse.

RUSSIAN-BYZANTINE PAINTING.

Andrew Rublev. The Holy Trinity. c. 1410 Great Church of
Troitsa.

*Reproduced by permission of the Delegates of the Clarendon Press from Kondakov's
'The Russian Icon,' translated by E. H. Minns.*

New standards were likewise introduced into literature. The provincial simplicity of earlier times was made to give way to an elaborate rhetorical style. All individual variety of fact was sub-ordinated to the general end of glorifying God and His ways in stately and noble language. The first models of this style were the Lives of St. Sergius and of Stephen of Permia, by Epiphanius the Wise. They are not so much narrative accounts of real men, as typical representations of the Holy Monk and the Holy Missionary. An historical work in the same style, which presented the History of Russia as the successive fulfilment of God's purposes, was also started under Cyprian. It formed the nucleus of the *Book of Degrees* completed in Muscovite times.

These works were only parts of a general movement to Byzantinise Russia and transform her into an Orthodox Kingdom that would be fit to lodge the Orthodox Church. It was the continuation of the work of Peter, Theognost and Alexis, except that Cyprian and his associates worked in the cultural rather than in the political field. It centred round the Metropolitan see of Moscow and St. Sergius' monastery of Troitsa, but everywhere, in the northern monasteries, in Pskov, and even in Novgorod, the intellectual *élite* contributed to the common cause. The spirit of liberty and anarchy ran riot in politics, but was unable to offer any opposition to the work of the Church. Gradually medieval Russia was being transformed into an Orthodox Autocracy.

The age of Cyprian introduces the Golden Age of Russian painting.* Up to the middle of the 14th century the history of Russian painting is still rather obscure. The painting of "icons" was practised by native masters, but all the better icons that have come down to us from those times, appear to be the work of Greek artists. Soon after 1340, a fresh wave of Greek influence introduced the neo-Byzantine style of the time, giving rise to several remarkable groups of paintings both in the Moscow and in the Novgorod areas. It culminated in the work of Theophan the Greek (fl. c. 1370-1410), which ushers in the golden age. His

*See *The Russian Icon*, by Kondakov, Oxford, 1927 ; *Les Icones Russes*, by Muratov, Paris 1927 ; *Denkmäler der Ikonenmalerei*, by Wulff and Alpatoff, Dresden, 1925 ; catalogue of the exhibition of Ancient Russian Icons at South Kensington, 1929 ; *Painting in Moscow in the mid-14th century*, by Zhidkov, Moscow, 1928.

work was continued by Andrey Rublev (c. 1370, d. 1430), a monk of Troitsa. This is the only name of an old Russian master that has been handed down to us by continuous tradition. Till recently he appeared rather as a symbol of old Russian painting than as a palpable artistic personality, but within recent years the uncovering of his works from later layers of paint (especially of the icon of the Trinity in the great church at Troitsa), has strikingly confirmed the traditional view and revealed him a painter of genius.

The impulse given by Theophan and Rublev was continued throughout the 15th century, reaching a second highwater-mark in the work of Master Dionysius who flourished c. 1500. These three names are about the only individual ones in the history of old Russian painting, which was not an individualistic art, and the effacement of the individual painter, whether he was a monk or a secular craftsman, was a sign of the collective spirit that, with the progress of the Church's work, was replacing the old individualism.

Old Russian painting is wholly Byzantine in origin. Its very close relation to that tradition goes far to explain the extraordinary achievement of Russian painters in an age that, all said and done, was barbarous and uncultured. Russian painting was the first, and, perhaps the most perfect, fruit of the grafting of Byzantine ideas on the Russian tree. It is in no way inferior to the highest Byzantine achievement. But it is, in a sense, more Byzantine than the Byzantines. It is less realistic, less picturesque, less emotional. Its colours are extraordinarily pure and clear, giving it a peculiarly rarified and seraphic air. It preserves the noble refinement of the Byzantine human canon and of the Byzantine rendering of movement. But it further emphasises the stateliness and majesty of the composition. Its dominant form of composition becomes the *deisus* (δεηόις)—symmetric rows of saints turned in adoration towards Christ. There is a peace and a harmony in these compositions that for the Russian mind symbolised the Kingdom of Heaven. This sacred painting stood in essential harmony with the spirit of the Orthodox liturgy. It was the static expression of the transcendent Ideal that sanctioned and consecrated the Orthodox Monarchy.

Architecture for a long time remained little affected by the new ideals. In Moscow, and in the Niz in general, the art was in a state of decadence, and the craftsmen unable to build high walls and large vaults. The few churches that have survived from the age of the great Metropolitans are small and insignificant. In Novgorod and Pskov the architects were more skilful. The churches there are usually small, but they are exquisitely proportioned, and their very smallness adds to their peculiarly intimate and homely charm. They all go back to Byzantine types, but Byzantine classicism in them has been ruralised and domesticated. The smallness of these churches is partly due to practical considerations—especially considerations of warmth—but it is also the outcome of the competitive individualism of medieval Russia. Each corporation must have its own church. Each citizen who could afford it aspired to build one, if he could not found a monastery. Pskov, small as it is, had as many as eighty-five churches. Architecture was little affected by the new spirit that inspired painting and longer remained dominated by a more medieval mentality.

Chapter V

THE MUSCOVITE PERIOD
(XVth-XVIIth Centuries)

1. THE GREAT RUSSIAN NATION.

2. THE MUSCOVITE TERRITORY.

3. THE THEOCRATIC MONARCHY.

4. MUSCOVITE SOCIETY.

5. MUSCOVITE GOVERNMENT.

6. THE MUSCOVITE REVOLUTIONS.

7. THE NATIONAL MINORITIES.

8. MUSCOVY AND HER NEIGHBOURS.

9. FEATURES OF MUSCOVITE LIFE.

10. ART AND LETTERS.

11. THE CRISIS OF MUSCOVITE CIVILISATION.

I. THE GREAT RUSSIAN NATION.

THE Great Russian nation is the Russian population of Muscovy, and Great Russian and Muscovite are interchangeable terms. It is a union of two ethnic groups—a northern and a southern— which are, ethnologically and linguistically, sufficiently different for Russian philologists to have proposed a division of the whole Russian people into four, instead of the usual three, main divisions. Each of the two branches of the Great Russian people would be thus accorded a status of equality with the two nations of West Russia. The classification is acceptable from the purely ethnological standpoint that would study origins rather than actualities, as well as from the "purely linguistic" which would limit itself to phonetics, to the exclusion of the vocabulary and of linguistic consciousness. As these were precisely the standpoints of late 19th century scholarship, and as they gratified Great Russian nationalism, they had a considerable vogue and the division of the Russians into four instead of three sections may still be found in ethnological and philological handbooks. Within the narrow limits of the ethnology of origins and of phonetics, the view is quite tenable. But for the historian the southern Great Russian group is essentially different from White Russian and Ukrainian, for it never had any distinct consciousness, never formed a separate unity, and is merely that part of the Great Russian nation which, in early Russian times, belonged to the sphere of influence of the three cities of the south, and not to that of Novgorod. In other words it is that part of the possessions of the house of Chernigov which was not absorbed into the making of the Ukrainian, or of the White Russian nation.

As long as Novgorod was the chief centre in the north, southern influence could extend very far north-eastwards, and the Chernigov frontier passed within a few miles of Moscow. But with the growth of the Suzdal power and the intensified occupation of the Mesopotamia, the Oka basin was irresistibly drawn into the Northern sphere of influence. Ryazan had recognised the suzerainty of Vladimir already before the Tartar invasion. When the Tartars devastated the parkland of the Don and Oka basins its population retreated northwards, drawing nearer to the Mesopotamian centres, and losing touch with their old metropolis of Chernigov, which now lost all importance.

Moscow stood near the old Suzdal-Chernigov frontier, and consequently on the very dividing line between north and south. From the outset her expansion went on in both directions *pari passu*. In the nation of which she became the centre the two sections were united roughly on an equal proportion.

The speech of Moscow which became the basis of standard Russian is neither northern nor southern. It combines elements characteristic of both, and occupies a central position among Great Russian dialects. Dialect, however, is hardly the word to use of the varieties of Great Russian speech. The difference between even the extreme north and extreme south is insignificant much smaller than between, say, London and Somerset. The Great Russian unity created by Moscow is, both politically and linguistically, a very complete unity. If there is a Great Russian group that may be detached from the rest, as a distinct unity it can only be the Cossacks; and their individuality is not due to any initial ethnical distinction, but to the peculiar character of the social conditions in which they lived since the 16th century

The territory occupied by the north Great Russians (with the probable exception of the Pskov district) and by the south Great Russians of Ryazan, was originally inhabited by Finno-Ugrian peoples. In the greater part the Finno-Ugrians have disappeared without leaving a trace, and it is logical to assume that they were absorbed by the new-comers. How great is the proportion of Finno-Ugrian blood in the north Great Russians it is impossible to say. There is every reason to believe that the Finno-Ugrian population was very sparse. Much of the Dvina basin, for instance colonised in the 13th-14th centuries, appears to have been virtually empty. The evidence of language is disappointing. The river names of north Great Russia are for the most part Finno-Ugrian though the Volga is Slavonic, just as most of the American river-names are Indian. But the number of Finno-Ugrian words in Great Russian is infinitesimal. Great Russian folklore and folk beliefs are certainly closely related to the Finno-Ugrian—sometimes more closely than to the Ukrainian—and I have already alluded to a number of ethnological traits shared by the Great Russians with the Finns, but not with the Ukrainians.*

Contacts with Turkic peoples go back to the earliest Bulgar-Chazar period. The presence of a number of Turkic words denoting agricultural objects is significant. Most of the south Great Russians were, for a time, subjects of the Chazars, from whom they received one of their most important crops, buck-wheat. In general, the Turkic element in the Great Russian vocabulary is very great. Apart from administrative terms and names of goods imported from the East, many of them ultimately Persian and even Arabic, they include terms used in various crafts (e.g. *kirpich*—"brick," while the Ukrainian word is borrowed from the German), and a very large number of words connected with horses, including nearly all the numerous designations of colour, and the word "horse" itself (*loshad'*). While both Great Russians and Ukrainians bordered on the Turks of the steppe, only the Great Russians were in touch with the agricultural Bulgars and in contant relation with the Turkic towns of the Volga. It is interesting in this connection, that the Cossacks, the oldest Great Russian inhabitants of the steppe, like the Ukrainians, use the Slavonic *kon'* and not the Turkic *loshad'*.

Many ethnological lines dividing Europe from Asia pass west of Russia or even between Great Russia and Ukraina. The subject has only recently begun to be given proper attention† and cannot be discussed here at any length. But it may be mentioned that Great Russian folk-music is the westernmost outlier of the " Indo-Chinese scale," common to most Asiatic peoples. The Russian folk-dances are also essentially connected with the East : they are either "one sex" dances, or if "two sex" dances, the man and woman do not form a pair, as in European dances, but the dance is the imitation of a wooing, the man and the woman performing entirely different movements.

*cf. page 62.
†cf. *The Problem of Russian Self-understanding,* by Trubetskoy, Editions Eurasie, Paris, 1927 (in Russian).

2. THE MUSCOVITE TERRITORY.

The unification of the original Great Russian territory under Muscovite rule was completed by Ivan III and Vasili III. Its principal stages were the incorporation of Novgorod (1478), Tver (1482) and Vyatka (1484), of Pskov (1511) and Ryazan (1517) the adhesion and subsequent incorporation of all the Eastern dependencies of Lithuania as far south as Chernigov (1500 and following years), and the conquest of Smolensk (1514).

In the 'fifties of the 16th century Muscovy went through an economic revolution that put an end to the feudal "natural economy" structure of society, made commercial capitalism the dominant economic force and the great commercial highways the vital arteries of the nation. Three groups of routes converged to Moscow*—the western group to the Baltic and North Sea countries of Europe; the Volga route, which became Muscovite in 1552-56, to the middle East; and the north-eastern routes to Siberia. The latter supplied the precious furs that served to make up the trade balance. The former two connected the country with the world-market, and formed together an important transit route from northern Europe to Persia. The greatest single event in the commercial revolution was the discovery of the White Sea route to Russia by the English in 1553. The English Russia company received extensive privileges in Russia, which amounted to a monopoly of foreign trade. The White Sea route was, however, a roundabout and perilous way to north-western Europe. A port on the Baltic would serve the demands of Anglo Russian trade much more effectively and accordingly, only five years after the coming of the English, Ivan IV began a war against the Livonian Order, then in the last stages of political decomposition. The war was at first successful, and the port of Narva bade fair for a time to replace the White Sea as Russia's principal outlet. But Muscovite aggression aroused general uneasiness in eastern Europe. Lithuania and Poland intervened to save Livonia from

*The actual geographical conditions created by the commercial revolution would rather have favoured the rise to the first position of Yaroslavl, Nizhni or even Vologda. But the accumulated importance of Moscow counteracted the geographical factor, and these towns became only secondary centres.

Russian conquest. The Muscovites suffered heavy defeats, and the war, which dragged on for a quarter of a century, ended in no gain and great impoverishment for Muscovy. It contributed to create a body of anti-Russian feeling in Poland, Sweden and Ger-

Fig. 11. Muscovy and her neighbours, 1560-1650.

many, which led to an effective blockade of Russia from the west. Novgorod lost its importance and began to decline. The annexation, in 1617, by Sweden, of what remained of the Russian Baltic coast completed the isolation of Russia on that side.

The Baltic blockade made the White Sea route Muscovy's only

125

outlet to the European market and the port of Archangel her only
seaport. The country between Moscow and Archangel became
commercially the most vital part of the empire. The great cities
of the Muscovite period were those of the great north road—

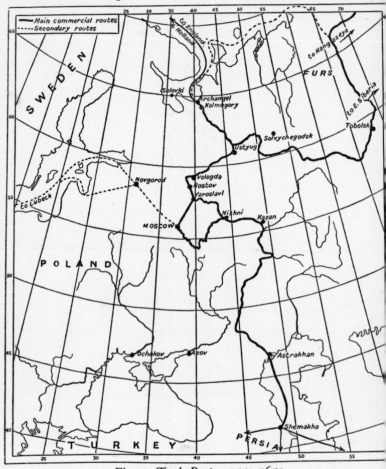

Fig 12. Trade Routes, 1550-1650.

Yaroslavl, where it crosses the Volga; Vologda, at the head of the
Dvina navigation; Ustyug, at the junction of the route to Siberia;
and, nearer Moscow, Rostov, and the great monastic town of
Troitsa. The flourishing state of even the smaller Northern towns,
Kargopol, Solvychegodsk, and Kolmogory, is testified to by their
wealth of 16th and 17th century architecture. The Volga towns

MUSCOVITE ARCHITECTURE.

Group of Churches in Yaroslavl with " tent " bell-tower.

Kostroma, Nizhni, Kazan and Astrakhan alone could rival those of the North road.

Moscow itself was a large city—larger, English travellers thought, than London. Its citadel, the Kremlin, containing the Tsar's palace, the cathedrals and the Patriarch's residence, was surrounded by lofty walls, built by Italian engineers. The adjoining "city"—*gorod**—the commercial centre, was also walled. This core was surrounded by the *posad*, the actual town and home of the citizens. It was a maze of crooked streets, unpaved, or paved with logs of wood. The houses were all of wood surrounded by vast courts and outhouses. The impression of a gigantic village was natural to the stranger, accustomed to the stone-built and compact towns of the west. But this was a superficial impression. Moscow was a very urban centre much more prevalently commercial and middle-class than later in the 18th and early 19th centuries. The Kremlin and city contained many substantial stone (or rather brick) houses, but even the palace remained partly wooden. The real ornament and glory of Moscow were her churches, of which there were supposed to be forty times forty. The country round Moscow was studded with residences of the Tsar and the richer boyars. The residences were invariably of wood; the owner's wealth and love of beauty was not testified to by his house, but by the church adjoining it.

The provincial towns were reduced copies of Moscow, with stone citadels, numerous and beautiful churches, and wooden *posady*. Besides the towns, the most conspicuous places were the large monasteries, also surrounded with stone walls and forming the nuclei of important commercial settlements. The walled monastery is the most characteristic feature of the Muscovite architectural landscape. They symbolised the political importance of the "black" clergy, and were quite effective from the military point of view. Troitsa, for instance, played a decisive strategic part in 1608-9. They were the Russian equivalent of the secular castles of Europe. In the Mesopotamia and in the commercial north there were many *posady* unattached to adminis-

---

*Gorod (town) in Muscovite Russian meant a walled administrative centre. English travellers translated it by " castle." The part of the town inhabited by the civil population was called *posad*.

trative "towns" but distinctly urban in character. In the South, on the contrary, the "towns" usually had no *posad* and were merely administrative posts.

The rural population lived in small and straggling hamlets. The parish centre was not as a rule a village, but an isolated church and parsonage. The most thickly peopled part of the country, the Mesopotamia, had a density of rural population o. about twenty to the square mile. Much of the forest still remained uncleared and served as a hiding place for brigands. Outside the Mesopotamia, and a few other districts (Pskov and Ryazan), the population was still sparser and concentrated in the river-valleys. The occupation of the land was still very extensive, and the wealthiest part of the country, the White Sea basin, was among the most sparsely peopled.

The commercial revolution made the Northern coast the most vital sector of the whole Muscovite frontier. Fortunately it wa little exposed to foreign attack. The Swedes of northern Finland (Kajana) were often aggressive, but the inhospitable nature o the intervening country did not call for a large defensive establish ment. The monasteries here played an even more active part than elsewhere. The most important was the great foundation c Solovki, in the White Sea. The abbot and monks, besides adminis tering vast possessions of their own on the mainland, acted as th representatives of the central government. They had regula troops at their disposal, and were responsible for the defence c the Karelian coast from the Kajana Swedes. By the end of the 16t century Solovki became a fortress of such strength, that when century later the monks refused to submit to the ecclesiastica reforms and rebelled against Moscow, they were able to hold ou seven years (1669-76) against the army sent to besiege them.

The century-long ruthless exploitation of the nearer Nort emptied it of its wealth of furs, and by the middle of the 16t century the nearest profitable fur-yielding districts were th Pechora basin and Siberia. Russia had access to them by the ol Novgorodian sea-route, but it was long and extremely dangerou The better routes into Siberia were controlled by a hostile powe the Tartar khanate of Sibir, which included all the best part c the Ob basin. It was a formation somewhat similar to the earl kingdom of Kiev. A group of armed merchants, Muhammadan and Kipchak-speaking, were organised under the leadership of the khan for the exploitation of the native Vogul and Ostyak hunters of the hinterland. The precious peltries brought in by the native chiefs were sent by river and caravan to the markets of Turkestan. Agriculture was practised, but on no extensive scale. The population was very sparse, the dominant race numbering no more than a few tens of thousands, and the subject races probably even less.

As the Kama route, even after the conquest of Kazan, remained exposed and precarious, the nearest route to Siberia led through Permia. Northern Permia, the land of the Zyryans, had become a Russian bishopric as early as 1400; southern Permia, the land of the Permyaks, was occupied under Ivan III. The Russians ignored the mineral wealth of the Urals, but exploited the rich saltmines of Solikamsk on the upper Kama. The district farther south was administered by a private family of merchants of Novgorodian origin, the Stroganovs, who had made their fortune in the salt trade. It was the gateway to Siberia, and the idea of adding that country to their sphere of influence naturally came to them. A band of Cossacks, former freebooters, in the pay of the Stroganovs, and led by one Yermak, sailed up the Chusovaya and down the Tura, attacked the Tartars and with unexpected facility conquered their kingdom (1582). The new acquisition was presented to the Tsar, who found it too profitable to be left in the Stroganovs' administration and sent governors with troops to take possession of it and to extend its boundaries.

As America was a land of gold, Siberia was a land of fur. All other aspects were negligible. The fur-less parkland and steppe were left to the nomads. The Russian advance proceeded northward and eastward through the Tayga along rivers and over portages. As far as the Yenisei it was conducted by the governors and by regular Cossacks in the Tsar's service. After that the initiative passed to the pioneers themselves, and the advance was more rapid. Yeniseysk, on the Yenisei, was founded in 1619; Okhotsk, on the Pacific, in 1647. The Siberian natives, hunters and reindeer-rearers organised into small tribal groups, could no more stop the advance of the Russians than the American Indians could the Spaniards. Firearms, in both cases, were the decisive factor. Enormous tributes of fur (*yasak*) were imposed on the natives, and much of its produce went into the pockets of the pioneers. The exploitation was so predatory that the immensely

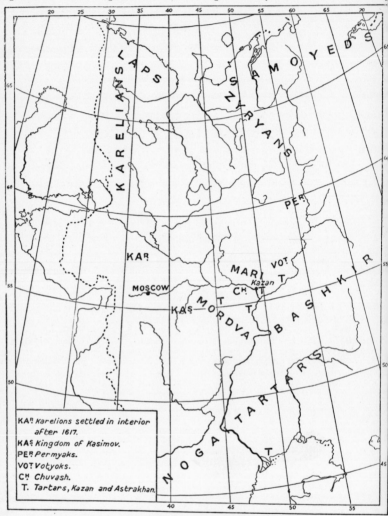

Fig. 13. Non-Russian population of Muscovy.

rich fur-district of Mangazeya (between the lower Ob and the Yenisei) was cleared of sables and ermine in some thirty years. Agricultural occupation was neglected, and grain for the pioneers and garrisons was imported from Vyatka and Permia. Only in

he second half of the 17th century the outer fringe of the Tayga
)egan to be effectively peopled by agriculturalists.

The Russian advance through the yielding wilderness of Siberia
topped only when it came against organised political power.*
The Mongol Empire of the Altyn-Khan prevented it from pene-
rating up the Tom and Yenisei further than Kuznetsk and
Krsanoyarsk. The advance of the Cossacks into the Amur valley
ed to conflict with China, which had just then, under the first
Manchu emperors, entered on a period of vigorous expansion.
The Chinese took and destroyed the Russian fortress of Albazin,
and by the treaty of Nerchinsk (1689), Russia withdrew from the
Amur valley. Dauria (Transbaykalia) remained the farthest Russian
possession in that direction till the middle of the 19th century.

In the end of the 15th century the Golden Orda disintegrated
nto several independent khanates: Kazan, Astrakhan and Krim.
Kazan sank before long to the position of a Russian dependency.
An attempt to assert its independence was followed by its final
onquest (1552). Astrakhan, the direct successor of the Orda, was
nnexed four years later. The Mordva country and part of the
parkland south of the lower Kama were gradually occupied and
olonised. By 1650 the Russian fortified *limes* reached the line
Tambov-Penza-Simbirsk-mouth of the Belaya. Russian forts were
ounded on the rivers of the Bashkir country (Ufa in 1586), but
he Bashkirs remained practically independent. The Muscovite
occupation of the lower Volga was purely naval. The fortresses
etween Simbirsk and Astrakhan were merely naval bases; the
teppe remained in the possession of the nomads. Though the steep
nd wooded right bank of the Volga offered many sheltered spots
or colonisation, this was spontaneous and outside government con-
rol. The Volga hills became famous as the repair of river-pirates.

But Astrakhan was a thriving colony and soon after its conquest
trading station was founded at the mouth of the Yaik (Guriev)
nd a fortress at the mouth of the Terek (Terki). Relations with
Persia were safe, except for Russian pirates, and constant. The
reat commercial centre of Shemakha, the terminus of the trans-
ussian route from London to Persia, supplied all Russia's
emands for silks, cottons, metalwork, precious stones and spices.

*See *Russia, Mongolia, China*, by Baddeley, Macmillan, 1919.

Russia was in close diplomatic relations with Persia, Georgia and Qabarda, then the paramount power in Ciscaucasia. A branch of the Qabarda dynasty settled in Russia, and the second wife of Ivan IV was a princess of Qabarda.

In the Western steppe the disintegration of the Golden Orda had changed the whole situation. The Peace of the Tartars was at an end, and Moscow's connections with the Genoese ports, which now became Turkish fortresses, were severed. The Khan of Krim became the vassal of Turkey. Muscovy was barred by the Turks and Tartars from the Black Sea, as effectively as she was held from the Baltic by the Swedes and Poles. The Krim Tartars were a military community organised for plunder, with the slave trade, fed by their raids on the Russian borderlands, as their economic mainstay. At first they remained friendly to Moscow and were content to raid the Lithuanian marches. But after 1520 they extended their raids to the Great Russian parkland. Life in the Muscovite south became entirely impossible and the Russian population was once more thrown back to the forest fringe. The parkland became a no-man's land. Every year the Tartars came in large numbers, penetrating into the inhabited woodland, sometimes even crossing the Oka. In 1571 Moscow itself was burned down by them, only the Kremlin remaining untouched. About 1550 Ivan IV's government took the business of defence seriously in hand. Armies were yearly concentrated on the Oka ready to advance at the first news of invasion. The fords over the rivers and the defiles between the forests were guarded by outposts. The whole population of the border districts was organised on a military basis with a view to meeting the Tartars. All this made the south unproductive, and an unmixed liability in the economic life of the country. The steady advance into the no-man's land did not at first change matters. District after district of fertile black earth was occupied, but immediately militarised. The great agricultural wealth of the newly occupied country lay fallow. To feed the southern garrisons the government had to organise State farms tilled by forced labour. It is no wonder that in the early 17th century the south was a powder house of social discontent. A more peaceful time began for the parkland only after 1650, when a continuous fortified *limes* (*cherta*) was erected which ran through Belgorod and Voronezh, and joined the Eastern *limes* at Tambov. At the same time the country farther south, of which Kharkov is the centre, was colonised by Ukrainians, escaping from civil war at home. By the end of the 17th century the South was no longer merely military and unproductive; Belgorod and Voronezh, its capitals, were prosperous towns prepared soon to become the rivals of Yaroslavl and Vologda.

South of the official frontier, Great Russian communities of Cossacks,* similar to the Ukrainian Sich, settled in the valleys of the Don, Yaik and Terek. The Don community was in existence by 1550, the other two soon after that date. They lived in fortified villages, subsisting on fishing, and still more on plunder. The Turks and Tartars were their lawful prey, but they did not always limit themselves to these. They recognised the Tsar as their sovereign, but as he did nothing to enforce his authority, the Cossacks were practically independent military democracies. A general assembly (*krug*), controlled as a rule by the richer and thriftier Cossacks, chose a commander (*ataman*). The poorer Cossacks (the "naked" as they were called—*golyt'ba*) were a constant element of unrest. They formed the bands of river pirates who infested the Volga, and took a leading part in the revolutionary movements of 1604-13 and 1670-72.

The structure of Cossack society was very different from the Muscovite. The spirit of freedom and spontaneous organisation makes them more like the old republican communities of the North, or their cousins the Ukrainian Kozaks. They developed a distinct individuality that marks them off from the other Great Russians, and has even led some enthusiasts among them to regard themselves as a separate nation, comparable to the Ukrainians.

*The word Cossack (Russian *Kazak*, Ukrainian *Kozak*) is borrowed from the Turki, where it means "out caste," seceder, "man who has become separate from his tribe." The Qazaqs of Qazaqstan were originally a federation of tribes who seceded from another federation. In Muscovy the word *Kazak* was not only applied to the autonomous communities of the steppe valleys. There were also *Kazaks* in the government service ; they were military servants of lower rank than the *pomeshchiks*. The word was used all over Muscovite territory. We have spoken of the Cossacks in Siberia; the northern monastery of Solovki too had its *Kazaks*. To prevent confusion three different forms of the name are used in the present book—" Kozak " of the Ukrainian, " Cossack " of the Great Russian communities, and "Qazaq" of the Turkic nation of that name.

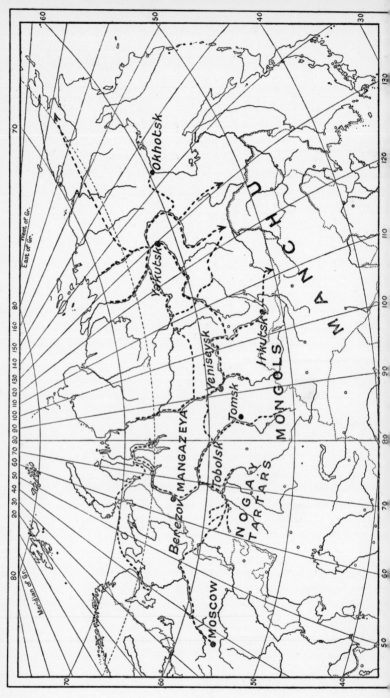

3. THE THEOCRATIC MONARCHY.

THE Muscovite Monarchy grew up as the political expression of the class of privileged landowning clergy.

Everything contributed, in the course of the 15th century, to the growth of monastic, at the expense of secular, landownership. The main cause for this was its religious nature which, by attracting a never-ceasing flow of donations, not only increased the acreage possessed by the clergy but allowed them to accumulate capital. The institutional, impersonal and as it were "immortal" character of monastic landowning increased its stability. The monks proved themselves far more efficient managers of rural property than any princeling or boyar. As, moreover, they were largely recruited from other classes than the feudal aristocracy, and had a different social consciousness, and different standards of life and conduct, the secular lords could not help regarding them as an alien and even hostile class.

In the course of the later 15th century the Great Prince who had previously been merely a secular prince of the ordinary type, if on a vaster scale, came to be transformed into something more definitely institutional and "religious." By becoming an institution comparable to the Church he ceased to form part of secular feudal society, which found itself as it were beheaded. The class of "institutional" and "religious" landowners now included both the Church and the Monarch. Their alliance, necessary for the fulfilment of the Church's ideals, was thus given a material foundation in social fact.

The political ideal, of which the Muscovite monarchy regarded itself as the fulfilment, was a product of the union of Roman and Biblical conceptions in Byzantine theory and practice. The Biblical idea of the Monarch as the Chosen of the Lord occupied the central place. His mission was the maintenance of the true Faith among his people. As long as he was Orthodox he stood by the side of the Church as an equally God-ordained and necessary institution against whom there was no appeal to any earthly court, not even to the Church. Only heresy made him liable to human judgment, and changed the duty of obedience into the duty (not the right) of insurrection. In the developed Muscovite system there was no opposition of a secular society with a secular king at its head to the spiritual society of the Church, but on the one side a subject secular society and the other the union of the Church with the Monarch, who partook in an equal degree of religious consecration.

Muscovy came to regard herself not only as an Orthodox Kingdom, but as the one Orthodox Kingdom and the one depository of the true Faith in the world. This was due to a succession of events that happened outside Russia, and which, coinciding as they did with the unification of Great Russia by the rulers of Moscow, made them, in Muscovite opinion, the successors of the Orthodox emperors. The first of these events was the Council of Florence (1439), where the Greeks, in the hope of obtaining Latin help against the Turks, agreed to a union with Rome and recognised Papal supremacy. The Metropolitan of Moscow, the Greek Isidore, gave his signature to the union, but he was deposed in Moscow where no need was felt of propitiating the Latins. After some hesitation, the Russian Church was declared autocephalous and independent of the Greek Patriarch (1446). This was a definite step towards national independence and towards a place at the head of the Orthodox world, but it diminished the independence of the Church in relation to the monarch. Alexis and Cyprian were forces at least equal to the Prince of Moscow. After 1446 the head of the Russian Church became *de facto*, if not in theory, the nominee of the secular sovereign. The date may be regarded as the moment when in the alliance between Church and Monarchy the former ceased to be the dominant partner.

When, in 1453, Constantinople was taken by the Turks, this was regarded by the Muscovites as a judgment of God on the Greeks for having betrayed their faith to the heretics. Muscovy was by now the strongest Orthodox kingdom in the world. She began to regard herself as the successor of both Israel and Rome. The theory of Russia—the New Israel—found its final expression in the *Book of Degrees* (c. 1550). That of the Third Rome was first formulated by the monk Philotheus of Pskov (c. 1480): the first

Rome had lapsed into heresy; the second Rome—Constantinople —had failed to preserve its Orthodoxy pure and was now delivered to the infidel. Moscow was the third Rome and the last, for there would be no fourth. Other apocryphal tales were devised, and a genealogy was later officially adopted, according to which the Russian dynasty was descended from a brother of Augustus Cæsar. Ivan III's marriage to Zoe Paleologe (a niece of the last Emperor) added the consecration of marriage to the transfer of primacy from the second Rome to the third. Tartar suzerainty incompatible with the new Roman status of Russia was discarded in 1480. The title of *Samoderzhets*—a translation of the Greek *Autokrator*—itself a rendering of *Imperator*—was adopted. The title of Tsar* began to be consistently used in literary works, and occasionally in diplomatic documents, but it was not officially adopted till 1547. The Muscovite rulers were more tenacious than hasty in their pretensions.

In completing the unity of the country they also acted leisurely. Ivan III preferred his apples to fall instead of having to pick them. He never embarked on an enterprise that was not a foregone success. So it was only his son, Vasili III (1505-1533), who gathered in the last autonomous Russian territories (Pskov and Ryazan). Nor was anything drastic done against the secular feudal lords. They retained their privileges and immunities, and much real power. During the minority of Ivan IV their factions for several years were in control of the central government, but their economic power was declining, and they were too illiterate and anarchic to be able to form an opposition that might cope with the superior organisation and culture of the clergy.

They found an unexpected ally in the northern hermits. A new wave of asceticism had spread over the Russian "wilderness" under the influence of the *hesychastae* of Mount Athos. The hermits denounced monastic landowning and the participation of the "unburied dead," as they called the monks, in the affairs of

---

*Tsar, from earlier *Tsisarĭ* is derived from Caesar. It was used in Church-Slavonic to translate the Greek Βᾰσῐλεύς. It consequently denoted the Kings of the Old Testament, and the (Eastern) Roman Emperor. It was also used of the Great Khan of the Tartars, and of his successors who retained independent power as the result of the partitions of the Empire. English writers of the sixteenth century invariably translate *Tsar* by *Emperor*.

the world. Ivan III himself was still sufficiently a feudal lord of the old type to be attracted by their attack on monastic land-owning. At the same time a rationalistic heresy, equally anti-clerical, that had sprung up in Novgorod, began to spread in Moscow. Ivan's daughter-in-law and even the Metropolitan favoured it, but the Church party displayed an energy that ended in the complete overthrow of both the heretics and the ascetics, whose principles of tolerance made them suspect of favouring heresy. Vasili III was a man of the new mentality, under whom all opposition was silenced.

The ideas of the new autocracy were formulated with particular vigour by the leader of the Church Party, St. Joseph, Abbot of Volok. The Tsar, he taught, was "similar to humans only by nature, but by the authority of his rank similar to God." The Church must be the loyal ally and helper of the Tsar, in their common work of establishing a divine order on earth. He derived his authority directly from God, and his judgment could not be overruled by that of any prelate.

All this time the evolution had slowly gone on, making the secular lords poorer and less important, and the monarchy and the monasteries stronger and wealthier. The Great Prince was gradually transforming himself from a feudal lord into an im-personal embodiment of the State, which was gradually becoming something different from an estate. But the social vocabulary re-tained old feudal terms, and in these terms the growing power of the autocrat could only be identified with the old conception of a feudal lord as the owner (*gosudar'*) of his "people" (*lyudi*). *Gosudar'* became the usual title of the Great Prince and remained the usual term to denote the sovereign till the fall of the monarchy.

When in 1547 the young Ivan IV (1533-84) was at last crowned Tsar the official transformation of the principality of Moscow into an Orthodox Empire was complete. It was followed and empha-sised by a Church Synod (1550) which codified the usages and the canon of Saints of the Russian Church, thus giving a fixed and final form to the outer body of Orthodoxy, by the conquest of Kazan and Astrakhan, the two Tartar states on whom had devolved the inheritance of the Golden Orda, and by a series of administrative reforms that put an end to the old feudal system of government. These events which coincided with an economic revolution of far-reaching importance, mark the final triumph of the theocratic monarchy and the achievement of the ideal for which the Church had striven ever since the 14th century. The only remaining step to secure complete independence was taken in 1589 when the Eastern Patriarchs, who had become largely dependent on Russian charity, were coaxed into conferring on the Metropolitan of Moscow Patriarchal rank.

The authority of both the Byzantine and the Muscovite monarch was regarded as derived direct from God, but the manner through which they came to power from the point of view of human law was different. The Byzantine Emperor was, in theory at least, elected by the people, but the Muscovite Emperor succeeded his ancestors. The idea of a hereditary dynasty was no integral part of the new Muscovite ideal, but part of the private-ownership complex that formed the essence of the authority of the medieval princes. It was subordinated to and utilised by the new theocratic conceptions, but it retained some of its old accompaniments. The Tsar's authority continued to be conceived as his property. The junior members of his family continued to be entitled to principalities only where they had sovereign authority, though this was reduced to quite insignificant proportions.

When, with the death of Theodore (1584-1598), son of Ivan IV, the old dynasty ceased to exist, recourse was naturally had to popular election. This was in complete accordance with the Byzantine tradition. But the elected Tsars supported their claims, apart from election, by their relationship with the old dynasty. Under the Romanovs the "patrimonial" nature of the Tsar's authority diminished, but never completely disappeared, and the confusion between the Tsar's property and his authority was never entirely overcome in Muscovite times.

This, however, was not only a result of the "patrimonial" point of view. The essence of the autocrat's power, according to the new theocratic conception, was that it was absolute. He alone possessed rights; his subjects had none, but only duties. As early as 1517 that remarkably observant writer, Herberstein, thought it possible to affirm that the power of the Prince of Moscow over his subjects was greater than that of any monarch in Christendom. It was still more so under Ivan IV and the Romanovs. The Tsar's freedom was limited by no human counter-rights, only by his own duty towards God and the Divine Law, but of that he was sole judge. Even the head of the Church (apart from questions of Orthodoxy) could only supplicate, but not advise him.

This does not mean that the Tsar took no account of the voice of the people. The first administration of Ivan IV was entirely governed by public opinion and the reforms effected by it resulted in a considerable amount of self-government for the provinces. After the restoration of the monarchy in 1613, parliaments (Zemski Sobor) were for some time convened almost yearly. But this was no concession to the people's rights. It was merely due to the fact that though absolute in law the Tsar was, in social fact, the representative of a given combination of dominating social forces, and in the absence of an efficient bureaucracy it was easiest for him to take direct counsel with his social supporters. The deputies themselves never regarded their functions as a privilege, but as a duty of the same kind as their military and fiscal duties. The growth of bureaucracy put an end to the convocation of parliaments.

The Church itself had no defined rights in respect of the Tsar. The head of the Church was in practice nominated by him, though formally elected by a council. But the social power of the Church was so great and the support it gave him so absolute that at first it was clearly in his interest to act in complete harmony with it. When the social importance of the Church began to decline and the military gentry became the really dominant class, respect of tradition and constitutional conservatism had become so profoundly imbedded in the Muscovite mind that the idea of reducing the importance of the Church never occurred to anyone. It was even in the 17th century, when the Church was no longer the real social force it had been under Joseph of Volok, that it gained the greatest outward recognition it ever received. Twice did the Patriarch become a real colleague of the Tsar, with the title of *Gosudar*. But both cases were exceptional. Patriarch Philaret (1619-1634) owed his position to being the father of the newly-elected Tsar, Michael Romanov. Patriarch Nikon, who aimed at achieving a lasting diarchy of Tsar and Patriarch, was successful at first owing to his personal ascendancy over Alexis, but was ultimately deposed and condemned by a synod for aspiring too high. Still the theocratic autocracy of Moscow could not belie an alliance that was the ideological keystone of the whole building and the moral justification of its authority. The last of the Patriarchs, Adrian (1691-1700), was one of the most influential. When, finally, the Church came to be deprived of its position, Orthodox Monarchy ceased to exist, and Russia became a secular autocracy, no longer sanctioned by religion, but by itself, by the interests of the governing classes, and by what support it could find in the doctrines of Natural Law.

But the landowning clergy had ceased to be the main foundation of the Tsar's power long before the official end of theocratic monarchy. Ever since the commercial evolution of the mid-16th century the dominant social forces were, in varying relationship, commercial capital and the new class of military landowners.

4. MUSCOVITE SOCIETY.

THE Muscovite body-politic was divided into three main "estates"—the Tsar, the Church, and the Tsar's *lyudi*, a word which it will be remembered when accompanied by a possessive case means absolute dependents—serfs or slaves. The *lyudi* fell into two classes: the "serving people" (*sluzhilye lyudi*) who served at court, in the army and in the administrative offices, and the "tax-paying people" (*tyaglye lyudi*) who paid and collected the taxes. The two classes were distinct in their functions, but not in their rights. The members of both were in an equal degree the *lyudi*, the serfs or slaves of the *Gosudar'*, whose power over them was absolute and unlimited by any rights of theirs.

The clergy alone neither served, nor paid taxes. They were not the Tsar's serfs, but his "supplicants before God" (*bogomol'tsy*). As in pre-Muscovite times, they were immune from civil jurisdiction, and constituted a social pyramid of their own. At the head stood the bishops and abbots of the great monasteries, collectively known as the "Powers" (*vlasti*). They took no direct part in civil administration, but besides being a dominant social and economic force as the possessors of about a third of all the land, they were the depositories of the national theocratic tradition and the highest moral authority in the country. When the whole nation (*zemlya=* "land") assembled at a Zemsky Sobor the Powers took precedence over the boyars and secular delegates.

The upper layer of the "white" (secular) clergy, the priests of the great city churches, were well endowed and as highly educated as the bishops and abbots. In life and outlook they were closely connected with the commercial class. Their social influence was considerable. One of the body, the priest Sylvester, was the head of Ivan IV's most brilliant and progressive administration in the middle of the 16th century. Others played the leading role in the great schism of a hundred years later. The rural clergy (except in the rich and commercial districts, especially

142

along the great north road) were poor and barely literate.

The serving class were primarily landowners. The privileged, feudal, or rather allodial landowning of the old boyars and serving princes disappeared in the course of the 16th century, but it was replaced by a type of landowning we may also describe as feudal, if we take the term in its widest meaning as denoting possession of land that conveys jurisdiction over the inhabitants. This new type of landowning was the *pomestie*, i.e. a holding given in conditional tenure in return for military service. The holder was called *pomeshchik*, a word that ultimately acquired the meaning of "squire." Lands in conditional military tenure began to be granted on an extensive scale by Ivan III, who disposed in this way of the estates confiscated from the Novgorod boyars. The accumulation of land in the Tsar's hands, and the necessities of defence led to the further extension of this type of tenure. In the course of the reign of Ivan IV the *pomestie* system became the prevalent form of land tenure in all the central, southern and western provinces.

The lower ranks of the *pomeshchik* class were scarcely differentiated from the domestic slaves, especially in the south, where they were most numerous, very poor and precariously provided for. In the early 17th century it was still not unusual to find a man mentioned one year as the slave of some high official, in the next as a military tenant of the Tsar. Their standard of living was very low, and western observers were amazed at the hardships and privations they were able to put up with in their campaigning, feeding on nothing but water and oatmeal, and sleeping on the ground in the winter with no other shelter than some improvised weather screen.

The *pomeshchiki* formed only the cavalry of the Muscovite army. The infantry (*streltsy*) and artillery were recruited from a lower class of serving people who did not receive *pomesties*, but only houses and gardens in special "liberties" (*sloboda*) adjoining the garrison towns. They formed a distinct class, socially inferior, but not always worse off than the lesser *pomeshchiki*, for besides their pay they were granted immunity from taxes and custom dues, and could thus engage in trade in particularly advantageous conditions. In the late 17th century the *streltsy* of Moscow were among the most conservative groups in the country, and Peter the Great began his reign by exterminating them.

The nucleus of the *pomeshchik* class was originally formed by the personal retainers of the Great Princes, many of them of servile descent, and later recruited, especially in the South, from the most various sources. When the serving princes and boyars lost their hereditary estates and their economic independence, they were, by degrees, incorporated in the class of "serving people," which thus came to include the most heterogeneous elements, from descendants of St. Vladimir to the sons of slaves. The old feudal families preserved a place of honour inside it and a system of precedence (*mestnichestvo*) was evolved at the still very feudal court of Ivan III, according to which no courtier, at court or in the field, could take precedence over another, unless he could show that his father, uncle, or other relative had taken similar precedence over the father or corresponding relative of the other man.

Till the middle of the 16th century Muscovite society remained, in the main, a congeries of self-contained rural units covered by the loose and sparse web of a trade that mainly dealt in articles of luxury for the very rich. The conquest of the Volga and the coming of the English marks a new era, when Russia ceased to be a land of natural economy, and commercial capitalism became a dominating economic force.

The greatest capitalist was the Tsar himself, and under his cover there flourished a great number of crown officials who made money out of their official positions. The richest men in Russia at the end of Ivan IV's reign were the Shchelkalov brothers, the heads of the two most important administrative departments. The monasteries were among the first capitalists and long retained a leading position as money lenders. The commercial capitalists of old Novgorod had been ruined and dispossessed by the Muscovite conquest. The only family of Novgorodian descent that survived were the Stroganovs, the administrators of vast and rich lands in the East, whose financial help to the government in the crisis of 1608-1613 was rewarded by exceptional privileges, and honorific distinctions that placed them on a level with the boyars.

A less privileged group was formed by the *gosti*, recruited from the richest merchants of Moscow and the provinces who were employed in the Tsar's financial service, so that though they bore a heavy responsibility, they had fine opportunities for increasing their fortunes.

The lower tax-paying people formed communities in each *posad*, and in each *volost'*. The communal authorities, recruited from the richest and financially most reliable members, apportioned the taxes of the community, but were also personally responsible to the treasury. Apart from the *gosti*, few townspeople were capitalists on any very large scale. Retail trade especially was exceedingly subdivided. A traveller says that eight Russian retail booths of the usual kind would go to make an average Amsterdam shop.

There was no sharp social barrier between the people of the *posad* and of the rural *uyezd*; least of all in the north where the former were few and the rural population, only partly agricultural, was largely commercial, industrial or engaged in fishing, forestry and trapping. The position of the peasants in these districts had considerably improved since medieval times, for the destruction of the Novgorod aristocracy freed many northern *volosti* from feudal overlordship. The free peasants of the north were not the least prosperous of Muscovite subjects.

In the more densely populated agricultural districts of the centre a three-year rotation was substituted in the course of the 16th century for the old predatory methods. But this did less to raise the status of the peasants than to increase their obligations to their landlords. For everywhere except in the north the 16th century was a period of rapid enserfment. At first its principal form was growing indebtedness, mainly to the monasteries. But the *pomestie* system gave vast masses of virtually free or loosely dependent peasants to the rapidly growing class of military tenants. This increased manyfold the burden that lay on the peasant. Light and traditional feudal dues were now replaced by the obligation of supporting a hungry *pomeshchik* who had to squeeze out of his peasants as much as he could, while the extension of the urban corn-market induced the larger landowners, monasteries and the upper layer of serving people to make every effort to increase the productivity of their lands and tenants. Unpaid work for his landlord did not exempt the peasant from crown taxes. It is no wonder that peasants began escaping from their grinding obligations into the south, where they might become free Cossacks or minor serving people, or into slavery, which at least exempted them from taxes.

The government made every effort to prevent the peasants from abandoning the estates of the rank and file *pomeshchik*. Tenants had the traditional right of "exit" (*vykhod*): they might leave their landlord and his holding on paying off their debts to him; this right could in actual fact be exercised only with the help of·richer landlords who alone could advance to the peasant the money he needed. It invariably operated against the interests of the smaller *pomeshchik*. The right of "exit" was consequently gradually abolished. All the governments that succeeded each other after Ivan IV contributed to increase the authority of the landlord over his peasants, till at last it was made absolute by the Code of 1649, which put an end to every means the peasant had of leaving his master's estate. It is from this moment that serfdom may be regarded as finally established.

Still the serfs remained distinct in law from the slaves (*kholopi*) who stood outside civil society, were not registered and paid no taxes. The majority were domestic servants and agricultural labourers, for a large percentage of the rural population were not newly enserfed peasants, but had been slaves for generations. The distinction between serf and slave gradually became nominal, but it was only Peter the Great who assimilated the slaves to the serfs to enable the former to pay the polltax.

5. MUSCOVITE GOVERNMENT.

THE political philosophy of the Muscovite State was a consistent whole, but the actual system of government which should have given flesh to that philosophy was far from reflecting its unity and consistency. It was a "natural growth." Except for the period of reforms of the mid-16th century and for the "summing-up" years of 1648-49, Muscovite legislation was never carried out according to plan. It left unchanged everything that it could and introduced reforms only under the stress of urgent necessity.

The traditional nature of Muscovite institutions is nowhere better seen than in the topmost institution, the Council of Boyars, which took form in the reign of Ivan III, when the "princelings" and old boyar families were still of paramount influence, and survived with hardly any change until discontinued by Peter the Great. All affairs of State passed through the Council and all acts of government bore the formula: "The Tsar has ordered and the Boyars have decided." Most of its work was done by the *diaki*, or "secretaries" as English writers called them. They were socially so inferior to the boyars that they did not sit, but stood, at the sessions. But the part played by them in the government was immense, and their opportunities for enrichment greater than any-one else's. The Shchelkalov brothers, who virtually ruled Russia in the seventh decade of the 16th century were plain *diaki*.

The technique of office work and official communications (including the postal service) was based on the Tartar model. It was a great advance on the chaotic methods of Kiev and medieval times, but it was cumbrous and slow, owing to the tendency to accumulate all administrative business in Moscow. Afterwards this was partly mitigated by the multiplication of administrative institutions in the provinces, but excessive centralisation always remained the vice of Muscovite administration. A fundamental feature of the Muscovite administrative system was the complete fusion of the administrative and judiciary powers. Old Russian law never crystallised into a system of procedure comparable to

147

those of medieval Europe. But a transition from medieval to modern conditions was effected in the conception of the judiciary powers of the State in criminal law. The conception of offences as torts to be righted by individual action was gradually replaced by the Roman conception—long familiar to the Church—of crime to be suppressed by the State in the public interest. This involved the disappearance of the old competitive forms of trial, wherein two private parties contested before the public authority, and the adoption of new legal methods including torture and brutal capital and corporal punishment. Russian penal law was different from the German and French law of the time, not in being more cruel, but in its cruelty being cruder and less refined. It was also more "democratic" and recognised no personal privileges connected with rank. If under the Code of 1649 the upper serving people were punished with exile, where lower ranks were given the knout, this was purely and simply an act of the Tsar's leniency, not a privilege inherent in noble birth or high position. When the occasion presented itself, a boyar might be tortured or scourged exactly like a serf.

Before the great reforms of Ivan IV, local government was carried on in a purely medieval way. Towns and districts were assigned to lieutenants (*namestniki*), recruited from the upper serving class, who collected the revenue, and after delivering a lump annual sum to Moscow were free to pocket the balance. This system of "feedings" as such appointments were called was officially regarded as a means of rewarding the lieutenants, rather than as a method of government. It was absolutely inconvenient to the people, and was abolished in the years following the commercial revolution, when self-governing corporations were created for the assessment of taxes and for the administration of justice.

The essence of the system was that the inhabitants were collectively responsible for crimes committed on their territory, unless they succeeded in discovering the individual criminal. They were likewise collectively responsible for the taxes, and the tax-paying communities saw to it very carefully that no one escaped his share. Self-government was the form of Muscovite administration that weighed most heavily on the liberty of the individual.

In the 17th century, however, crown governors (*voevoda*) were once more established in all the provinces. They were salaried officials and their posts were not regarded officially as "feedings." But the extent of their powers and the difficulty and costliness of appeal against them gave them and the *diaki*, who acted as their secretaries, such opportunities that they soon acquired a universal reputation for illegal acquisitiveness. In this, however, they were not different from the boyars and *diaki* who sat in the central offices.

The rural land-commune, a social feature that has received particular attention from students at home and abroad, goes back to Muscovite times and is mainly the outcome of Muscovite administrative conditions. It is quite essential to distinguish between the old rural community, the *volost'*, a self-governing body which did not affect the property rights of its members, and the modern land-commune, which is called *mir* by non-Russian writers, and is primarily an organisation for the equal repartition of communal land between the individual holders, with periodical readjustments to the changing number of the population. The *volost* survived, more or less, in the north, but in the centre, south and west most of the *volosti* were broken up to form *pomesties* for the serving people and ceased to exist as units. The first traces of the modern commune appear in the later 16th century. It was primarily intended to meet the tax-paying obligations of the community by distributing them equally among the householders, which entailed the equality of holdings and their periodical redistribution. By the end of the 17th century the "egalitarian" commune was the prevalent form of landholding in all the more densely peopled districts where the pressure of space had forced the peasants to adopt three-year rotation. It remained unknown in the north till the following period.

6. THE MUSCOVITE REVOLUTIONS.

A STRIKING feature of Muscovite history is the contrast between the stability of its political philosophy and the frequent instability of its social fabric. Four times in the course of a little more than a century was Muscovy shaken by movements that cannot be described otherwise than revolutionary.

The first of these movements was started by the Tsar himself, and began (1564) by Ivan IV dividing the whole country into two sections: the *zemshchina* was to continue governed by the constituted authority, the *oprishnina* ("peculiar"), was to become the private affair of the Tsar. To administer it Ivan formed a new household, whose members received the name of *oprishnik*. All persons who were not made members of it were expelled from the *oprishnina*, their lands were confiscated and distributed to the *oprishniki*, while they were given small holdings in the *zemshchina*. This implied the confiscation of a great amount of land belonging to old families and its distribution to men of the lower and middle serving class. All the more commercial districts were incorporated in the *oprishnina*; the English merchants too were included in its sphere of business. The whole proceeding was an attempt by the Tsar to eliminate not only the influence of the boyars, but also that of the Church; an attempt to establish a purely secular absolutism that would draw its sanction from its military and financial power, not from theocratic theory. There was a strong anti-traditional and xenophile tendency in the movement. Foreigners, especially German mercenaries, were welcome in the ranks of the *oprishnina*. The Metropolitan Philip, who protested against the cruelties that followed the *oprishnina*, was deposed by a servile synod and put to death. The *oprishniki* established a reign of terror in the course of which many boyar families were exterminated to a man. But the lower and middle classes suffered as much as anyone from the savage caprices of the Tsar and his retainers, and the whole system was muddleheaded to a degree. Public opinion of all classes grew hostile to it, and in 1571 the system was discontinued. Politically the effects of the *oprishnina* were nil. Muscovy remained a monarchy based on the alliance of Church and State and the subsequent canonisation of the martyred Metropolitan amounted to an official condemnation of Ivan's attempt to secularise it.

The second Muscovite Revolution is known in historic tradition as the "Time of Troubles" (*Smutnoe Vremya*).* Boris Godunov, a very able ruler who had governed the country for fourteen years as "Lord Protector" under the last Tsar of the old dynasty, and after his death (1598) had been elected Tsar by a Zemsky Sobor, was defeated by a revolt headed by a young man who was supposed to be Dimitri, the son of Ivan IV. There ensued a period of anarchy, during which new Pretenders appeared, Poland and Sweden intervened, and the Poles occupied Moscow, which ended only in 1613 with the election to the throne of Michael Romanov.

In all this succession of events the policy of the boyars and upper layer of the serving people was, for the most part, purely self-seeking and factious, merely favouring this or that personal combination. In the country much of the movement was mere brigandage, but some events and policies stand out with a greater social significance. In 1610, some of the junior boyars and other members of the upper serving and tax-paying class of the capital framed a consistent class policy, which found expression in the election of Wladyslaw, son of the Polish king, on condition that he would become Orthodox and guarantee certain political and personal rights to the upper classes. This was a clear revival of the medieval spirit of aristocratic and municipal liberty: the heads of the movement were a boyar, Michael Saltykov, and a merchant of Moscow, Theodore Andronov. It came to nothing because the nation refused to accept an alien Tsar, while the Poles preferred to conquer Muscovy for their king, rather than give away their Prince to the Muscovites.

The middle layers of the serving class, especially in the south, for the most part espoused the cause of the first and second Pretender, partly from loyalty to the old dynasty, and partly from

*See especially *Studies in the History of the Troubles* by Platonov, 1st edition, St. Petersburg, 1899 (in Russian), which is one of the classics of Russian historical literature. The introductory chapter contains a valuable survey of the social geography of Muscovy.

a vague dissatisfaction, the fruit of the general critical condition of the country on the eve of the Troubles. The lower serving people were more definitely opposed to Moscow and more definitely desirous of change. For a moment they took part in the great rebellion of the lower classes raised in 1606 by Ivan Bolotnikov. Bolotnikov was a real revolutionary, having as programme the spoliation of the boyars and of the rich in general, in favour of their slaves. The movement, which was short-lived, was not primarily a peasant movement. Peasants, no doubt, joined it, but in the south, where the movement originated, peasants were few. Its nucleus was formed by slaves and the lowermost and poorest serving men. It is significant, however, as the earliest movement in Russian history with a definite programme of social Revolution.

The first social force to organise resistance to anarchy and foreign invasion was the Church. The Patriarch Hermogen and the authorities of Troitsa initiated a movement to secure the triumph of the conservative and national forces, which was taken up by the towns of Nizhni and Ustyug, and supported by the whole population of the relatively prosperous and stable North. The serving people, who had oscillated for a long time between many policies and many loyalties, and the more regular Cossack troops, representing the propertied elements of the Don community, joined it. The election of Michael Romanov was due to the popularity of his father among what might be called the left wing of the movement—the Cossacks and serving men that had supported the second Pretender. The net social result was the victory of the alliance of the two middle classes, who accepted the leadership of the Church, and restored the monarchy. The lower classes were suppressed; the aristocracy greatly weakened. The *Zemsky Sobor* became, for a time, an almost permanent institution, but this implied no limitation of the Tsar's power. The conservative mind of the middle classes refused to conceive any form of government other than Orthodox autocracy.

Still the ruling groups, the boyars, *diaki* and high clergy, resented the increased importance of popular opinion, and worked towards the establishment of purely bureaucratic government. The *Sobory* came to be convoked less frequently. Administration by *voevoda* and *diak* was now extended to all the provinces. The growth and corruption of the bureaucracy became the cause of the third Muscovite Revolution (1648). It was started by the Moscow *posad*, and taken up by other *posady* especially in the north. The disorders were suppressed, but the fact that it began in the capital and was taken up by such centres of conservatism as Ustyug and Solvychegodsk appeared threatening. The Tsar convened a new *Sobor*, which was fully representative of the middle classes, and was allowed to draft and pass a great Code of Laws that embodied all the demands of the two middle classes. After the Code became law the convocation of the *Sobory* was discontinued, and bureaucratic government was restored in all its power. Yet the middle classes were appeased; they were content to forego all political initiative, as long as their social interests were safeguarded.

The last of the Muscovite revolutionary movements originated in a band of freebooting Cossacks, which had grown so strong on the plunder of the Persian coasts that it succeeded in seizing Astrakhan and the Muscovite posts of the lower Volga. Its leader, Stepan Razin, unfurled the banner of revolt against the boyars and *voevody*, and promised the extension of Cossack democracy with its *krug* and elected chiefs to all Russia. He was supported by the poorer townspeople and lower serving people of Astrakhan and the other Volga stations. He moved north; and as he approached the agricultural districts in the middle Volga, the Russian peasants, who were groaning under the weight of the newly crystallised serfdom, and the natives, crushed by taxation and robbed by degrees of their lands by the invading *pomeshchik*, rose in arms and acclaimed the cause of Razin. His army was defeated under the walls of Simbirsk, and the peasant revolt was quenched in blood. The upper classes were victorious, but the rebellion of Razin marked, much more than that of Bolotnikov, the beginning of a class-consciousness among the peasants. For it spread over the most purely agricultural districts of the country, and was openly and avowedly directed against the whole social and political system that enforced serfdom and tolerated the administrative fleecing of the population by the new ruling class of *pomeshchiki*.

THE Finno-Ugrian population of the Mesopotamia, of a great part of the Novgorod territory and of the Dvina and Onega valleys was tracelessly absorbed in the Great Russian people, but in the northern districts of Novgorod the Finns retained their identity. They belonged partly to minor nations of the West-Finnish group (several of whom have survived, in insignificant numbers, to this day), partly to the Karelian branch of the Suomi or Finnish people. The Karelians of Russia were not ethnologically different from their kinsmen over the Swedish border, and have preserved much of the national inheritance even better than the Finns of Finland; the Finnish epic *Kalevala*, for instance, was extant only in Russian Karelia when it was written down by Lönnrot in the eighteen 'thirties. But they early adopted Orthodoxy, and in their mode of life and outlook became quite similar to their neighbours, the Novgorodian peasants. After the cession of the Baltic coast to Sweden whole districts of them emigrated to inner Russia, where they were given crown lands in the basin of the Mologa and formed their own *volosti*. There they still preserve their language, though in all other respects they are indistinguishable from the Russian peasants.

Of the two branches of the Permian nation, the Zyryans were evangelised and incorporated in Russia about 1400, and the Permyaks under Ivan III. Both peoples opposed little resistance to Russian civilisation, and adopted Russian ways. The Zyryans retained a strong racial consciousness, and developed into a vigorous pioneering and commercial people, who came to play a leading part in the economic life on both sides of the northern Urals.

In the case of the Samoyeds of the tundra and of the peoples of Siberia, Muscovite domination was limited to predatory exploitation. The obligation of paying the *yasak* (fur-tribute) marked off the aborigines from the invaders. They retained their old clan organisation, and their mode of life remained what it had been before the Russians came. In so far as they did not die out, most

f them retained their primitive civilisation in virtual integrity
ill long after the 17th century.

The conquest of Kazan incorporated into the Muscovite body-
politic a territory with a relatively dense population of non-
Russians, Moslem and pagan. The dominating race, the Kazan
Tartars, were the descendants of the Muhammadan Bulgars, with
some admixture of nomad blood. They called themselves *bul-
arlyk*, but spoke the Kipchak dialect of the conquerors.

An aristocracy of nomadic origin formed the ruling class at
Kazan, while individual Tartar nobles were dispersed over the
country as the feudal lords of pagan peasants. The peasants of the
districts nearest Kazan were "tartarised," i.e. adopted Islam
and the Kipchak speech, but the social groups most characteristic
of Kazan, as the successor of Bulgar, were the merchants, who
monopolised all the commerce of Eastern Cisuralia. The conquest
of the Khanates of Astrakhan and Sibir gave Muscovy more Tartar
subjects, of the same type as those of Kazan, but these two groups
were numerically insignificant.

The migration of Tartar princes and lords to Moscow began in
the 15th century. Some of them adopted Christianity and amalgamated with the Russian serving-class, but those who remained Muhammadan were also given fiefs on special conditions of tenure. The
most important of these was the kingdom (*Tsarstvo*) of Kasimov on
the Oka. From about 1450 this district began to be given to members of Tartar royal houses, who were kept in reserve and made use
of as pretenders to the thrones of Kazan or Krim. Their subjects,
the Kasimov Tartars were used as Muscovite envoys to Oriental
countries. The position of the kings and princes of Kasimov was
very high, and they took precedence over all subjects of the Tsar.

The pagan nations subject to Kazan were the Chuvash (in the
hilly country south of the Volga and east of the Sura); the Mordva
(south of the Chuvash and as far west as the lower Oka); the
Votyak, or Ud-murt (in the Vyatka basin); and the Mari, or
Cheremis (between the Volga, the Vyatka and the Vetluga, with a
small section on the right bank of the former).* They all had what
was practically the same civilisation, which, though most of them

*See *Les Populations Finnoises de basstns de la Volga et de la Kama*, by I. N.
Smirnov, Paris, 1898.

spoke Finno-Ugrian languages, was entirely different from that of other Finno-Ugrians. The Chuvash, the only non-Finno-Ugrian of these nations, are the direct descendants of that section of the Bulgars that had not adopted Islam and had preserved the old Bulgar language. All these peoples were, more or less, agricultural, though the collecting of wild wax and honey and other pursuits connected with the forest were, in some districts, as important as agriculture. The Mari derived more from hunting than from tillage, and paid their tribute to Kazan, as afterwards to Moscow, in peltries. They were the most independent of the four nations, and were not the vassals of Tartar lords but had their own communal organisation under village elders. Among the Mordva there were remains of a national aristocracy, but on the whole the four nations were purely peasant.

The taking of Kazan was followed by the confiscation of the lands of the Khans and of the Tartar aristocracy. They were extensively made use of to endow monasteries and still more extensively distributed to serving-people as *pomesties*. A Russian squiredom arose in the districts round Kazan and Simbirsk, and in the Mordva country. The surviving Tartar nobles were gradually Christianised and amalgamated with the main mass of the Russian gentry. Many of the Mordva were enserfed to Russian landlords or remained serfs of Tartar nobles, but the other pagan nations for the most part escaped serfdom. Russian immigration began as soon as the country was annexed, breaking up the originally compact blocks of native population, and pushing the natives into the backwoods, away from the arterial waterways. The Mari alone offered serious resistance at first, but the encroachments of Russian immigrants, the growing burden of taxation and the general oppressiveness of the Muscovite administration made the peoples of the middle Volga, especially the Mordva, ready to rise whenever they saw an opportunity. They revolted in 1606, and took a prominent part in the peasant rising of 1671.

At the time Kazan and Astrakhan were taken, Muscovy was passing through a particularly intense phase of Orthodox consciousness; the crowning of Ivan IV as Tsar, and the Synod of 1550, had just taken place, and the victorious Muscovites felt it incumbent on them to signalise their victory as a triumph of the

Cross over the paynim. Mosques were destroyed and turned into churches; new churches were built and monasteries founded; bishoprics were established in both conquered capitals. But this zeal for conversion did not last long and after the first flush of victory Islam was allowed to live on unmolested. No serious attempt was even made to convert the pagans before the second half of the 17th century. Only under Tsar Alexis an intensive missionary campaign was started, in which the bishops and monasteries were freely given military assistance. The pagans offered a spirited resistance which culminated in the battle in which a bishop of Ryazan was killed by the Mordva. But it was the Mordva, too, who first gave in. The Mari and Votyaks were more resistant and a large section of them have preserved their paganism to this day.

8. MUSCOVY AND HER NEIGHBOURS.

MUSCOVY was self-contained, if not economically, at least in her consciousness. The Muscovites were convinced "know-nothings." In the west, Muscovite merchants were quite an exceptional sight In the east they were more numerous, but as a rule they did not go further than the great Persian mart of Shemakha Afanasi Nikitin, the merchant of Tver, who lived in India for three years (1468-71), and wrote an exceedingly interesting account of his travels, was an exception. Except for a few pilgrimages to the Holy Land, the only records of Muscovite travel are the reports of persons sent on diplomatic missions. Moscow was well informed of Persian and Turkish affairs, but the discovery of the Chinese Empire was quite a surprise, and when envoys from Akbar came to the Muscovite court, the Foreign Office refused to receive them, on the grounds that it did not know whether Akbar was an independent prince and whether it was not beneath the dignity of the Tsar to treat with him. Nor was the Orient much better informed of Moscow : an official 17th century Bokharan historian speaks of Moscow as of a "Frankish Sultanate." The Muscovite system of conducting diplomatic relations with all Muhammadan powers exclusively through the Kasimov Tartars, was not conducive of increased familiarity Astrakhan contained numbers of Persian, Bokharan and even Indian merchants, and Eastern goods poured into Russia; but all said and done, Russia stood in no closer contact with the Moslem East than with the Latin West.

The Greeks themselves, after the Council of Florence, became very suspect to the Muscovites. Greek clerics in Russia did not feel at home. The sad fate of the humanist, Maxim the Greek, invited to Russia under Vasili III to revise the Slavonic translations of the Holy Books, and who spent the twenty last years of his life in a monastery prison, is typical of the early Muscovite period. In the 17th century the Greeks began to be viewed less critically. The Patriarchs of the first Romanov reigns and Tsar

Alexis himself were Philhellenes. But public opinion resented this, and the great schism of the sixteen 'fifties was largely due to the excessive authority conceded to the Greeks by the heads of the Russian Church.

The cultural contact with Lithuanian and Polish Russia in the 16th century was very loose. The Ukrainian Kozak was a hostile alien—as hateful during the Time of Troubles as the Pole, as whose subject he came. There can be no question of West Russian influence in Muscovy before 1650. Muscovite influence in the West was, if anything, stronger. Thus, the Muscovite printer, Ivan Fedorov, was the first to found a permanent press in West Russia; the Muscovite oligarchic statesman, Prince Andrew Kurbsky, became a leader of the West Russian Orthodox revival, and the Muscovite heresiarch, Theodosius the Squinter, one of the heads of West Russian Anti-Trinitarianism. But these were all refugees who left Moscow with bitterness and became easily converted to the different ways of the West Russians. Only in the middle of the 17th century did Moscow begin to open her doors to Ukrainian scholars, and this was one of the immediate starting points of the great cultural crisis that was to be the end of Muscovite civilisation.

With the Latin West, Muscovy kept up continuous diplomatic relations ever since she was "discovered" by the Europeans in the reign of Ivan III. The profound difference of mentality made contact difficult and distant. Commercial interests obliged England, Holland, Denmark and Lübeck to be consistently pro-Russian. But the general feeling in Europe was certainly one of hostility and contempt, mingled with an increasing degree of fear. At the time of the Livonian war much anti-Russian propaganda was published in Germany, and reports were presented to the Emperor how best Muscovy might be utterly destroyed. Muscovy was hardly regarded as part of Christendom, and Muscovite ambassadors appeared as exotic to the European public as any Persians or Siamese.

Poland occupied a place apart in Russian relations with the West. The Poles were the hereditary enemy. But the presence of numerous originally West Russian elements in the Polish ruling classes, constant (if usually hostile) contact, and a considerable similarity of language, made the Poles different from the other

Latins. Polish prisoners of war were pressed into the Muscovite service, and easily amalgamated with the natives. The Tsars were constantly intriguing to be elected Kings of Poland, and a Polish Prince was actually elected Tsar of Russia and recognised for two or three years by a considerable minority of Muscovites. But Latin Catholicism erected an insuperable barrier between the two nations.

Apart from the Poles the first Europeans to frequent Russia were the Italians and Germans, who came as ambassadors, artists, physicians, or engineers. Muscovite civil architecture was for long time largely in Italian hands. But in the course of the early 16th century, Muscovy became practically barred to Roman Catholics, and Protestants alone were allowed to establish themselves in Russia. Of these the English were the first to acquire firm footing, and remained to the end economically the most important. They cannot be accused of taking no interest in the Russian people. Giles Fletcher's book (1588), is a masterpiece of intelligent, if distinctly unsympathetic, observation. An Englishman, Richard James, was the first man to preserve and hand down to us texts of Russian folk songs.* But the fact remains that the English have left singularly few traces in Russian civilisation. Of all the Eastern nations (except Spain and Portugal) Russia, in her assimilation of European civilisation, owes least to England.

The Germans came chiefly as mercenaries and adventurers. There was quite a number of them in the *oprishnina*. In the 17th century the inadequacy of the tactical equipment of the *pomeshchik* cavalry obliged the Muscovite government to invite increasing numbers of German, Scottish and Swiss mercenaries to form army units after the European model. Together with engineers and other specialists and tradesmen they were assigned a special suburb of Moscow which received the name of the German Liberty (*nemetskaya sloboda*).† Though unprotected by treaty,

*Seven songs written down for him in 1618-19 at Kolmogory and preserved in the Bodleian.

†"German" (*nemets*) was applied in Muscovy to all the Germanic nations including the Swedes and the English. It is misleading to say that it ever meant foreigner in general. The Latin-speaking nations were called " Franks" (*fryazi*).

was practically ex-territorial and autonomous. Its population was mainly Protestant, and Protestant Churches were allowed there. Outside the "Liberty," foreign soldiers of fortune, German and Scottish, settled all over Russia, were given *pomesties*, took Russian wives and became amalgamated with the main mass of the serving class.

9. FEATURES OF MUSCOVITE LIFE.

MUSCOVITE society was theocratic and its consciousness wa:
religious. The same religious ideal gave its sanction to Muscovit(
autocracy and transfused the life of the individual Muscovite
It was essentially an ideal, searching for the meaning of existence
not in the works of this world, but in the life to come. Thos(
who could not devote their life to ascetic effort often took th(
cowl at the approach of old age, or even on their deathbed
But in the affairs of this life the religious ideal was equally presen
to the mind of the Muscovite. To practise the forms of religion
to declare oneself an Orthodox Christian by every act was ar
essential duty. It tended to transform all life into a ritual and t(
impress on human behaviour the same ordered stateliness as tha
which inspired the sacred painters. The Orthodox liturgy in th(
great cathedral and monastic churches reflected the divine orde
and harmony of the Kingdom of Heaven. It was in this "goo(
orderliness" (*blagolepie*), that the essential message of Orthodoxy
as conceived by the Muscovites, resided.

The ethical element played a secondary part in the teaching
of the Russian Fathers. They laid small value on the natural anc
" pagan " virtues. Charity, of course, was a duty, fulfilled b
every good Muscovite, but it was still more praiseworthy to con
tribute to the upholding of the "good orderliness" that sanctifiec
human society. This implied, first of all, unquestioning loyalty t(
the Orthodox Monarch, strict observance of fasts and feasts, attend
ance at the services of the Church, and, for the head of a house
hold (or of a monastery) the maintenance of good order anc
discipline.

To aspire to a higher stage of Christian perfection meant t(
aspire to sanctity, the highest ideal of old Russia. The only ulti
mate test of sanctity was a holy death. Miracles wrought by hi
relics revealed the Saint to the world. By far the greater numbe
of saints canonised in Muscovite times were holy hermits, practi
cally all of whom lived in the two centuries of the great monasti(

162

age—between 1350 and 1550. St. Sergius of Radonezh and the great Metropolitans of Moscow, who had created the monarchy, were the most reverenced. A kind of holy man peculiar to Muscovy was the *yurodivy*—the "fool in Christ" (literally "defective"), who combined the severest mortification of the flesh with a grotesque and humorous behaviour, which was intended as a mortification of the spirit, since it brought contempt and ridicule. But under the cover of assumed folly the *yurodivy* could prophecy God's wrath and denounce the wickedness of the great.

Muscovite religion was not inclined to reason. Only in the early Muscovite period was there any inclination towards heresy of the questioning and rationalistic type. This died out by the middle of the 16th century, and the schism of a hundred years later was a characteristically Muscovite movement, traditional and ritualistic.

The Muscovite ideal was not equally alive in all classes. Among the peasants there still persisted beliefs and practices that went back to pre-Christian times. Pre-Christian (or non-Christian) elements were able to adapt themselves to the Orthodox ideal—and some districts of the north where they have been best preserved have also most faithfully kept the traditional forms of Muscovite Orthodoxy. The lower and middle layers of the serving class cannot be regarded as good representatives of the Muscovite spirit. The rank and file of the serving men were rare visitors at home. Their standard of life was low, their income either small, or ill-gotten. They had much of the mentality of a *lanzknecht* or janissary, and were not, on the whole, a conservative factor. They formed the bulk of the blasphemous and anti-traditional *oprishnina* and in the days of Peter they were the most eager to adopt the new European ways.

The realisation of the Muscovite ideal is to be looked for at court, among the boyars and higher *diaki*, the upper layer of the commercial class, the "white" clergy of Moscow and of the great commercial cities, and very generally in the more prosperous parts of the country. The most complete expression of the stately ceremoniousness and "good orderliness" of every moment of life will be found in the elaborate ritual that surrounded the Tsar, especially at the courts of Theodore I, of Boris Godunov, and of Michael and Alexis Romanov. But the classes that best preserved the Muscovite ideal, when it was betrayed by Tsar and gentry, were the merchants, especially in the north and on the Volga, and the peasants of the north. Indeed, it is only in the farthermost rural districts of north Russia that the Muscovite traditional forms have survived to our own times.

There was another side to the Muscovite medal that was coarse and crude, and it was that side that most struck the foreigner. All Western accounts of Muscovy are patently hostile, due in part to political hostility especially in the case of German writers, who never forgot the horrors of the Muscovite invasion of Livonia, and to the profound incompatibility of the Puritan and Muscovite standpoints (this applies particularly to the English travellers), but also to the fact that even judged by its own standards Muscovite behaviour fell short of the Muscovite ideal. Its crudity was largely due to the very low general standard of life, and also to the lack of those influences that tend to soften and refine human relations. The lack of respect for human personality was inherent in the Muscovite outlook. Absolute obedience took the outer form of servility and was not necessarily inseparable from genuine loyalty. The Muscovite more frequently displayed unquestioning loyalty to an idea or to a cause, especially to one sanctioned by religion, than the personal loyalty fostered by European feudalism and by the Turanian clan system. The small stress laid on worldly ethics by the Church found reflection in the low standard of common morality prevalent in Muscovy. The Muscovite administration was openly and blatantly corrupt, and the level of commercial morals, especially in relation with foreigners, deplorably low. The heavy pressure of tax and service bred a propensity to shirk obligations. The absence of recognised personal rights tempted people to prefer roundabout to straightforward ways, except in dealing with inferiors and dependents.

A European feature conspicuously absent in Muscovy was the chivalrous cult of woman with all the poetry adherent to it. The relations of the sexes might assume only one of two forms—patriarchal marriage or gross carnal intercourse. Mixed company was as rigorously excluded from Muscovite as from Muhammadan life, and men's company, even among the upper classes, as soon as liquor appeared, was inclined to lose the stately decorum that gave the Muscovite his nobility. The two basic units of Muscovite society were the monastery and the private household.

In the former the degree of ascetic severity varied greatly. In the great monasteries, the seats of power and wealth, it was not very high, yet presence at the almost continuous services was essential even in the least strict houses. Monastic life attracted many active people who had no particular inclination to asceticism, for bishops were recruited exclusively from the "black" (regular) clergy and the office of abbot was one of the highest and most gratifying to which a Muscovite could aspire. That of abbess was the only career open to a woman that allowed her to lead an active and independent life. The monasteries were also a refuge for all those who fled the grinding burden of their obligations to the state. But the poorer monks were often little better than the serfs of the monastic authorities.

The Muscovite family was strictly patriarchal and subject to the absolute authority of the head of the house. Among the upper classes, including the merchants, it was isolated and self-contained. The women were secluded in the *terem* (gynæceum) and did not appear in public. The father retained his authority over his sons when they were grown up and married. In the serving class this was largely counteracted by the official duties of the young serving men; as soon as they were able to serve they were entered in the service registers and given a *pomestie* of their own, thus becoming economically independent of their fathers. Here again we find that in the lower and middle serving class Muscovite conditions were less conservative and the Muscovite style of life less stable. In the commercial class the authority of the father over his sons was much more effective, for the son could not start a business of his own except with his father's capital, and thus had to remain in the family business. A father with his sons, or an elder brother with his younger brothers, or an uncle with his nephews is the typical form of business association in Muscovite times, the younger members of the family acting as assistants rather than junior partners.

The Muscovite family was distinctly more patriarchal and self-sufficient than the family of early Russian times. Between the Kiev and the Muscovite period the growth of the patriarchal family was continuous. Ecclesiastical influence was a decisive factor in its development. In Novgorod the upper classes were already quite "Muscovite" in their ideals or behaviour at home. It was in Novgorod that the *Domostroy* (*The House-Orderer*) was composed, that remarkable monument of Byzantine-Russian worldly wisdom which prescribes the way in which the *paterfamilias* must rule his wife, his children and his servants. But its final version belongs to the Priest Sylvester, the head of the "liberal" administration of the mid-16th century. The importance of relationship and kinship also increased between Kiev and Moscow times and reached its high watermark in the 17th century. *Mestnichestv* gave kinship a very practical importance, for the precedence of the most distant cousin might affect the precedence of all his kinsmen. In the application of the *pomestie* system too, it gradually became the rule, if a *pomeshchik* died without male issue, to hand over his land to the nearest kinsman in the male line. All these factors contributed to develop, in the 17th century, a strong sense of family among the serving people.

The Muscovite woman was secluded in her *terem* and subordinated to the patriarchal rule of her husband. On the other hand, her economic independence towards the end of the Muscovite period became complete. The Code of 1649 already established the principle that a woman's rights of property are not affected by marriage and the complete separation of property between husband and wife. The origin and initial stages of this institution, which seems so opposed to the patriarchal structure of Muscovite life, are somewhat obscure. It affected very profoundly the subsequent status of the Russian upper and middle class woman. Only in the lower classes where there was no property to keep separate, did woman become the complete subject of her husband.

THE Golden Age of Russian painting, the first and purest achievement of the Russian Byzantine revival, coincides roughly with the 15th century. Only its last phase belongs to Muscovite times. The masterpieces of this later phase are the frescoes executed in 1500 by Master Dionysius in the Monastery of St. Therapon, in the White Lake district. In the course of the 16th century the delicately severe style of the Golden Age gave place to a manner whose principal representatives, were from Ivan IV to Michael Romanov, the Tsar's painters and illuminators. They continued to conceive sacred painting as a representation of transcendental realities and consequently to reject all earthly naturalism. But they substituted for the majestic harmony of the 15th century a filigree minuteness of design and colour, that gave their work a jewel-like richness and often made it look fitter for the treasure-house than for the church. Excessive attention to the rich brocades in which the saints (especially the holy kings and bishops) are clothed, marks the growth of a more worldly and materialistic spirit, while their love of detail and chequered colour-schemes raises the problem of their relation to Oriental, especially Persian, painting—a problem that has not yet been seriously approached.

About the middle of the 17th century European influence began to appear in Russia, largely through the medium of Dutch engravers. The painters began to replace the severe and abstract Byzantine faces by the more sentimental types of the northern Renaissance painters. This was the end of old Russian painting. Sacred painting (*ikonopis'*) gave way to realistic painting (*zhivopis'*). The traditions of the former were preserved in the mass-production of icons, but degenerated into mere artisanry. The impersonal reproduction of traditional and abstract types, which in the Golden Age had been the integral part of a complete religious outlook, became, in the hands of the icon-craft, the mechanical preservation of an ossified convention.

Muscovite architecture is not a continuation of the provincial Byzantinism of Novgorod and Pskov, but a complex product of the metropolitan Russian-Byzantine tradition as preserved in the churches of Vladimir; of native developments that cannot be explained from Byzantine sources; and of Italian engineering technique. The excellent Italian architects who worked in Moscow under Ivan III and his successors, left a profound trace on Russian civil architecture: the walls of the Kremlin are their work, and the Banqueting Hall in the Kremlin (*Granovitaya Palata*) erected in 1484-91, by Marco Ruffo and Pietro Antonio Solario is a typical building of the early Italian Renaissance. But in church architecture their æsthetic influence was very small. The Assumption Cathedral, built by the Florentine, Fioravanti (1479), is a direct continuation of the Vladimir churches, which he carefully studied. The technical influence of the Italians was, however, immense, and they taught the Muscovites to build large churches that would not collapse. For even the Pskov engineers, who, in the 15th century were the best in Russia, could not build on a scale sufficiently vast to gratify the imperial ambitions of the Third Rome.

The Byzantine plan, used in the Vladimir churches and in Fioravanti's Cathedral at Moscow—a Greek cross, with the corners filled in, four pillars supporting the central cupola, and four smaller cupolas over the corner spaces—became the officially sanctioned type of church. Deviations from it were discountenanced by the ecclesiastic authorities, and most of the larger churches of Muscovy comply with it. But a group of churches built between 1529 and 1560 present a quite un-Byzantine type, known as the "tent" plan, and consist of superposed octagonal pyramids and octagons resting on a cube. The "tent "churches are among the most remarkable monuments of old Russian art. Their origin is obviously native and it has been ascribed to wooden architecture. But though all the north of Russia is studded with wooden churches of a very similar type, none of them can be proved to be earlier than the 17th century. In Moscow the "tent" plan was discountenanced by the Church, as not in conformity with tradition, and it came to be used only in belfry towers, which are still a familiar feature of the Moscow landscape.

In the ordering of the interior, a Russian innovation which gradually imposed itself in the course of the early Muscovite period was the *iconostasis*, a high partition consisting of superposed rows

RUSSIAN-BYZANTINE PAINTING.

Manner of Master Dionysius. The Crucifixion. Early 16th century.

Reproduced by permission of the Delegates of the Clarendon Press from Kondakov's
'The Russian Icon,' translated by E. H. Minns.

f icons, and dividing the sanctuary, with the altar, from the
entral nave. The *iconostasis*, though not Byzantine in origin, was
ertainly Byzantine in spirit. But in the details and ornamentation
f the Muscovite churches Byzantine elements early began to give
vay to a less severe and more picturesque style. The outer walls
egan to be treated with a view primarily to pictorial effect. Ornament became profuse, varied and free, and independent of struc-
ural demands. Polychromy asserted itself, glazed tiles and paint
overed the walls. Muscovite architecture became what foreign-
rs like to describe as exotic or Oriental, and what the Russian art
istorians of to-day, more particular in their choice of words, call
'baroque." The term is quite apposite, for Western influence,
hough destructive of old Russian painting, gave fresh vigour to
Muscovite architecture. Baroque ideas, mainly of Northern origin,
ound a ready soil in Moscow. They strengthened the existing
ictorial tendencies, but also quickened the constructive imagination and gave new life to the spirit that had evolved the "tent"
orm. The last remains of the severe Byzantine style went overboard
and "Muscovite baroque" was free to revel in unbridled construc-
ive and pictorial freedom. It consecrated the "bulbous dome"*
and gave their final form to the towers of the Moscow Kremlin.†

The few brick houses that have survived from Muscovite times
in the provinces are simple and sober, with no ornament but
elaborate mouldings round the windows. But the wooden architecture patronized by the Tsar and the boyars in the second half
of the 17th century is a veritable orgy of unbridled imagination,
a chaotic forest of pyramids, gables and bulbs.

The general appearance of the architectural landscape of
Moscow is mainly due to the "baroque" period of the later 17th
century. In a view of the Kremlin the Byzantine nucleus is hardly
apparent behind the outer coating of baroque and Renaissance.
Purer and earlier ensembles are to be looked for outside Moscow,
especially among the walled monasteries of the north, many of

---

*The Russian " bulbous dome " has obvious western affinities, and is a
close relation of the South German bulbous spiretops that are so prominent
a feature of the Bavarian landscape.

†The first to introduce a definitely " exotic " and " baroque " note into the
severe structure of the Italian engineers was Christopher Galloway, a Scots-
man who, in 1624-25 built the top of the Saviour's tower in Jacobean Gothic.

which have preserved the severe aspect they were given in the 16th and early 17th centuries.

The severity of the pure Byzantine tradition dominant in early Muscovy must be kept rigorously apart from the picturesque tendencies of the later Muscovy. These had, of course, native roots, but were mainly due to the development of the taste of the rich, which found itself in sympathy both with Oriental and with European baroque taste. Polychromy and picturesqueness, the love of jewels and brocades, are not inherent in the main tradition of Russian art. The older "tent-churches" and the wooden churches of the north are free from them (the polychrome coating of the Blessed Vasili church is of later date) and their freedom of imagination is entirely structural. Oriental and baroque motives dominate the decorative arts of the Muscovite court, often combining in a pleasing and unexpected manner. But the artistic handicrafts of the northern peasants are much closer to the genuine and fundamental Muscovite tradition. The wonderful wood carvings and embroidery that still survive in the north are purely, though freely and imaginatively, geometrical. The stylised animals of an embroidered towel from Totma or Vaga are the product of a mature and conservative art, itself the reflection of a stable and self-content civilization. They are much closer to the spirit of Rublev and Dionysius than to the capriciously picturesque art of the upper classes of decadent Moscow.

Old Russian Church music stands by the side of sacred painting, as strictly belonging to the innermost Byzantine core of her tradition. Indissolubly connected as it was with the Liturgy, it was impersonal and unemotional, and as severe in style as the painting of the Golden Age. In the later 16th century it also developed a taste for greater colour and virtuosity, and in the middle of the 17th century it began to be replaced by European polyphonic music. Except among the Old Believers, it survived only in a few churches, and in the "spiritual songs" of the north.

Muscovy was schoolless. All literary and general knowledge was either transmitted by the clergy, or acquired by reading. Books not relating to the Church had a certain circulation, but they were such as belonged to the lowest strata of Byzantine and European culture—the *Physiologus*, for instance, and various books on divination and the black arts. These last were severely proscribed by the Church, but remained popular among the literate. The reading public consisted of the clergy and of the upper layers of urban society. The *diaki* were, naturally enough, inclined to be great bookmen. Though in their administrative work they used the official language which was that of the town of Moscow and was simple and primitive in its syntax, many of them were masters of the most complicated and hellenized literary Church-Slavonic. Several of the Tsars, especially Ivan IV and Alexis, were among the best educated men of their time. But education was limited to a knowledge of the Scriptures, Liturgy and Lives of the Saints, of the better-known Fathers and of Russian history, as told in the Chronicles and official compilations.

Printing was introduced into Russia under Ivan IV. The first printed book appeared in Moscow in 1564. For a long time only books for the daily use of the Church were printed. The first book to be published in the Russian of the offices, and not in Church-Slavonic, was the Code of 1649, but manuscripts remained in general circulation till well into the 18th century.

Literature was not a distinct pursuit. Only such books were written as were necessary, lives of new Saints, vindications of the true doctrine against new falsehoods, or historical records of recent events. The literary style continued to be the same as had been introduced by Cyprian and the Bulgarians. The most ambitious literary works of the Muscovite period were the official history of Russia (*Book of Degrees*) and the *Saints' Calendar*. Both were compiled in the middle of the 16th century under the direction of the Metropolitan Macarius, who also formulated the decisions of the Council of 1550. Lives of Saints were the most widely read of all books. An unofficial compilation, called the *Prologue*, including much semi-apocryphal matter, is the book that has come down to us in the greatest number of copies. Polemical literature was extensively cultivated during the disputes between the Hermits and the dominant Church party, and during the political disputes of the age of Ivan IV. The Time of Troubles, though it produced a series of historical works of considerable interest, produced no political literature, as it produced no ideas to oppose to the theocratic conception which was by that time alone vocal, and dominated all the historical literature of the period. A new stimulus was given to polemical literature by the Schism of the Old Believers. Their leader, the Archpriest Avvakum, was one of the greatest writers ever produced by Russia; he began his career as a preacher and introduced into his written works the spirit of popular preaching and the language of the street. He was the first to use colloquial Russian for literary purposes.

Imaginative literature formed no part of Muscovite civilisation. It included neither poetry nor fiction. The function of the latter was fulfilled mainly by Lives of Saints and other edifying stories, contained in the *Prologue* and similar collections. Fiction began to be introduced in the 17th century, when romances imported from the East or West, but transformed into fairy tales to suit the Russian reader, made their first appearance. The wholesale importation of novels which began about 1675 was one of the forerunners of the disintegration of Muscovite civilisation.

The function of verse was mainly fulfilled by oral poetry. Its most interesting manifestation, from the historical point of view at any rate, are the narrative poems, which were intoned but not sung and which were known by the name of *byliny*. The oldest evidence of their existence is a manuscript made for Richard James in 1619, and they survive to the present day in various parts of Northern Russia (especially on the north-east coast of Lake Onego and on the lower Pechora). In subject matter they fall into two groups, one dealing with historical events of the Muscovite period, and the other with the exploits of legendary heroes—*bogatyri* (a word derived from the Turki *bahadur*), who are grouped for the most part round the court of a Prince Vladimir of Kiev. The poems are leisurely and repetitive in manner. The metre is accentual with a varying number of unstressed syllables; there is neither rhyme, nor arrangement into stanzas. Though some of the heroes appear in several different poems, the poems are not grouped into cycles. The subject matter of the *bogatyr* poems is partly of the fairy-tale, partly of the *fabliau* type. The heroic spirit, in the sense the term is used of the *Iliad*, of the sagas and of the Serbian *pesme*, is conspicuously absent. The subject matter of the other group of poems is historical. The earliest event commemorated is the taking of Kazan (1552). The narrative poems contained in Richard James' manuscript are all of the historical, not of the *bogatyr* class, and one of them refers to an event of the year in which it was written (the return of Philaret Romanov to Moscow in 1619). Later texts of the historic poems, as might be expected, confuse events to a greater extent; still the facts are quite recognisably historical, and free from all fantastic and fairy tale elements.

The subject matter of the *bogatyr* poems is entirely unknown to Ukrainian folklore, but a cognate metrical form, combined with a very similar poetical style and vocabulary, are clearly recognisable in the songs that are sung in honour of the bridegroom at weddings in the Carpathian valleys. These Ukrainian poems are regarded as having belonged to the repertory of the strolling jugglers and singers (*skomorokhi*) who appeared in the South-West in the 14th-15th centuries, coming from the Balkans *via* Moldavia. They spread to Muscovy and in the 16th-17th centuries were widely popular among the aristocracy. Like many other elements of Muscovite civilisation they were preserved in the North after they ceased to be fashionable in the capital. In this last home of theirs they passed from the *skomorokhi* to trained reciters recruited from among the local peasants. The problem of their literary origin, however, is still obscure. The existence of a continuous oral tradition going back to the real Vladimir of Kiev was postulated by the romantic ethnologists of the 19th century and is still upheld in text-books, but this view is exceedingly improbable. The existence of the metrical form and absence of any trace of the subject matter in Ukraina would appear to indicate that the two became united only on Muscovite soil, where the *skomorokhi* began to compose poems in a style that had developed elsewhere, on subjects taken partly from Muscovite historical literature (Vladimir and his court) and partly from the international stock of wandering fairy tales and fabliaux. The Oriental and Byzantine origin of some of the subjects has been demonstrated. The late Muscovite origin of the poems is further corroborated by the absence of historic poems dealing with events prior to 1550, and the absence of all trace of either the style or subject matter of the *byliny* in pre-Muscovite and early Muscovite literature, contrasted with the frequency of such traces in the 17th century. Besides the North, songs in the same style, but sung and not intoned, have been preserved on the Volga and among the Yaïk and Terek Cossacks. A few of them are about the same *bogatyri*. Others are about the great Cossack leaders and pirates of the Volga, who are romantically idealised, Stepan Razin being a special favourite.

It has sometimes been affirmed that the Church condemned epic poetry. This is entirely false, the enactments of the Council of 1550 are against ribald dancing songs and survivals of pagan ritual. The period immediately following the Council was precisely a time of great progress for epic poetry and all our knowledge of it comes from the later Muscovite period. Its survival among the Old Believers of the North, who have preserved all the severe ritual enactments of the Muscovite Church, is sufficient to prove that it was never discountenanced by the Church. Even in their capacity of jugglers, dancers and acrobats, the *skomorokhi* survived well into the 17th century and disappeared because of the introduction of European fashions and not because of the condemnation of the Church.

In style and music the *byliny* are closely allied to the "spiritual verses" (*dukhovnye stikhi*) that were performed by itinerant mendicants, usually blind or crippled. Their subject matter is taken partly from the canonical literature of the Church, partly from the more apocryphal legends of South Slavonic and Byzantine origin, some of which (as for instance the remarkable *Visit of the Virgin to Hell*) are, however, known only in their Russian form. Most of the spiritual verses are epic and impersonal in tone, but others have a more lyrical accent. One of the latter is the supremely beautiful *Praise of the Wilderness*, impersonating the Prince Josaphat of the Indian legend, which was as popular in old Russia as it had been in Byzantine Greece, and owing to which the Buddha became a Saint of the Orthodox Church. Poems like the *Praise of the Wilderness* are the starting point of the intensely lyrical and emotional poetry of the Dissenters which reached its full development in the 18th century. Spiritual verses might also have become the starting point for a written poetry, but the anonymous 17th-century poem of *Gorë-Zloschastie* ("Woe-Misfortune") is the only specimen of this kind that has been preserved.

11. THE CRISIS OF MUSCOVITE CIVILISATION (1654-98).

FROM the standpoint of social history the second half of the 17th century was a period of steady and continuous movement in one direction—the ascent of the *pomeshchiki* to social supremacy. Their right of property over their serfs was confirmed by the Code of 1649, and, undeterred by the rebellion of Razin, serfdom steadily and irrevocably approached to slavery. The *Zemskie Sobory*, in which the influence of the commercial communities counterbalanced that of the serving people, were discontinued and crown administration run entirely by men of the *pomeshchik* class became the only form of government. Monastic landowning itself was drawn under the control of the *pomeshchik*-governed state. *Mestnichestvo*, the last survival of old feudal privileges, was abolished in 1682 and the way was open for the serving class to acquire full rights and privileges after the model of the Polish *szlachta*. It was precisely in the years following the abolition of *mestnichestvo* that the *pomeshchiki* began to regard themselves not merely as a class of military servants, but as a hereditary "noble" caste of administrators and governors. The Tsar, by the end of the century, had definitely become a *pomeshchik* Tsar. The Church and the commercial class, the two most conservative and traditional forces, were losing their importance; the *pomeshchiki*, culturally the least conservative and socially the most pushing of the ruling forces of old Muscovy, were growing and expanding. Such was the social basis of the cultural transformation Muscovy underwent between 1650 and 1700.

Of all the causes that hastened the decline of the Church, the Schism that broke out in 1654 was the most effective. It was provoked by the pro-Greek tendencies of the upper clergy, which came to a climax in the Patriarchate of Nikon (1652-1658). Almost immediately after the enthronement Nikon ordered the substitution of ritual forms current in the Greek Church for those to which the Russians had been accustomed for centuries, but which Nikon and his party regarded as corrupt. The reforms were a direct blow at the idea of Muscovy as the vessel of Orthodoxy and the metropolis of the Orthodox world. They implied that the Greeks, subjects of the infidel though they were, and notoriously suspect since the council of Florence in matters of Orthodoxy, were henceforth to be regarded as a higher authority than the tradition of Moscow the Third and only surviving Rome. These implications were immediately realized by a number of prominent churchmen, who refused to accept the innovations. The leaders were a group of "white" priests who, in the middle of the seventeenth century had started a movement of revival and regeneration in the Church. With the support of the Patriarch they abolished abuses, pursued remissness in liturgic matters, and revived the practice of preaching that had been in abeyance since the 16th century. They were the élite of the Church; the most prominent of them, Avvakum, was a man of iron will and unbending conviction, and a writer of genius. Nikon and the Tsar, who at that time was entirely in the hands of the Patriarch, struck against the opposition; the leaders were deported to Siberia or confined in monasteries. The fall of Nikon, deposed for his papalistic tendencies, was followed by the return of the exiles, and by an attempt made by the peace-loving Alexis to come to an understanding with them. But Avvakum refused to consider anything short of an unconditional return to pre-Nikon usages accompanied by a condemnation of all the innovations. The council of 1666-7, presided over by two Greek Patriarchs, condemned Nikon for his love of power, endorsed his ritual innovations, and anathematised Avvakum and his followers, who became known as Raskolniks (schismatics) or Old Believers.*

The serving class, apart from a few members of the upper court families, proved impervious to their ideas. But among the merchants and among the peasants of the North, in a word among the conservative core of the tax-paying classes, loyalty to the old tradition found a very favourable soil.

The persecution of the Old Believers by the government was ruthless, but it only heightened their fanaticism. They came to believe that the apostasy of the official Church from true Orthodoxy announced the coming of Anti-Christ (whom they after-

*See *Life of the Archpriest Avvakum*, by himself, tr. by Jane Harrison and Hope Mirrlees, with a preface by D. S. Mirsky. Hogarth Press, 1924.

ards recognized in Peter the Great), and sought martyrdom at
he hands of the triumphant "Nikonians." Though essentially a
onservative movement, Old Belief became a restless and revolu-
onary factor in Russian life, and a rallying centre for all anti-
overnment forces, however little conservative. The monks of
olovki defended their monastery for seven years against a besieg-
ng army. Old Believers were prominent among the followers of
azin, while others, deported to Siberia, took part in the rising of
he Yakuts against Muscovite oppression.

The Church was purged of Raskolniks, but not without diffi-
ulty, and not without disastrous results for itself. The secession
f the most conservative and most religious elements greatly
ndermined its significance in the state and its force of resistance
o secularising currents. Its position was henceforward precarious,
ependent on the goodwill of the sovereign and on the inertia
f tradition, not on any real strength of its own.

The Schism coincided with the beginning of an immigration
nto Muscovy of West-Russian clerics whose Orthodoxy, though
ure enough in dogma, was much less traditional in ritual and
utlook, and imbued with Latin cultural influences. Gradually,
nd at first imperceptibly, their influence began to conquer the
hurch. In 1685 an Academy was founded in Moscow on the Kiev
odel where Greek and Latin were taught. Ukrainian, Polish, and
enerally Latin influences slowly transformed the whole fabric
f ecclesiastical civilisation. In painting, architecture, and music,
ld styles were abandoned and European models adopted. The
hurch still remained the leading influence in all matters of
ulture. There still might be a reaction against the growing tide
f novelties as there was under the Patriarch Adrian (1691-1700)
nd a Muscovite disciple of the Ukrainian doctors might even be
urned for holding Latin views (Sylvester Medvedev in 1692),
ut when Peter took up the reins of government he found in the
krainian prelates a willing instrument in his work of secular-
ation.

The year in which the Schism began, 1654, was also the year of
he adhesion of the Kozak state of Ukraina to Muscovy. This
roved the beginning of a succession of wars, in the course of which
Muscovy's military and financial efficiency was shown to be en-

tirely inadequate to her ambitious policy. Crushing defeats were inflicted on the Muscovites by Poles, Turks and anti-Muscovite Kozaks. This necessarily led to reforms in the army, to an increased appeal to foreign specialists, and to attempts to create a national industry that might at least meet the demands of the army. It began to be realised in high circles that, far from being the Third Rome and a model to Christendom, Russia was rather in need of becoming the pupil and apprentice of Europe in all things of this world. The first openly phileuropean administration was that of Artamon Matveyev, who came to power in 1669. His policy was continued under Alexis' successor, Theodore II (1676-82). After Theodore's death, when his two brothers, Ivan V and Peter were proclaimed co-Tsars, the Regency was assumed by their unmarried sister Sophia (1682-89), a fact hardly consonant with strictly Muscovite ideas. Her time was one of rapid transformation. The predominant influences for the moment were Roman, Polish, and Ukrainian. The state remained theocratic, but ecclesiastical culture was profoundly Latinised. The deposition of Sophia by the young Peter was followed by an Orthodox reaction. This stemmed the tide of Ukrainian and Catholic influence, but only to open the doors to the Germans and Protestants. The tide of europeanisation was coming in, and nothing could stop it.

The only really fierce opposition came from the Old Believers. Under their influence the *streltsy* garrison of Moscow, who were jealous of the new model army units, attempted to act as the champions of the old order, and even to impose themselves as kingmakers. But the gentry were willing to accept the new ways. The younger generation of courtiers and *diaki* and some of the young generation of Moscow merchants, formed a clique that was most ready for the reception of "German" ideas.

The first success of secular civilization was in 1672, when German players produced for the Tsar the first play ever acted in Muscovy. A few years later romantic fiction began to be regularly turned out and circulated in manuscript in very clumsy Russian translations. Amorous rhymes began to be written. But all these scarcely fused into a coherent whole. The order and style of life remained Muscovite, and defended itself from these first

MUSCOVITE ARCHITECTURE.

Iuscovite Baroque " style. Tower of Novo Devichi Convent in Moscow. End of 17th century.

attempts at secularisation. It is characteristic that the earliest Muscovite love verses have been preserved in a criminal suit, where they were produced as evidence against the author. But the "German" crept in from all sides and the fortress of Muscovite civilisation was doomed to destruction. Its best defenders—the Old Believers—had realised this and abandoned their posts on the ramparts, to start a guerilla war of despair in the open country. When Peter, after nine years of reigning without governing (during which he left the administration of his Empire to his mother and her reactionary friends), returned in 1698 from England and started his Reforms by the wholesale execution with his own hands of the restless *streltsy*, the stronghold of theocratic civilisation fell before him without more than a murmur.

Chapter VI

THE PETERSBURG PERIOD (1698-1861)

THE europeanisation of Russia took place within the twenty-seven years that Peter the Great was actual ruler of Russia (1698-1725). The process began before Peter was born, and went on after his death, but the turning-point, when the consciousness of the upper classes ceased to be Muscovite and became European, falls in these years. The classes affected by the change were the serving gentry, and a section of the commercial classes; the main mass of the tax-paying classes remained unaffected. The difference found external expression in enactments about dress and personal appearance: the gentry alone were obliged to wear "German dress" and shave their beards, but the tax-payers might let their beards grow and dress as they liked.

In matters of form and style the Reform was drastic. Besides European dress and clean-shaven faces, European forms of social intercourse were prescribed. The women were made to appear in mixed society, and dance with men at public balls. German, Dutch, French or Latin names were given to all ranks and things in the army and navy, and to all the numerous new offices and boards. Such was the outer shell of the "Reform." Its essential content was the adoption of European technique and technical instruction, the encouragement of essential industries, the creation of a modern army and navy, and the radical secularisation of the body-politic.

The Church ceased to be a power commensurable with and sanctioning the power of the sovereign, and became a department of the administration. The Patriarchate was abolished, and the government of the Church was vested in a "Most Holy Synod" of prelates and priests appointed by the Emperor. The new order was essentially similar to that introduced in England and in the Lutheran North by the Reformation. Peter himself was inclined to Protestantism, but as the new princes of the Church, the Ukrainian prelates, were for the most part so pliable and subservient that they made Protestant Reform superfluous, liturgy and dogma were permitted to remain unchanged. It was an Ukrainian prelate, Theophan Prokopovich, who produced the most complete and learned vindication of the new secular monarchy. Thus, with the approval of the higher clergy, the Russian theocratic monarchy was transformed into a secular absolutism of the Western type. The substitution of Western for Byzantine political thinking was symbolised by the assumption of the title of Imperator instead of Tsar in 1721, and in the name of Senate given to the supreme council of government instituted in 1711.

The secularisation of the State was accompanied by the secularisation of culture. The Church ceased to be the sole depository of learning; secular schools, technical for the most part, were founded ; secular books were published in increasing quantities. Russian replaced Church-Slavonic as the literary language and, to emphasise the break with ecclesiastical tradition, a new "civil" alphabet was introduced with letters approaching in form to Latin characters (1703). The old *kirilitsa* and the Church-Slavonic language survived only in ecclesiastical publications.

Another aspect of Peter's Reform was militarism. The great war with Sweden for the Baltic coast filled twenty-one of the twenty-seven years of the reign (1700-1721), and most of his financial and administrative reforms are to be explained by the stress of war-time conditions.* The army and navy absorbed all the resources of the country. The upper classes were, to a man, under the obligation of continuous military service. The lower classes, besides being crushed with a heavier burden of taxes and *corvées* than they had ever borne, were subjected to the new burden of conscription.

The enemy, Sweden, was the most efficient military power in Europe, and began the war by utterly routing the Russian army at Narva (1700). But at the price of colossal effort an army and navy were created which won the decisive victories of Poltava (1709), and Hangöhud (1714), and which, by the end of the war were second to none in Europe.

That the country as a whole was not permanently crippled by

---

*On the connection between the Reform and war-time exigences, see *Russian Finance in the first quarter of the 18th century and the Reform of Peter the Great*, by Milyukov, St. Petersburg, 1892 (in Russian).

the Swedish war, was due to the successful effort of industrialisation. The development of shipbuilding, of the iron industry in the Urals, of the leather, cloth and cordage industries in the centre, were the most important aspects of this "industrial revolution." The conquest of the Baltic coast with the ports of St. Petersburg and Riga, gave Russia a new and more advantageous outlet to the world market, and greatly increased the volume of her trade. But the economic progress of the Empire only contributed to increase the subjection and exploitation of the people.

The reforms of Peter the Great met with considerable opposition from various quarters, but it would be wrong to imagine him either as a hero struggling against fearful odds to civilise a stagnant country, or as a tyrant arbitrarily imposing an alien civilisation on an unwilling nation. The most active and vigorous forces in the land were on his side. He had the backing of almost the whole serving class, of the Ukrainian clergy, and of a small, but active, minority of the commercial class. The opposition came chiefly from the lower middle classes—urban and rural—that gravitated towards the Old Believers. The main mass of peasants was too downtrodden to do more than try to escape from taxes and forced labour into the unoccupied steppe. Nor did the opposition of the more substantial classes take a very active form. The reign of terror maintained during the whole of this period by the secret police had innumerable victims, but few of them were guilty of anything more than words. Only in the south the *streltsy* and townspeople of Astrakhan, in 1705, and the Don Cossacks, two years later, attempted to rise in arms, but were suppressed without much difficulty and with ruthless cruelty.

The social results of Peter's reform were twofold. The policy of industrialisation and commercial development implied legislation that favoured the productive middle classes. A succession of reforms, begun as early as 1699, gave the urban and commercial classes almost complete independence from the crown administration, that is to say, from the serving class, and a predominant place in the financial government of the country. But this did not last. Peter's "bourgeois" policy was continued by Prince Dimitri Golitsyn, but the fall of that remarkable statesman in 1730 left the serf-owning and military gentry the only class of any account in political life.

It was during the reign of Peter that the serving class finally became a corporate gentry, with a definitely aristocratic class-consciousness. The transformation was not retarded by the obligation, enforced more rigorously than ever under Peter the Great, of devoting all their life to military service, for the militarism of the reign made the army and navy officer, socially and politically, a dominant figure. It was in their military capacity that the gentry were able to play their most active role. Nor did the great number of foreigners and new men admitted into the service under Peter in any way "democratise" the gentry or the administration. The famous "Table of Ranks" that divided the service into fourteen grades, open to all persons irrespective of their birth, provided for the regular infusion of new blood into the gentry, but did not diminish its corporate or hereditary character. As for the old feudal families, their influence had long ago become entirely contingent on the royal favour and their successes in the administrative career, and not in the least on birth or hereditary wealth.

The political gains of the gentry became fully apparent only after the fall of Prince Dimitri Golitsyn, but their social gains were immediate and obvious. Their estates, by the assimilation of *pomestie* to *votchina*, became unconditionally hereditary property. Their serfs were assimilated with slaves, for though the law put this the other way round and transformed slaves into serfs to enable them to pay taxes, in reality their legal condition remained unchanged and that of the serfs deteriorated. Large areas of crown land were given to members of the gentry in reward for services, and the free inhabitants reduced to slavery. But the losses of the peasant class were even greater than the gains of the gentry; non-noble capitalists were given, in conditional possession serfs to work their mines and factories; peasants supplied the forced labour used for the construction of St. Petersburg and of the canals; they paid the poll-tax (which under Peter the Great replaced the older land and house taxes), and provided the main bulk of recruits for the army and navy. All burdens were heaped on them, with no corresponding advantages; they were the slaves of both the squires and the State.

2. TERRITORIAL SURVEY OF THE EMPIRE.

THE conquest of the Baltic coast from Viborg to Riga revolutionised the whole economic geography of Russia. St. Petersburg, founded in 1703 at the mouth of the Neva, became the seat of government. The new capital was no artificial creation. If we consider the orientation of Russia towards the European market, and the direction of trade routes, St. Petersburg was as natural a metropolis as New York or Buenos Ayres. All the principal articles of export—flax, hemp, timber, and tallow—were produced by the northern and north-western districts that gravitated to Petersburg. Canals connecting it with the Volga basin strengthened its hold on the economic life of the country. All the north and east, up to and including the Volga valley, were drawn into its sphere of influence, and the upper Volga towns, Yaroslavl and Tver, though much nearer to Moscow, became tributaries of Petersburg. The commercial function of the new capital was partly shared by Riga, which became the commercial focus of the flax and hemp districts of Pskov and Smolensk. Archangel lost its national importance, but remained a secondary outlet for Ural iron and Siberian furs. The commercial vitality of the north declined, though at first only gradually.

The Urals were the district most affected by the "industrial revolution." Iron and gold made it one of the most vital spots of the national economy. The expanding forces of mining imperialism led to the occupation of the South Urals, where the native Bashkirs had to give up much land to the mining magnates, and to the advance from Siberia into the Altai where a secondary mining centre sprang up. It was chiefly to protect the mining districts from the Qazaq nomads that a fortified frontier running in a semi-circle from Orenburg to Omsk and thence up the Irtysh, thus cutting off the Urals and the Altai from the steppe, came into existence.

The opening-up of the Altai and the establishment of the new frontier shifted the centre of gravity of Siberia to the south. The

187

relative importance of the fur-producing *tayga* diminished. The outer forest-fringe and the parkland began to be filled in by peasant colonisation. A new high-road running from Kazan, *via*

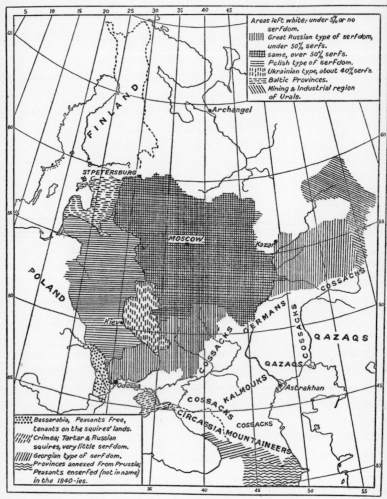

Fig. 15. Russia in the first half of the 19th century, showing the distribution of serfdom.

Tyumen, Tomsk and Irkutsk to Kyakhta on the Chinese frontier, became the commercial axis of Siberia. Its terminus became a lively place of exchange as the great point of entrance for tea. In general, as long as the Black Sea coast remained in foreign hands,

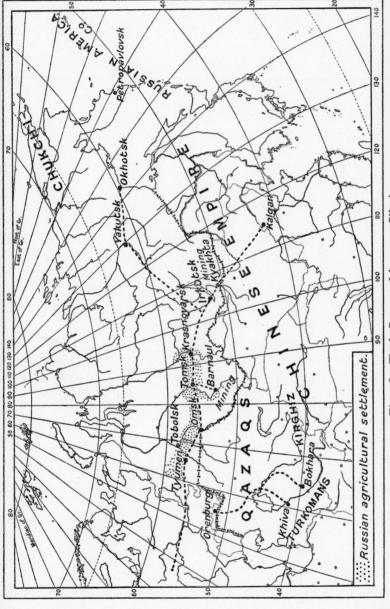

Fig. 16. Trade Routes, 18th century Siberia.

189

Russia's Oriental frontier came next to the Baltic coast in commercial importance. Kyakhta, Orenburg (the terminus of the caravan route to Bokhara) and Astrakhan were points of entry second only to Petersburg and Riga. Persia and Turkestan long remained important furnishers of manufactured goods—all East Russia, for instance, dressed in Bokharan cottons. The greatest markets in the interior were also connected with the East; the fair at Makariev on the Volga (transferred in 1817 to Nizhni, where it is still held annually), became the great meeting place of Europe, Iran and Turan; and the fair of Irbit, the focus of all commerce between Siberia and Cisuralian Russia.

As a producer of fur Siberia receded before new territories further east. The conquest, under Peter the Great, of Kamchatka, inaugurated a new phase of Russian Imperialism—the occupation of the sealskin coasts of the North Pacific. In the end of the century a chartered company was founded for the exploitation of the Kurile and Aleutian islands and of the mainland of North-West America. Its naval base was at Abo in Finland, and the nearest way to the North Pacific colonies round the Horn.* Settlements were founded in California and in Hawaii to serve as watering stations and to grow corn for the sealers.

The exploitation of the North Pacific coasts and islands was purely predatory. For a time it brought in enormous dividends, but by 1850 the sealskin Eldorado was as depleted as Mangazeya two hundred years earlier, and the United States senators who, in 1867, opposed the purchase of Alaska were not far wrong in describing it as a mere "ice-box."

If Petersburg was the capital of the commercial north and east, Moscow remained the metropolis of the rural south and centre. The shifting of commercial routes had made the old capital lose much of her importance. Her population remained stationary, and she tended to become a "big village," a vast congeries of nobles' residences. She was the capital of serfdom, the social centre of the provinces most densely inhabited with serfowners and serfs. With the rise of the textile industry in the early 19th century

---

*The circumnavigation of the Antarctic continent by a Russian expedition under Admiral Bellingshausen, who actually discovered its mainland, was connected with the development of this route.

Moscow once more began to be urbanised, but she grew into a real economic rival of Petersburg only in the latter half of the 19th century, by becoming the centre of the Russian railway system.

The parkland of the middle south, colonised in Muscovite times and contained within the 17th-century *limes*, was now the

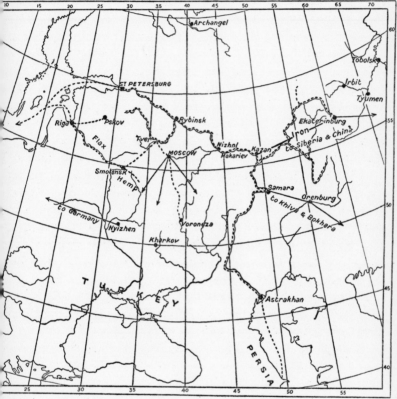

Fig. 17. Trade Routes, 18th century.

principal producer of grain, and the part of the country where serfdom assumed its most extreme and characteristic forms. The districts adjoining the Volga (Kazan and Simbirsk) were the grain furnishers of Petersburg and the north. The parkland south of the Oka, a still more typically "peer-and-peasant" country, grew the grain for the consumption of Moscow. The outer belt of the parkland, between the old *limes* and the steppe, was colonised in the early 18th century. Here serfs were fewer, but as many of the free peasants were gradually given away as serfs to magnates and favourites, very large estates became characteristic of all the belt running from Kursk to Samara. The parkland east of the Volga, especially after it was protected, towards 1740, by a fortified frontier running from Samara to Orenburg, was intensively colonised, partly by free peasants—Russian, Mordva, Mari and Chuvash—partly by squires, who appropriated large expanses of land belonging to the native Bashkirs at the same time as the mine-owners invaded Bashkiria from the north.

The extreme south-west of the Muscovite parkland was colonised in the mid-17th century by Ukrainians. Kharkov became the economic capital of the country between the Don and the Hetmanshchina, which formed the transition from the land of serfdom to the freer steppe. The fairs of Kharkov, the focus of the horse and cattle trade, were inferior to those of Makariev and Irbit alone. Autonomous Ukraina, the Hetmanshchina, was less closely connected with the Russian economic system. Nizhen (Nezhin), her commercial capital in the 18th century, had closer relations with Germany than with Moscow. It was only gradually that the Muscovite merchant became a familiar figure at the Ukrainian fairs. Cattle and pigs, rather than grain, were long the principal produce of this country.

The occupation of the steppe took place in the second half of the 18th and early part of the 19th century. Only east of the Don it could proceed without international wars, for there it was occupied by Kalmoucks and Qazaqs, who had not behind them the support of any organised power. They recognised Russian suzerainty in the early 18th century, but it was only in the 19th that Russian posts were established in the interior of Qazaqstan, and that the steppe east of the Volga began to be turned over to agriculture.

Farther west, the advance into the steppe was due to a succession of wars with Turkey (1736-1791), which resulted in the annexation of all the Black Sea steppe, of the Crimea and of Ciscaucasia as far as the Kuban and Terek. They were rapidly colonised, mainly by Ukrainians. For a long time sheep and cattle occupied more space in the new territories than arable land, and even when the wheat fever gained the steppe, only from one seventh to one fifth of the land was ploughed at a time—the rest remaining grazing ground. It was not, however, till the second quarter of the 19th century that the export of wheat from the southern ports became a paramount item in Russian trade. The paucity of waterways reduced the possibilities of the steppe. The Crimean war showed with what difficulty the new South was accessible from the centres. Only railways made it a real part of the Russian economic system.

The conquest of the Black Sea gave Russia, for the first time since the Kiev period, a commercial front looking south-west. But without the control of the Dardanelles, access to the Mediterranean was at the mercy of a foreign power. Catherine II and her successors made every effort to complete the conquest of the Black Sea. They dreamed of a great Euxine Empire with control of the Dardanelles and hegemony over the Greco-Turkish East. But neither the appearance of the Russian fleet in the Ægean nor the repeated occupation of Roumania and Bulgaria was enough to break the Turkish power. The annexation of Bessarabia (1812) was the only stable result of the Russian campaigns on the Danube.

Between the Black Sea and the Caspian, Russia's advance was more successful. Peter's attempt to take advantage of the anarchy in which Persia found herself during the decadence of the Sophies, and to make a Russian lake of the Caspian, only led to a ruinous war that ended in no gain for Russia and in the reassertion of Persian power by Nadir-Shah. But in 1783 Georgia was declared a protectorate, and in 1800 (after Russian protection had failed to save her from the terrible invasion of Aga-Muhammad, the first Kajar Shah) the King of Georgia was induced to abdicate and the country annexed to Russia. This gave a convenient *place-d'armes* for the conquest of the adjoining Persian and Turkish dependencies, but also led to a long-drawn war with the Caucasian mountaineers, which was brought to an end only in 1864. The conquest of Transcaucasia and Caucasia added a secondary market for the budding Russian industries and increased Russia's commercial hold on Persia, but it was not till the opening up of the Baku oil-fields in the later 19th century that the country became a vital part of the Russian economic system.

In the west, as in the Caucasus, Russian expansion was the outcome of political rather than economic imperialism. Its effect was greatly to increase the European character of the Empire by linking her to the centres of western civilisation, by introducing larger proportions of European elements into her population, and by making her not only culturally and politically, but geographically, a European power and a natural member of the "European concert." The western provinces remained very imperfectly incorporated. They retained considerable political and complete cultural autonomy, and remained outside the Russian economic system. Poland retained her own customs frontier till 1850, Finland till her separation from Russia.

3. ECONOMIC STRUCTURE.

In spite of the "industrial revolution" of the reign of Peter the Great, Russia remained a predominantly agricultural country. The proportion of crops grown for the market was larger than in Muscovite times, but for a long time only flax and hemp were exported abroad in any considerable quantities. Rye and oats were supplied for the home market, but by far the greater part of the crop was consumed by the producer. In the immense majority of cases the peasant grew his rye, buckwheat and oats merely to keep his family and horse alive. Even the money he required to pay his taxes had often to be obtained from non-agricultural sources. Grain for the market was grown mainly by the squires.

The whole economic system rested on serfdom. Though only about half the peasants were serfs, serfdom gave its colouring to the whole social structure. In most serf-inhabited estates the arable land was divided into a landlord's part and a peasant's part. The former was worked by *barshchina*, that is to say by the unpaid labour of serfs, who derived their livelihood and paid their taxes from work on their own holdings. As the majority of the landlords produced for the market, modern Russian serfdom was not limited, as medieval serfdom was, in Marx's phrase, by the capacity of a stomach. This made the Russian serf more akin to the American or West Indian slave than to the medieval villein. But in another respect conditions were distinctly medieval—the squires invested no capital in their land and it was worked with the serf's live stock and equipment. In the early 19th century the landlords in the more densely peopled districts attempted to raise their incomes by increasing their part of the arable land at the expense of the peasants and by substituting for the old three-field rotation more intensive systems of farming, after the English model. But agricultural progress proved incompatible with serfdom, and the attempts were abandoned. In the meantime in the wheat belt there was little or no serfdom, and the wheat was grown either by free farmers, or with the aid of free, wage-earning labour. The profits of the wheat growers were immense. Under the influence of all these facts the serf-owners in most districts realised, by the middle of the 19th century, that serfdom was unprofitable, and it was consequently abolished in 1861.

The *barshchina* system remained prevalent till the end of serfdom in the black-earth belt and in the principal flax and hemp districts, but in the greater part of the forest belt, and on the larger latifundia all over the country it tended to be replaced by the *obrok* system under which the serfs did no work for the landlord, but paid him dues in cash. The size of the payment was conditioned by the financial possibilities of the individual serf, for it was an essential feature of Russian serfdom that it was regulated by no customary law, and the obligations of the serf depended entirely on the pleasure of the master. But *obrok*-paying serfs were free men in comparison with their *barshchina* class fellows.

The industries that grew up under Peter and his successors were likewise based on serfdom. In some cases the workmen were simply serfs; in the majority they were "possessional" peasants, who were not the property of the owner of the works, but, as it were, hereditarily lent to him by the State, and might be made use of for no other purpose than to work a specified mine or factory. Legally this made a difference; economically the "possessional" workmen were among the most exploited and miserable of Russian serfs. They were especially numerous in the mines and foundries of the Urals. The industries worked mainly for the State, the army and navy being the principal consumers of iron, cloth and cordage. Many of the most important works were state-owned and state-managed. The technical level was low. In the flax and hemp industries machinery was almost unknown and the workers worked in common rooms under supervision, as they might have worked at home. This low technical level, inseparable from servile labour, explains why Russian industry came to be so badly out-distanced by the West between 1800 and 1860.

The old industries, in so far as they were not State-owned, early became concentrated in the hands of the gentry. The merchants who had not free access to servile labour devised in the course of the 18th century another system : instead of having factories they advanced raw materials to peasant home workers, buying up the produce at prices fixed by themselves, which were of course very low. This was the origin of the Russian home industries, which received a great development among the "free" peasants and *obrok* serfs of the Central and Northern Provinces. Whole districts became thus industrialised. The hardware industry of Pavlovo, near Nizhni, the ikon-painting of Khòluy, near Vladimir, the pottery of the Gzhel district, near Moscow, and the boot-making of Kimry on the upper Volga obtained a national importance.

A new phase of industrial development began about the turn of the century, when non-noble capitalists (many of them serfs) founded the Russian cotton industry. At first it was as primitive in technique as the old industries (modern machinery from England was first introduced in 1840), but from the outset it worked exclusively on free labour. The rise of the cotton industry, together with that of the wheat export, was the principal symptom of the approaching end of the period of serfdom.

As in agriculture and industry, transport conditions were dominated by the extreme cheapness of labour and by the complete subjection of the working classes. The canals which played such a part in the commercial development of Petersburg were built by forced labour. Grain was brought to Moscow and other markets of the south-east sector carted by the producer's serfs, who had to supply the sledges, the horses and the escort without remuneration. The up-river shipping and all the shipping on the canals was drawn by human labour and gangs of *burlaki* (towers) dragging a barge were a familiar sight on every river-bank.

The export trade remained, as in Muscovite times, in the hands of foreigners, among whom the English came first. In the 18th century the principal articles of Russian export were flax and hemp, iron, timber and tallow. In the 19th century the rise of new techniques in the West put an end to the Russian iron export, and wheat became of predominant importance. The principal articles imported from the West were articles of luxury and semi-luxury from England (high class textile goods) and France (wine, furniture, toilet articles) and colonial produce. Till the middle of the 19th century Russia depended on the West for no other goods than luxuries for the rich.

SECULARISED by Peter the Monarchy became even more absolute than it had been. If by absolute we mean free to legislate without any formal consent of the nation, it remained so till 1905, but in the second half of the 18th century, it began to be limited by the personal rights of subjects, primarily of the gentry, which came to be recognised as independent and inalienable.

The attempt made in 1730 to give a group of subjects legislative as well as personal rights proved abortive. Its initiators were not the gentry but the members of the Supreme Privy Council, whose leading spirit was Prince Dimitri Golitsyn, the successor of Peter the Great in his policy of industrial and bourgeois progress, distasteful to the gentry. Some of the latter were inclined to support a constitution that would provide for a governing Council elected by the whole body of the gentry. But the bulk of the gentry petitioned the Empress Anne to leave things as they had been. So she "resumed autocracy," and dissolved the Supreme Privy Council. The bourgeois policy of Peter and Golitsyn was discarded, and the monarchy became the political expression of the social hegemony of the gentry.

Though the gentry had no constitution to appeal to, they had at their disposal an effective weapon, the regiments of the Guards that formed the garrison of Petersburg, and where the majority even of the privates were nobles. When in 1741 the Guards deposed the German Emperor, Ivan VI, and proclaimed Elizabeth, the daughter of Peter the Great, Empress, they did not demand of her any formal recognition of rights. The gentry preferred real advantages to abstract rights, and though from the constitutional point of view the reign of Elizabeth (1741-61) was a simple continuation of the absolutism of Peter the Great, in practice the Monarchy became entirely subservient to the interests of the gentry.

Elizabeth's successor, Peter III (1761-2) did not appreciate this realistic attitude of the dominant class, when he hoped to restore his popularity with the serf-owners by the " Liberty of the

Gentry" Manifesto of 1762. He was deposed a few months later by the Guards, who substituted for him his wife Catherine II, the mistress at that time of one of their most popular officers. Nevertheless the Manifesto of 1762 is an "epoch-making"document, for it definitely limited the Monarchy by recognising a group of subjects as having absolute and inviolable rights. It described itself as a "fundamental and unalterable rule for all time," and made the gentry an inalienably privileged class. Their rights were further confirmed and extended by the Charter of 1785, when less extensive rights were also granted to the townspeople. Russian Absolutism was no longer constitutionally different from the Absolutism of French or Prussian Kings.

The gentry were quite content with this state of things. In the first years of Catherine II there was some agitation in favour of an oligarchic constitution, but the rebellion of Pugachev (1773), which showed all the lower classes unanimous in their hatred of the gentry, put an end to all these plans and confirmed the loyalty of the serf owners to their faithful watchdog, the sovereign.

When the monarchy attempted to emancipate itself from the dominant class it was invariably called to order. Paul I was murdered by a conspiracy of courtiers (1801) for preparing war against England—the principal consumer of serf-produced goods, and after the peace of Tilsit (1807), the progressive bourgeois and pro-French administration of Speransky was allowed to carry on for four years only under the immediate stress of military defeat.

The constitutional movements that grew up under Alexander I, did not count on the support of the bulk of the gentry. They had the support of only that sector of the class who were no longer economically satisfied with serfdom, and sought an entente with the nascent industrial bourgeoisie. Speransky's constitutional reform, calculated for the transformation of the gentry along modern "English" lines failed to materialise. The next constitutional movement was that of the Decembrists, which assumed a distinctly revolutionary character. The Decembrists were for the most part nobles, but intellectuals rather than serfowners (most of them were officers living on their pay). They wanted freer and more bourgeois forms of life where there would be more room for their intellectual energy. The gentry, as such, were solidly hostile to the Decembrists, whose defeat by Nicolas I (1825) meant not only the victory of autocracy, but a reaffirmation of the whole social and political system based on serfdom.

The absolutism of Peter the Great and his successors was inclined to borrow its phraseology from Roman and Natural Law, and to justify itself by its utility to the nation. The view of power as an object of property and enjoyment was no doubt, in practice, the view of most of the 18th century rulers, especially of Anne and of Elizabeth. But even then the monarchy paid lip-service to civilisation and the public weal. The most efficient Russian monarchs of the 18th century, especially Peter, were in advance of most contemporary European sovereigns in the consciousness of their public duties and in the "enlightened" character of their despotism. But they were singularly free from moral inhibitions and a strong contrast, in this respect, to the first Romanovs. The abandonment of all tradition had meant for them abandonment of all restraint. The open and shameless disorders of precisely the two most progressive 18th century monarchs, Peter I and Catherine II, have become notorious.

The untraditional, and as it were, "illegitimate" character of the Russian monarchy after Peter is strikingly expressed in the absence of any law of succession. Peter, to free himself from his heir, the reactionary and clerically inclined Alexis, enacted that every monarch should appoint his own successor. But of the eight sovereigns who ascended the throne between 1725 and 1797 only four were thus appointed and of these four three were promptly deposed by the gentry. The two rulers that ruled longest and were most popular, Elizabeth and Catherine II, were both carried to the throne by a revolt of the guards, the latter without the ghost of a legal pretext.

"Illegitimate" monarchy came to an end with the publication by Paul of a fixed law of succession (1796), inspired by the dynastic pacts of the German ruling houses, which marked the adhesion of Russia to the Western doctrine of legitimism and Divine right, and made the Russian Emperors the champions of the cause of monarchy in all Europe.

Parallel to the transformation of the dictatorial absolutism of

Peter the Great into the more "legitimate" autocracy of the 19th century, the arbitrary and personal administration of the early Empire was transformed by degrees into an organised and disciplined bureaucracy.

Peter had attempted to organise the administration after the Swedish bureaucratic model, then the most progressive in Europe. But the collegial system introduced by him proved in practice a mere decoration, and throughout the 18th century the administration was carried on by independent and practically irresponsible individual administrators.

Judiciary and executive power remained fused. In spite of the "Table of Ranks" the civil service formed no regular pyramid; between the administrators and the minor clerks (*podiachie*) there was a social gulf almost as deep as between serf and squire. The army of *podiachie*, uneducated, unrespected and underpaid, living on bribes, were a universal pest. This was aggravated by the state of legislation, which was a maze of unrepealed and uncodified decrees. Individual administrators did some useful work, but the majority of the high officials regarded their offices as an opportunity for increasing their fortunes by more or less open peculation. The administration had all the vices of bureaucracy—secrecy, corruption, slowness—without any of its safeguards and advantages.

Reforms began under Catherine II, inaugurated by the convocation in 1767 of a "Commission of Deputies" regularly elected by all classes of the population, except the serfs and the clergy. The impossibility of reconciling the interests of the gentry with those of the other classes made the Commission a failure, but its committee-work became the basis for the reforms of 1775-85. These were dictated by a desire to regularise and modernise the administrative machine, in the interests, primarily of the gentry, and secondly of the commercial class. The judiciary was separated from the executive. The provincial governors retained very extensive powers, but greater regularity was introduced into the subordinate offices. The administration of the rural districts was placed in the hands of the local gentry who nominated the executive officers and members of the inferior courts.

The work of regularisation was continued under Alexander I. The Speransky administration created ministries where work was

organised on the French Napoleonic model, and welded th
bureaucracy into a united corps with a regular pyramid of ascen
All its members were now in the same sense officials—*chinovnik*
The latest achievement in the way of regularising the goverr
ment was the publication of the Digest of Laws in fifteen volume
a remarkable work of codification, under the supervision of th
greatest of Russian bureaucrats, Speransky, after his return fror
exile (1832).

The Digest proclaimed the principle that the Empire w
governed "on the firm foundation of the Law." This was no doul
truer in 1832 than in 1760. Nevertheless, apart from the fa
that the great majority of the people were in the strict sense devoi
of all rights, the element of arbitrary and personal power remaine
very prominent. The Emperor took a personal part in the ac
ministration of justice. Political offenders (e.g. the Decembrist
were invariably tried by special courts created *ad hoc*.

In the 18th century, not only favourites like Potemkin, who
power was in practice equal to the Empress's, but even th
rank and file of provincial administrators, paid little or no atter
tion to Petersburg, and ruled their provinces like feudal baror
or Chinese war-lords. The " last of the barons " was Gener
Ermolov, "proconsul" of the Caucasus in 1816-1826, one of th
most cultured and gifted men of his time, a friend of the Decen
brists and of Griboyedov, but who ruled his province with th
independence and cruelty of a Sulla. He was quite expected
move his army against Petersburg after the suppression of th
Decembrists. His removal was the beginning of the era of con
plete subordination that marks the reign of Nicholas I.

It was also the era of absolute suppression of all public opinior
when no question of current political or administrative intere
might be discussed by the Press. Its most typical institution w
the Third Section of His Majesty's Own Chancellery, and i
instrument the Corps of Gendarmes. It was the most efficier
and perhaps the least corrupt of all the administrative institution
and its head, Benckendorff, a man of considerable organisir
ability. There were other efficient men among Nicholas I's ministe
but irresponsibility in its dealings with the private citizen, endle
procrastination, peculation and bribery were the inevitable a

ompaniment of bureaucratic secrecy. The picture of the pro-
incial administration drawn by Gogol, though inexact in detail,
true to the spirit of the bureaucracy of Nicholas I.

The darkest spot in the administrative machine were the law
ourts. Though separated from the executive by Catherine II,
ie judiciary remained purely bureaucratic—secret and in-
uisitorial. The slowness of the law courts was greater than that
f any other office, the corruption of the clerks proverbial, and
ie reputation of the judges worse than that of other officials.

The penal system remained virtually unchanged since Musco-
ite times, except that deportation to Siberia became a more
niversal measure. Though torture was abolished by Catherine,
nd capital punishment for non-political offences by Elizabeth,
he *knout* was often a more cruel form of death, and even after its
bolition in 1845 public whippings remained the most usual form
f punishment until 1863. As the gentry were exempted from
orporal punishment in 1762, and the exemption was by degrees
xtended to the other propertied classes, justice in Russia had
ecome what it had always been in Europe, a system of intimida-
ion of the lower classes.

The army and navy were recruited by conscription, which was
ne of the heaviest burdens that weighed on the common people,
or a soldier's service, even after it was shortened to twenty-five
ears, was practically for life.

Before the reign of Paul, the army was intensely national and
lominated by the gentry. Discipline was loose, and soldiers were
llowed a considerable degree of liberty. Commanders acted by
ersonal influence and courted the favour of all ranks. In war-time,
ooting was allowed and even countenanced. Victorious wars made
he army popular and self-confident. Even the private soldier had
he pride of his profession and felt himself a privileged and glori-
us personage. Under Paul and his sons more severe Prussian
orms of discipline were introduced. The Napoleonic wars pre-
erved for a time the old spirit, but under Nicolas I the new drill-
naster system became exclusive. The private soldier became the
nost oppressed and voiceless of Russian subjects while the Russian
rmy surpassed the Prussian for its clockwork evolutions. An
xtreme expression of this militarist spirit was the establishment

of "military settlements," under which several hundred thousand crown peasants were turned into hereditary soldiers, submitted in every detail of their life to a brutal and meticulous discipline.

In the 18th century and under Alexander I the Russian army and navy were not in general inferior to any in Europe. Russia was not alone in having a great number of general officers that were incompetent and incapable of co-operation. The fighting qualities of the lower ranks were exceedingly high. The tactical tradition developed by Field-Marshal Suvorov (died 1800), and tested in the French wars, was based on the preference of cold steel to fire. It was not entirely unsuited to the times, but it bred a contempt for military technique which in conjunction with the parade-spirit resulted in gross technical backwardness. The disaster of Sevastopol was largely due to Russia having neglected to introduce either ironclads, or steam, or rifles.

5. THE GENTRY.

RUSSIAN society after the Reform of Peter the Great was divided into two main sections: the "masters" (*gospoda*) and the "people," or, in 18th century parlance, the "noble" (*blagorodny*) and the "low" (*podly*). The former became a legally distinct class, similar to a French *état* or a German *Stand* (the Russian statutory term *sosloyanie* is a translation of the latter), before the division into such legally constituted classes was extended to the "low." The legal distinction was emphasised by a cultural difference that was not one of degree but of kind: the gentry accepted European standards while the people lived on what they had preserved of the Moscow inheritance." German dress" and a shaven face marked off the nobles from the "low." The "low" did all the taxpaying and, after the Manifesto of 1762 exempted the gentry from obligatory service, alone had obligations towards the State. The gentry were "free"— the only obligation of a Russian gentleman was to shave his face.

The possession of "inhabited estates," that is to say, of land with the serfs living on it, was an exclusive monopoly of the gentry.* The sale of serfs without the land they lived on, a practice going back to the sale of slaves in Muscovite times, was allowed and practised extensively. The majority of the serfs were peasants, and had plots of land to till. But the squire could deprive a serf of his land in order to make him a landless domestic servant, and the houses of the gentry were full of crowds of servants, sometimes overworked (especially the maids), but more often distressingly idle. The powers of the squire over his serfs were limited by the rights of the State alone. He had not the right of capital punishment, but he might banish a serf to Siberia, and a law passed under Catherine II provided for the squire's compensation for the loss he incurred by thus depriving himself of his property. A serf could not petition the authorities against his master, and the administration never intervened between squire and serfs, except in

*Under Peter it was partly extended to non-nobles, but the squirearchic government of Elizabeth restored the monopoly of the nobles.

flagrant cases of cruelty bordering on insanity. In the extent of his rights over his serfs, as in the economic nature of the connection, the Russian serfowner came nearer to a planter of Louisiana or Jamaica than to a medieval lord of the manor.

Besides ruling the country as officers of the crown, the gentry had local self-government. They elected all the local executive officers in the rural districts (*uyezd*), and in each "government" a Marshal of the Gentry, who was the principal notable of the province. The opinion of the local gentry was the only public opinion with which governors had need to count.

At the top of the gentry there stood the great court families who had received the largest grants of land, and held the best posts in the government. Some of the families of this upper layer were descendants of princes and medieval boyars, but it was continuously recruited from the lower ranks, for it was one of the essential features of 18th century Russia that the poorest gentleman stood a fair chance of catching the eye of the monarch and becoming a "favourite." The fortunes of the great families were all due to those tremendous grants of "inhabited estates" that were the usual form of expressing the sovereign's favour in the 18th century. The greatest fortune of all was that of Count Sheremetev who, in 1860, owned about 300,000 serfs of both sexes. Fortunes of over 5,000 "male souls" (i.e., of over 10,000 of both sexes) were counted by the dozen.

The European consciousness of the Russian upper classes was inseparable from an intense patriotism. The Russian patriot was proud of his mighty monarchs, of their splendid residences, of the vast Empire ruled by them, of the wealth of its mines, of the victories won over foreign nations, but he never imagined that the Russians were a "God-bearing" people or that Russia was destined to create a new type of civilisation. The political circumstances of the europeanisation of Russia differed greatly from those under which the same process was traversed by other non-European nations. Russia was always economically and politically independent of Europe. From Poltava to the taking of Paris, Russia was almost invariably victorious in her wars and her weight in the councils of Europe continued to grow. The Russian

mperor ultimately found himself at the head of a European
oalition. All this naturally inclined the Russian gentry to regard
hemselves as a leading European nation rather than to oppose
hemselves to Europe. The first joint expression of europeanism
nd patriotism was the cult paid in the 18th century to Peter the
reat, the Culture Hero, owing to whom, in the words of Theo-
han Prokopovich's funeral oration, "Russia had come out of
on-existence into existence."*

The europeanisation of the gentry proceeded, of course, by
egrees. The army and navy were the first schools of european-
m; mathematics and engineering the first gentlemanly accom-
lishments. The provincial gentry and the women long retained
any Muscovite traits, usually in a more or less debased form,
nd remained illiterate and devoid of genteel manners.

Already under Elizabeth the Court was greatly influenced by
rench customs, but the rise to high office of favourites belonging
the provincial gentry allowed it for some time to preserve a
ther un-european raciness. The Orlov brothers and Potemkin
ere picturesque and representative figures of the semi-euro-
eanised, tremendously vital and absolutely uninhibited " bar-
arism" of the age of Catherine. It was only by the very end of
e 18th century that French manners conquered the main mass
the Russian gentry.

Russia's interpretation of European civilisation passed through
veral phases. Under Peter and his first successors Europe was
e home of higher techniques, and higher forms of economic
e; education was technical and practical, and the countries
ost imitated were Holland, Sweden and Germany. The age was
cular and utilitarian, inspired by a real will for enlightenment
d progress. It was prepared to admit a reasonable Christianity
it was fundamentally undenominational and non-mystical.

Under Elizabeth and Catherine II Europe became primarily
e land of elegance and pleasure, of the arts and of literature.
seful knowledge became the exclusive property of specialists,
d French the language of civilisation.

*What extreme forms this cult could assume is illustrated by the epithet of
Russian Bethlehem " given by the poet Sumarokov to Peter's birthplace, the
lace of Kolomenskoye.

Voltaire became the god of a large section of the gentry, Voltaire understood as a smiling philosopher of pleasure who ha freed human conscience from the bogey of other-world retributior The élite of 1770-1810 followed the more emotional and mystica forms of enlightenment. Freemasonry, with its undenomination piety and humanitarian ethics was a school for all that wa best in the Russian gentry. It degenerated, however, after th French wars, into a fantastic and bigoted mysticism that cor tributed to produce a reaction in favour of a more materialisti and worldly attitude. Liberalism of an Anglo-French type, wit a mixed admiration for Napoleon and for the House of Con mons, with Adam Smith and Bentham for principal text-books an Byron for favourite poet was the creed of the generation of 181; 1825. It is reflected in the poetry of the young Pushkin and in th political ideas of the Decembrists.

But all along, ever since the first appearance of the ideas of th *philosophes*, there was growing a conservative body of opinio which idolised Peter and Catherine, and had no idea of rejectin European civilisation, but detested the new Europe of Voltai and the Revolution. It remained more or less formless unt Karamzin, a Liberal Freemason in his early work, was converte to Conservatism by the peace of Tilsit and the policy of Speransk His ideas found favour in high quarters and became the offici doctrine under Nicholas I. This "official nationalism" place Russia above Europe, because the Russian people had bett preserved the old virtues of faith and obedience than any othe and because the national spirit was a spirit of devotion to th Monarchy and of detestation for all innovation. The nation. Church was restored to honour as the guardian of the people conservatism. "Orthodoxy, Autocracy and Nationality" becan the official formula expressing the "Russian idea."

Of European countries, Germany now became the most i fluential. To the Government it was a kindred land of absolutisn militarism and bureaucracy; to the intellectuals the home idealistic philosophy. The intellectual movement, stimulated German idealism, was at first purely metaphysical, but befo long it assumed a political colouring and crystallised in the two rival doctrines of Slavophilism and Westernism. Bo were liberal and opposed to the system of bureaucracy and serf-dom, both advocated "bourgeois" reforms, both were profoundly imbued with German thought, the former with Schelling, the latter with Hegel. The Slavophils insisted on the originality of the Russian cultural type, regarded its freedom from European in-dividualism and rationalism as things to be cherished and pre-served, and preached a return to "pre-Peter Russia," which they idealised into a kingdom where real justice reigned instead of formal law. The Westernisers on the contrary denounced Musco-vite Russia, exalted Peter as a great civiliser, and saw no other course than to become once more the pupils of modern, bourgeois, liberal and scientific Europe.

The Westernisers were conscious of the great betrayal of the traditions of Peter by the Russian monarchy. 18th-century Russia had modelled itself on 18th-century Europe, and at least in its aspiration had often been ahead of it : Peter was the first in time of the "Enlightened Despots." Catherine was a disciple of the most advanced French thinkers; her political treatise had been prohibited by the French censorship. As long as Europe was, like Russia, a land of privilege and absolutism, Russia had no difficulty in being European. But since two great revolutions, the French and the industrial, had produced a new Europe, European ideals ceased to be acceptable to the ruling class; new European tech-niques could no longer be introduced into a country where labour was servile, ignorant and oppressed. Russia remained on the level she had reached by 1800. But forces were maturing under the archaic crust that would inevitably break it. The Westernisers were the principal mouthpieces of the demand that 19th-century Russia should model herself on 19th-century Europe.

6. THE CHURCH AND DISSENT.

WE have hitherto emphasised the secular character of the Peters
burg Empire and scarcely mentioned the Church. It would be
wrong, however, to exaggerate the anti-clericalism of Peter and
his successors. They deprived the Church of all independence
and of every means of influencing secular government, but they
left it a sphere where it retained extensive authority as the repre
sentative of the State in religious matters.

The State did not regard Orthodoxy as necessarily the one true
religion; dissent and heresy were politically dangerous, but all
constituted religions were good in so far as they inculcated into
the common people the duty of obedience to the powers that be
Roman Catholicism, Protestantism, Armenian Christianity, were
all useful instruments of government. Even Islam and Buddhism
were at times given support as first stages for the more lowly
savages. The special function of the Orthodox Church was to
teach Christian obedience to the Russian lower classes, to conver
the peoples of the East from their dark heathenism, and above
all to suppress the Old Belief and the dissenting sects that repre
sented the national and plebeian opposition to the europeanised
and noble-owned State. The Church was given full facilities to
fulfil its duty towards the State, and the Holy Synod retained
most of the old episcopal jurisdiction. Under Elizabeth especially
the Church was in high favour. Bishops were prominent at court
monastic and episcopal estates, placed under secular adminis
tration by Peter, were restored to their owners. And the Church
did what the State demanded of it, pursued the Old Believers and
converted the heathen in hundreds of thousands.

With the death of Elizabeth the state of affairs changed
Catherine II began her reign by the wholesale confiscation of all
monastic and episcopal estates. The subservience of the high
clergy had become by this time such that only one prelate—Arsen
Matsievich, Metropolitan of Rostov, protested against the meas
ure. By order of the philosophical Empress he had to expiate
the crime of independence by solitary confinement for life.

WOODEN ARCHITECTURE OF THE NORTH.

Church at Kizhi, on Lake Onego. 18th century.

It was in the reigns of Catherine, Paul and Alexander I, that the policy of inter-confessional equality was most consistently followed. It found an external symbol in the row of Churches, Roman Catholic, Protestant and Armenian that lined the principal street in Petersburg, the Nevsky. After 1810, in connection with the general growth of conservatism and nationalism, an Orthodox reaction began to make itself felt. In its extreme forms it opposed all secular knowledge and culture, denouncing with particular fierceness the non-denominational piety and broad-Church ideas of the Freemasons. In a mitigated form, it became under Nicholas I, an official doctrine, and an integral part of the whole system of "official nationalism."

Under the Erastian constitution of Peter the Great, the Church had at its head a "Holy Synod," whose members were appointed by the crown, and whose authority over the bishops was unlimited. The higher clergy was recruited from the class of "learned monks," exclusively Ukrainian till the middle of the 18th century. For the most part they were sons of secular priests, as only these were as a rule admitted to the clerical schools. The clergy thus grew into a closed caste; parishes were handed over from father to son, or son-in-law, for priests' daughters were invariably married to prospective priests. The clerical class formed a sort of exotic growth in the midst of secular society; their very appearance—they wore beards and preserved the ample and flowing dress of Muscovite times—distinguished from the German-clad gentry. Isolated from modern life, imperfectly rooted in the Orthodox tradition, dependent on and subservient to the secular authority, the Church, by the middle of the 19th century, seemed well to justify the verdict of the Slavophil Khomyakov, a profoundly religious Churchman and a great theologian, that "the Russian Church was in a state of paralysis."

What preserved it from spiritual extinction was only the revival of asceticism in the later 18th century. St. Tikhon of Zadonsk, ex-Bishop of Voronezh; Païsi Velichkhovsky, abbot of Neamţu in Moldavia, and St. Seraphim of Sarov, were its principal figures. Païsi was the first of a succession of "elders" (startsy), men of high ascetic achievement who devoted their lives to the spiritual guidance of whoever came in search of it.

The hold of religion on all classes of the Russian people remained strong. The middle and lower classes remained untouched by scepticism, or irreligion. Rigorous ritual observance proclaimed, as in Muscovite times, the piety of the merchants and richer peasants. Pilgrimages were, for the poorest classes, the principal form of religious life. The roads were full of wayfarers bound for one of the great sanctuaries, Kiev or Troitsa, or even to Mount Athos and Jerusalem. But the Church was not alone in commanding the allegiance of the religious. Non-denominational pietism (and, in the 19th century, Roman Catholicism), among the gentry, Old Belief and new forms of Dissent among the merchants and peasants, attracted a large proportion of the most actively religious elements.

Old Belief was an essentially conservative form of consciousness, but as it was exclusively plebeian and as it was the only organised form of opposition to the gentry-ruled State and the State-ridden Church, it was inevitably connected with all movements of opposition, and might assume a quasi-revolutionary aspect. Old Believers played a prominent part in the rebellions of 1705 and 1707, and again in the great Pugachev rebellion. But from the outset the bulk of them settled down quietly to preserve the old faith in its integrity and to make themselves as comfortable as they could in an Antichrist-ruled world. Peter allowed them the exercise of their faith, subject to the payment of double taxes. Under Anne and Elizabeth persecution was resumed, many Old Believers fled the land and settled in Poland and in unoccupied parts of Siberia. Catherine II restored the policy of toleration which remained in force till the reign of Nicholas I.

Old Belief did not remain united and by successive splits fell into a number of distinct communities. The main dividing line was between the groups that had priests, and the "priestless" (*bespopovtsy*). The latter maintained that the world was in the hands of Antichrist and consequently the visible Church was no more. In principle they were adventists, expecting the present coming of Christ. In practice, however, many "priestless" communities were as conservative and as ready to make good in the world as the others. The centres of Old Belief were the monasteries situated for the most part in more or less remote districts, such as

Lake Vyg, near the White Sea. Here they preserved the old traditions of ritual and religious art, preserving untouched old Russian Church music and unspoiled icons of the 16th century and earlier. In secular affairs the Old Believers developed the puritan virtues of thrift and frugality and preserved the old patriarchal family law in all its purity. They became one of the principal nuclei of capitalistic accumulation. The percentage of Old Believers among the pioneers of the cotton industry and afterwards of steam shipping on the Volga, was singularly high.

During the period of toleration the official Church did not abandon its efforts to return the Old Believers to its fold. The idea was adopted (1800) that they should be allowed to submit to the Church, while retaining their ritual practices, so as to form a sort of United Church of the Old Rite, after the model of the United Churches of the Oriental Rite in the Roman communion. Many Old Believers accepted this arrangement. Nicholas I subjected those who refused to a new persecution in the course of which all the principal monasteries of the Old Faith were destroyed. Toleration was only re-established by Alexander II.

The more extreme adventist and apocalyptic wing of Old Belief became the soil out of which there grew a number of mystical sects. Recognising that the world had fallen in the hands of Antichrist, they announced new revelations that were to supersede the New Testament. The most notable of these sects were the *khlysty* and the *skoptsy*. The name of the former is a corruption of *Khristy*—"Christs," for their central tenet was that Christ and His Mother are constantly reincarnated in the heads of their community. Their principal form of worship was communal ecstasy to which they worked themselves up by dancing and whirling.* They kept their faith secret and outwardly conformed to the rites of the Church.

The *skoptsy*, or eunuchs, preached castration as a second baptism, "the baptism of fire," baptism by water alone being no longer efficacious. The teaching arose in the middle of the 18th century, and showed a remarkable spirit of proselytism. It was, of

*The idea that these communal ecstasies are an occasion for promiscuous intercourse is entirely due to the writings of official missionaries. All unbiassed students of the sect reject it as unfounded.

course, vehemently persecuted by the authorities, and survived only in exile—in the Yakut country whither they were deported and in Roumania, which became the sanctuary of the castrated adepts of the sect. Both sects were closely connected with South Great Russia and recruited their adherents from the richer agricultural class. The *khlysty*, for instance, were particularly numerous among the Don Cossacks.

The ritual and religious songs of these two sects are among the most remarkable, and certainly the most intensely lyrical manifestation of Russian folk-poetry.

Two other sects of a different kind are also connected mainly with the Great Russian South and with the richer peasant class. These are the *Molokane* and the *Doukhobors*, two communities of "spiritual Christians" who consider the revelations of the Holy Ghost as more binding than the Gospels. Their origin is ascribed to Anabaptist and Quaker influences, and goes back to the second half of the 18th century. They rejected the State and the Church, refused taxes and military service and drew on themselves much persecution. They were transported to the Caucasus, where the Molokane formed a flourishing community, thrifty and rich, of a definitely bourgeois type. The Doukhobors developed a form of peasant communism which is perhaps the only one that answers more or less to the traditional conception of the Russian rural commune. As is generally known, they migrated to Canada in 1899, where they form to-day a rigorously segregated and self-contained community.

7. THE MIDDLE CLASSES.

THE main bulk of the bourgeoisie was formed by the class of "merchants" (*kuptsy*). Though by degrees a number of personal rights, privileges and exemptions were extended to them, they remained socially inferior to the gentry. They were "uneducated," spoke no French, wore "Russian dress" and grew beards. They had no "ranks" and took no part in the crown administration. So from the governing class's point of view they belonged to the "subject race." By the bureaucracy they were treated with little respect. In the "non-noble" provinces of the north and east the administration was notoriously more corrupt and more arbitrary than in those where there existed corporations of the gentry. Merchant opinion did not count, but their wealth allowed them to make use of the administration for their profit. It was a widely accepted usage for the administrators to receive fixed payments from the merchants, and these readily accepted an arrangement that guaranteed them from superfluous intervention and gave them full liberty to dictate prices to the common consumer, and practise fraud on a large scale.

There was no sharp dividing line between the merchants and the richer peasants; the former were constantly being recruited from the latter. In the 19th century the majority of the richer merchant families were sons, or grandsons of peasants. For a serf there was the difficulty of having to "buy himself off" from his master. A rich serf was a hen with golden eggs. The *obrok* he paid might run into many thousands of roubles, and the master would not sell him his freedom for less than all he could afford to pay for it. So by the side of the merchant class proper there grew up a *bourgeoisie* of more or less rich serfs. The cotton industry, in particular, was very largely built up by them. Ivanovo, a manor of Count Sheremetev, produced a whole galaxy of industrialists and became the nucleus of the "Russian Manchester" Ivanovo-Voznesensk.

An essential feature of the commercial class was its conservatism. Many merchant families belonged to the Old Belief, and in their private life most merchants preserved the patriarchal despotism of Muscovite times. Their conservatism was part of their bourgeois philosophy of life : new-fangled customs, fashionable dress, European education, everything showy and up-to-date was expensive and consequently to be banned. It was only towards the end of the period that the Russian merchant began to develop the bold initiative and love of risk inherent in the capitalistic *entrepreneur*.

The urban clergy were closely connected with the commercial class, and formed, as it were, its intelligentsia. The plebeian cultural milieu that gravitated towards them was less æsthetic and more realistically inclined than that of the gentry. It is no chance that the two pioneers of modern Russian rationalism and radicalism, Chernyshevsky and Dobrolyubov, were both the sons of priests of the big churches of two commercial towns. This nonnoble civilisation had most vitality in the more commercial towns of the North and on the Volga. A "town" (*gorod*), however, remained primarily the administrative centre of an *uyezd*. All over the country, especially on the Volga and in the industrial Mesopotamia, there were "villages" where bourgeois Russia was more vigorous, and more money was made than in most "towns."

Neither of the two capitals was a really bourgeois city. Petersburg was mainly official and its merchants were more europeanised than elsewhere. Its streets and markets were a great melting-pot of the lower middle classes where serfs on *obrok*, domestic servants, minor government clerks, small traders, artisans and soldiers formed a mixed but characteristic population, "detribalised" and "unrooted," more open to new ideas than in the interior of the country. The Petersburg crowd was largely on the side of the Decembrists in 1825, and the government troops suffered more from the stones thrown by these civilians than from the ineffective fire of the mutineers.

Moscow was for the most part a metropolis of squires. But south of the Moskva river was the *Zamoskvorechie*, the citadel of conservative merchants who despised genteel ways and kept their wives, daughters and assistants under a rule of terror—the characteristic world of the plays of Ostrovsky. In the commercial

City, in the taverns and tearooms that surrounded it, there moved a crowd as mixed as in Petersburg, but less modern and with deeper roots in the conservative provinces.

The merchants and the clergy were legally constituted classes, *sostoyania*, and so were the petty townspeople—*meshchane*—traders and artisans, whose capital was not sufficient to qualify them as merchants. But there was also a large section of society that belonged to no class at all—merchants' sons without capital, sons of civil servants not in the civil service, priests' sons without holy orders, "free artists," freed serfs. These *raznochintsy* ("men of various rank") were not socially very different from those serfs that were neither peasants, nor incipient bourgeois. The *raznochintsy* became one of the principal sources of the modern intelligentsia. The domestic serfs also developed an intelligentsia of their own. It is sufficient to name the actor Shchepkin, the architect Voronikhin, the painter Kiprensky, the historian Pogodin, the great Ukrainian poet Shevchenko—all of them serfs or sons of serfs, to show the part played by this class of men in the formation of the intelligentsia.

8. THE PEASANTS.*

ABOUT half the peasants were "free," that is to say, they were no
the serfs of individual owners; but their freedom was a very
relative one. Besides being generally devoid of personal rights and
exposed without defence to the arbitrary actions of the adminis
tration, the "free" peasants lived on land that was not theirs, and
"belonged" to the owners of that land. The *odnodvortsy*, descend
ants of the smaller serving people who had failed to obtain the
rights of gentry, were the only Great Russian peasants who owned
their land, "belonged" to nobody, paid no dues but the poll-tax
and might be described as "yeomen." The "crown peasants" be
longed to the State and, besides the poll-tax, paid an *obrok* to the
treasury, exactly like the serfs did to their masters. The peasant
of the Imperial Family were in all respects similar to serfs, except
that their work and their payments were not regulated by the
arbitrary will of an individual, but by a bureaucratic board.

In most cases the position of the "free" peasants was better than
that of the serfs. The bulk of the *barshchina* serfs, and the "pos
sessional" peasants stood at the bottom of the economic scale
The *obrok* serfs of the industrial provinces, of commercial village
adjoining the highways, or of the *latifundia* of the southern park
land might be as well off as the crown peasants of the same dis
tricts. In the wheat belt, in the industrial centre, and on the Volga
and other big rivers, the peasant had a variety of means to make
money. The classical land of peasant poverty was the agricultura
district south of Moscow and the more purely agricultural dis
tricts of the woodland.

The "egalitarian" land commune became the prevalent form
of peasant landholding in the course of the 18th century. It wa
convenient to the State, for it was collectively responsible for the
taxes, and replaced the individual peasant. It was convenient to
the squires for it shifted on to the peasants much of the work o

*See *The Peasants under Catherine II*, by Semevsky, St. Petersburg, 1901 (in
Russian).

administration without giving them any independence. It was convenient most of all to the better-off peasants, for it equalised payments, without equalising incomes. In the greater part of the country the peasant's holding was no source of wealth, it was barely sufficient for him to live and to pay his taxes. Outside the wheat-belt, peasants could make money only in so far as they were something more than agriculturists. *Kulak*, which has come to denote a rich peasant in general, originally meant "usurer." It was only in the present century that the possibility of passing from three-years' rotation to more intensive forms of farming made the richer peasants interested in the abolition of communal tenure. In the 18th and 19th centuries the commune was a means in the hands of the richer peasants to shift the burden of dues and taxes on to the poor.

The commune implied no community of labour. Each peasant farmed his holding and neither got nor gave help to the others. It is clear that such a form of tenure could have formed itself only in a country where the rights of the individual were nil, and where the exploitation of the plain man by the State, by the upper classes and his better-off class-fellows, was limited neither by law nor custom. The possession of a holding was not even a safeguard against starvation, for it was of little use without the necessary live stock and equipment. It was a pure liability from which the peasant was not allowed to escape. Neither should the commune be too indiscriminately compared with another form of Russian "communism"—the *artel*, or gang of workmen. The *artel* is different from the commune in being a voluntary association, and not imposed from above, in that it does imply communal work, and payment for it to the *artel* as a whole. Moreover the money received is not equally distributed between all members, but according to a complicated scale.

Still there can be no doubt that both the commune and the *artel* did breed in the Russian people a different and less individualistic spirit than the European farmer's, and a more clearly felt class consciousness. The individualism, inherent in all peasants, did not come to full light in Russia before the Revolution. It was the commune that educated in them that capacity for mass-action which made Russian peasant movements so formidably singleminded. A Russian peasant crowd is a real collective organism, conscious of its strength and its capacity for resistance with which it is not easy to argue. But what contributed most to make the peasants' class-consciousness so intense and clear was the profound legal and cultural rift between them and their masters, whether squires or administrators.

The peasants did not always remain quiet and passive. Riots and disorders grew very frequent towards the end of the period and their cumulative effect was one of the principal causes in the abolition of serfdom.

But the one great rising of the period, the Pugachev rebellion of 1773-4, did not begin as a rebellion of serfs. It was started by the Yaïk Cossacks, who were being robbed by degrees of their autonomy. The "possessional" workmen of the Urals and the non-Russian Bashkirs were the first to join the Cossacks. But when Pugachev's forces approached the middle Volga country, the Russian serfs, as well as the Chuvash and Mordva peasants, were not slow to rise. The movement spread like wildfire and hundreds of squires were massacred. The class-consciousness of the Cossack leaders was very different from that of the serfs, and they did nothing to organise or support them. When in 1812 Napoleon invaded Russia, there were many who feared a general rising of the serfs. But Napoleon did nothing to win them to his side. France had long ago betrayed the Revolution, and the French felt more alien to the savage *moujik* than to the French-speaking *boyard*. The marauding ways of the Great Army soon made the peasants as fiercely patriotic as the gentry. That there were, however, opportunities for foreign revolutionary propaganda is shown by the fact that numbers of Russian soldiers deserted to Persia and to the Caucasian mountaineers, and fought against the armies of the Tsar.

Illiteracy, starvation and narrowness of outlook made the Russian peasant politically conservative. The monarchism of the peasants was largely due to the influence of the clergy, who thus fulfilled the mission, entrusted to them by Peter, of making the people harmless. Even when the peasant rose against the gentry and administration he believed he rose for the Tsar, and even Pugachev had no political idea to substitute for monarchism—he

PEASANT ART OF N. RUSSIA.

Embroidery. "Young Ladies and Gentlemen." 18th century.

(From 'Peasant Art of North Russia,' in Russian by Sokolov and Tomsky, Moscow 1924)

ave himself out to be the rightful Tsar, Peter III, and made of
is headquarters an imitation of the Court of Petersburg.

Their profound legal, economic and cultural difference from
ne other classes, made the peasants develop into a sort of nation
aside a nation, a "subject race" with a life of its own, beneath the
aperficial strata of "alien" upper classes. The division was not
absolutely water-tight. Domestic and military service could bring
ne peasant into close, if unequal, contact with the "dominant
ace" and transform him into an intermediate being, a sort of
altural and social "half-caste." If not legally, at least socially
nd culturally, servants and soldiers had more in common with
ne *raznochintsy* than with the peasants at home. The commercial
nd industrial centres were another "zone of contact." The peasant
ader rose into the ranks of the bourgeoisie, the industrial work-
an became "detribalised" and acquired an unconservative and
dependent mentality which had in it the germs of revolution.
he literature and journalism of the gentry are full of lamenta-
ons on peasant traders and workers losing their rural virtues and
suming wicked urban ways.

Even the purely agricultural village, especially the *barshchina*
llage, did not remain uninfluenced by the upper classes. The
rect action of the serf-owners played a considerable, if not quite
finable, part in the formation of peasant law and usages. It
as owing to such direct action that the outer appearance of the
reat Russian village was transformed, and the straggling houses
the 17th century gave place to broad, regular streets or greens,
ned by parallel rows of houses, facing it at right angles and stand-
g at equal distances. Through the domestic servants, words of
e genteel and urban vocabulary, and songs in new metres, with
w tunes, insinuated themselves into the thick of the agricultural
asses.

But on the whole, the main mass of peasants grew increasingly
lf-contained and segregated from the upper classes. The peasants'
entality became conservative, and strongly but passively class-
nscious. Peasant society assumed stable and stagnant forms,
ominated by a spirit of social and technical routine. The statutory
w of the land ceased to apply to the peasants. Their relations
me to be regulated by customary law, and administered by the

communal authority. The greater landowners promulgate
elaborate criminal labour and revenue codes for their serfs, bu
on the whole peasant law developed by itself beneath the supe
ficial layer of squiredom. Its essential feature is the conception o
the family as a unit of work and ownership. It was correlative to th
unit of work and payment established by serfdom, which con
sisted of a man and woman. There followed the complete sub
jection of the woman to the head of the working unit, and th
absence for her of all personal possession. A striking contrast t
the position of woman in the upper classes, who, though place
under the effective moral authority of her husband, retained con
plete independence in the disposition of her property.

The peasants of the serfdom provinces were conservative in tha
they assimilated little that was new, rather than that they pre
served much that was old. Songs, wedding customs, rites of th
year-cycle, female dress, went back to Old Russian times, but o
the whole the cultural possessions of the agricultural village wer
poor and few. Only in the north, which had been the great con
servative background of Muscovite civilisation and became
backwater in the course of the 18th century, were conditions mor
favourable for the preservation of an independent tradition. Her
the peasants always remained free from serfdom, and depende
less on the unprofitable pursuit of agriculture than on the fre
trades, home industry, hunting and trapping, commerce, lumbe
ing, and fishery. The arts and crafts developed types of the 16t
and 17th centuries, and folklore survived in unusual abundanc
The forms of life preserved the stable harmony of Muscovite man
ners, and here Old Belief had some of its principal citadels.

The valley of the Dvina remained a secondary but well-trodde
thoroughfare that kept in touch with the outer world. The peop
who largely lived on the production of artistic handicrafts pre
served old techniques, and the refinement and originality
the old styles, without being blind to the new: it is amusing t
see their embroideries of ladies and gentlemen in 18th centur
dress treated in the severest geometrical style. But as they pr
duced for a wider market they adopted new styles too. The greate
sculptor of the period, Shubin, was the son of a walrus-bone carve
of the neighbourhood of Kolmogory and had been original

rained to his father's craft. It is characteristic of the active and
rogressive spirit of the Dvina country that Lomonosov, the
reatest pioneer of European civilisation in Russia, was the son of
deep-sea fisherman from the same neighbourhood of Kolmogory.

In other fishing districts, farther away from the highways, a more
onservative though no less creative spirit prevailed. The north-
astern coast of lake Onego is the wonderland of Russian art and
ore. Here, within near reach of Lake Vyg, the citadel of Old
elief, we find concentrated in the same villages the best preserved
nd most elaborate specimens of wooden church-architecture, the
ncient laments for the dead still intoned at funerals by professional
male wailers, and the reciters of *byliny** who developed and per-
cted that type of poetry in the 18th century and have preserved
hem to this day. Similar refuge places of Muscovite civilisation
re to be found elsewhere in the North—on the lower Pechora
nd in the north of Siberia, but nowhere on a scale equal to that
f Lake Onego.

*The village of Kizhi which possesses perhaps the best wooden church in the
orth, was also the home of the best reciter of *byliny*, Trofim Ryabinin.

9. LEARNING, LETTERS AND ART.

THE intellectual and æsthetic culture of the upper classes wa drastically secularised by the "Reform of Peter the Great," bu ecclesiastical influence was not immediately, nor was it eve entirely, eliminated. The diocesan seminaries turned out at leas as many lettered men as the secular schools. "Seminarists" formec the bulk of educated plebeians, so that "seminarist" becam almost synonymous with "non-noble intellectual."

Secular schools were first founded under Peter the Great. Th first were purely technical in character. Less special and mor generally "genteel" schools for the gentry began to be foundec only under Anne. Peter made education compulsory for the gentry The Manifesto of 1762 exempted them from the obligation, but a minimum of education remained socially obligatory. The non noble classes had access to the "district schools" and "gymnas iums," where all classes (except serfs) could mix to form the futur intelligentsia; but nothing was done for the primary education o the peasants.

The first learned foundation was the Academy of Science founded by Peter the Great (actually opened after his death, i 1726), with the advice and help of Leibniz. The Academy lon remained mainly, and always largely, a German body. It i impossible to speak too highly of the work done for the study o Russia in the first half century of its existence. The two Academi Expeditions for the study of the Empire were scientific enter prises on a larger scale than anything attempted before or since and the publications due to them are still a treasure-house o geographical, botanical, mineralogical, ethnological and historica observation.

The University of Moscow was founded in 1757, but the uni versities did not become important centres of learning till the second quarter of the 19th century. Throughout the perioc Russian science owed much to foreigners, but from the outse Russia began to bring forth her own "quick-witted Newtons," in a phrase of the first and greatest of them, Michael Lomonosov (1711-65), the father of Russian Literature, and a chemist who came into his own at the end of the 19th century. The greatest of his successors were two professors of Kazan, the chemist Zinin, and especially the mathematician Lobachevsky, the creator of non-Euclidean geometry.

Literature was at first in the hands of the learned profession. The plebeian *literati*, closely connected with the Church and its schools, were inclined to keep Russian as close as possible to Church-Slavonic, which was still an actively cultivated language —the Authorised version of the Slavonic Bible was only completed in 1751. The real founder of secular literature and legislator of its language was Lomonosov, a plebeian, educated in the Moscow ecclesiastical academy. Owing to him, literary Russian was able to preserve a high proportion of Church-Slavonic words and forms which gave it a flexibility and richness approaching that of Greek.

The gentry, with their military training and ignorance of Latin, thought the new language and style pedantic. They cultivated the lighter literary kinds and used a language modelled on the colloquial speech of Moscow society. The greatest poet of the later 18th century, Derzhavin, though a man of the gentry, was a disciple of Lomonosov. His poetry is a magnificent mixture of racy and humorous realism, with the loftiest flights of pindaric lyricism. It is the splendidly adequate expression of the somewhat rude vitality of a class that had attained to undisputed power and was headed by an aggressive and victorious monarchy. But the "genteel" tendency gradually gained ground. The reform of the literary language by Karamzin in the seventeen 'nineties, which introduced a less pedantic and more "drawing-room" style into literature, marks the victory of the gentry over the *literati*. For a generation or two, literature fell entirely into the hands of the former, which did not exclude a highly conscientious and workmanlike attitude towards form and technique. The generation that came of age between 1815 and 1825 was the most artistic literary generation ever produced by Russia. Its general character is distinctly classical, rational and unromantic; it shunned rhetoric, emotion, and excessive imagery, and submitted to a severe formal discipline but at the same time commanded an air of ease that gives its work a unique charm and distinction. The greatest man of the generation, and the greatest of Russian poets, was Pushkin.

The Pushkin phase of Russian literature stands in close relationship to the Decembrist movement, and like it, was the expression of a gentry that retained all the aristocratic culture of pre-revolutionary Europe, but at the same time aspired towards freer, bourgeois forms of society and civilisation. It was as yet quite untainted by any kind of emotional or philosophical idealism. But on its heels, following the defeat of the Decembrists there came a new generation, no longer vigorous and extraverted, but neurotic and introspective. Its great creative artists were Gogol, Lermontov and Tyutchev. The hyperbolic satire and imagery of Gogol, the rhetoric and "Byronism" of Lermontov, the philosophical pessimism and dualism of Tyutchev indicate a profound crisis in the consciousness of the cultured gentry, and the approach of a new age.

Meanwhile the bourgeois element in literature had been growing. As early as the seventeen 'eighties, owing to the pioneering work of the Freemason Novikov, a reading public and a market for books were created, and publishing became a business The great fabulist, Krylov, Pushkin, Gogol, made comfortable incomes out of the sale of their works. In spite of the fierce censorship, journalism developed and grew profitable. At the same time a new "intelligentsia" was being produced. It was an amalgam of two social groups: there were the educated young nobles, who profoundly dissatisfied by the serfdom system, and unable to adjust themselves to the bureaucratic régime, desired a freer bourgeois world, not that they might make good in it, but that they might be able to meditate at leisure without being bothered by the *gendarmes*—idle, rich, dissatisfied and unemployed. Their representative man is Turgenev. On the other hand, there were the eager, undisciplined, iconoclastic and enthusiastic *razno chintsy*, sons of priests and small officials, who had to work for their living, and could make money only by journalism, private tuition or teaching in the government schools. The chief of the *raznoch intsy* was Belinsky who, from 1834, to his death in 1848, was the most influential and ardently modern of journalists. Censorship conditions made him a literary critic, for only literary topics were allowed to be discussed in print. His was the greatest single influence that formed the new intelligentsia, who, in the second half of the 'forties invaded literature with a succession of works that were the beginning of the great age of the Russian novel.

The social evolution of music was somewhat similar, on a smaller scale, to that of literature. It traversed two main stages: in the 18th century it was produced for the Church, and dominated by Italian and German models. This phase is represented by the magnificent compositions of the Ukrainian Bortnyansky (1750-1826). In the 19th century music passed into the hands of the gentry—unprofessional dilettanti who cultivated the "romance" form. One of them was Michael Glinka. To his contemporaries he was only a pleasing dilettante and a prodigal, from whom nothing very serious might be expected. It was only by the following generation that he was recognised as a great composer, a pioneer, and the founder of a Russian school of music.

The social status of artists, architects and actors, was not so high. They were the servants of the great, and were not as a rule given ranks as the scholars were. Many of the most remarkable architects and painters of the age were serfs or freedmen. Towards the end of the period a famous painter like Karl Brüllow had a social position equal to his earnings. But in general, artists and actors belonged to the intermediate class of *raznochintsy* and not to the gentry.

The first permanent theatre was founded under Elizabeth and very soon the stage became one of the most popular institutions in the country. The Imperial theatres drew crowds of gentry and of the intermediate classes. Private companies travelled the provinces, attracting big audiences while rich squires rivalled each other in forming castes from their serfs. The style of acting was governed by the canons of French classicism introduced by the first of the great actors, Dmitrevsky. The years that followed the end of the Napoleonic wars constituted the golden age of the Petersburg stage. Classical tragedy with the great actress Catherine Semenova, and the classical ballet, organised by the Frenchman Didelot, with the famous dancer Istomina—all of them glorified

by Pushkin—shared between them the public enthusiasm. Unde
Nicholas I the leadership passed to Moscow, and the classical wa
superseded by the more realistic style of the great comedia
Shchepkin, and by the emotional romanticism of the tragedia
Mochalov ("the Russian Kean"), the two idols of the young in
tellectuals and city clerks, and the harbingers of a new taste an
a new society.

Modern Russian painting was not a further development of th
later, semi-europeanised phases of icon painting, but an a
newly imported from the West in the early 18th century. Sculptur
which had hardly been practised in Muscovy was equally nev
But though Russia produced several excellent painters and sculp
tors these arts never attained to that organic independence whic
can alone produce a national school of art.

The most vital of the arts of Imperial Russia was unquestionabl
architecture. The Russian Emperors and the Russian nobles we
great builders, who were capable of choosing the best architec
and employed the best they could afford. Up to the middle of th
18th century, foreign masters, Dutch, German and French, worl
ing in Petersburg, produced work that is not in any sense Russia
but contributed to create the wonderful city-landscape of Peter
burg. In Moscow the old tradition of "Muscovite baroque" wa
continued, complicated by new influences, Western and Ukrainia
The architects were employed mainly for building churches, ar
produced work of even greater structural and picturesque fre
dom than that of the late 17th century. This art culminated in th
work of Bartholomew Rastrelli, the Russian-born son of an Itali
sculptor. He was brought up on Russian and Western mode
and while his palaces are consonant to the general spirit of co
temporary European architecture, his churches are a person
version of the native tradition. A characteristic feature whi
makes modern Russian architecture superficially unlike m
European, is the use of brick covered by coats of painted plast
This polychromy gives a very peculiar air to the Russian capita
Rastrelli and his predecessors and successors were not afraid of th
brightest colours, but in the following period, together with
severer style of architecture, a severer colour scheme prevaile
yellow and white being the only colours admitted. From abo

1770 to 1835 classicism was the prevailing style. We may distinguish in it—from the social, rather than from the stylistic point of view—two main types: the official classicism of public buildings dominant in Petersburg, but reproduced on a smaller scale in every town of the Empire; and the "private" classicism represented in the residences of the gentry—in Moscow, in the provincial capitals and in the country.

Owing to the unity of purpose that presided over its making, Petersburg presents a remarkable unity of appearance: it is perhaps the most remarkable architectural whole produced during the period of classicism. The architects who took part in the building of Petersburg—Thomont, Rossi, Voronikhin, especially Zakharov, the maker of the beautiful Admiralty and of the "Admiralty needle"—knew how to conform to a common idea without surrendering anything of their personality. The architectural landscape of Petersburg is the sublimation of the idea of a military and bureaucratic Empire.

Moscow too, was built with the help of great artists—Bazhenov, Kazakov, Beauvais, Gilardi. She never aimed at the unity of Petersburg, but grew into a chaos of old churches and new private residences, each habitation a separate organism, with its own yards and outhouses, as it should be in a "big village." Classicism in Moscow was less severe and more homely than in Petersburg and its snugger forms were adopted by the gentry in the innumerable country houses, most of them wooden, that stud all the serfdom provinces.

The residences of the greater magnates were on a very different scale. As Petersburg is surrounded by a semi-circle of Imperial residences—Peterhof, Oranienbaum, Gatchina, Tsarskoe, Pavlovsk—so is Moscow by a ring of private houses of the rich and great. For while the Muscovite boyar proclaimed his wealth by building a church in his country-place near Moscow, the "magnate" of the Petersburg period built a house for himself which might challenge comparison, if not with Versailles, at least with Potsdam or Caserta. Kuskovo, the seat of Count Sheremetev, mainly in mid-18th century baroque, and Prince Yusupov's Arkhangelskoe—reflecting the early and most magnificent phase of classicism—are the most sumptuous of these residences.

The intermediate classes had a literature and art of their own which developed in the 18th century mainly out of late 17th-century models. Chapbooks reproducing old fairy tales and the lives of famous criminals, were exceedingly popular, but by their side lives of saints and other edifying matter were also published and read. Books on divination and dreams were naturally another important type of publication and woodcuts with rhymed inscriptions also had a large circulation. Some of them were satirical as the famous picture of the mice burying the cat, which is a satire on Peter the Great. The public for whom all this was produced were the small townspeople and the servants, but it reached far into the villages and was for a long time the only printed popular literature in Russia.

THE Ukrainian Hetmanshchina preserved its autonomy till 1764. Though its independence was greatly curtailed by Peter, the country remained culturally and economically quite distinct from Great Russia, and for a long time Ukrainian influence was stronger there than Muscovite influence in Ukraina.

A systematic policy of Russification and assimilation was started by Catherine II, who put an end to the Hetmanate and the military organisation of the Kozaks. The Kozak gentry were only too willing to support it, for in return for political autonomy they received all the rights of Russian gentry, and a full share in the common pie. The gains of the Ukrainian gentry were entirely at the expense of their compatriots: the most important advantage obtained by them was the transformation into serfs of the peasants settled on their lands. The plain Kozaks lost their privileges, and became more or less assimilated to the Great Russian *odnodvortsy*.

The Ukrainians took a prominent part in the great colonising movements of the 18th and 19th centuries. In the south-east they settled in the midst of Great Russians, but the Black Sea steppe was almost exclusively settled by them. This was old Ukrainian territory and the Sich stood in its very centre. But the Sich as a last vestige of Ukrainian independence was abolished and dispersed by Potemkin in 1775. The Zaporoh Kozaks were allowed to settle in the newly annexed Kuban district and formed into a new military community on the model of the Great Russian Cossacks, but another section migrated to Turkey and formed a new Sich on the Danube, which became a sanctuary for fugitive serfs and other dissatisfied elements.

The partition of Poland gave Russia all the remaining Ukrainian lands (except Galicia and the Moldavian and Hungarian districts), as well as all White Russia. Catherine took steps towards the Russification of the new provinces, but Paul reversed her policy and restored the Polish gentry to their place at the head of the local administration; it was only after the Polish rebellion of 1831 that a policy of Russification was resumed.

The partitions had been preceded in the districts south of Kiev (which had been autonomous Kozak territory before the *z-hin* of 1714) by a furious anti-Polish jacquerie. The rebels, who called themselves *haydamak*, massacred Poles and Jews on a scale that recalled 1648. The jacquerie was put down by the Poles with their customary savagery, and with the aid of the Russian army. This showed the Ukrainian peasant that he had little to expect from the Tsar, and, in fact, the Russian policy in the annexed provinces was as aristocratic and squirearchic as anywhere. Numerous estates confiscated from anti-Russian Poles were given to Russian magnates, who were no less alien to the peasants, and treated them in the same way. The West Ukrainian provinces stood out among all Russian lands for the enormous size of the estates, which ran into hundreds of square miles of densely peopled land. The holdings of the peasants were infinitesimal. The squires were more progressive and capitalistic than elsewhere in Russia; in the 19th century they developed an advanced type of farming based on complex rotation, and the production of beet-sugar. From the outset the refineries preferred wage labour to *barshchina* which was unprofitable in a machine-using industry.

The general structure of society was thus very different in West Ukraina from that in the Hetmanshchina and the newly colonised steppes. Here there was a great semi-proletariat of Ukrainian serfs under a small number of alien landlords, Polish and Muscovite, with an equally alien intermediate layer of Jewish middlemen and artisans, and Polish or polonised stewards and retainers; there was a fairly regular pyramid of landowners with, at the bottom, a relatively small proportion of serfs (from one-fifth to one-third of the rural population).

Before the centralising reforms of Catherine, Ukrainian civilisation remained very distinct from Great Russian. The people had their rich store of folk poetry, their professional itinerant singers, their popular puppet theatre, their highly developed artistic handicrafts. Wandering scholars strolled the land; churches were built in the old native and in the "Mazeppa" baroque style. The one language spoken was Ukrainian and the *moskal* was an xotic figure so seldom seen, that the name was synonymous with oldier. In the second half of the 18th century the gentry began o adopt the Russian language and look to Petersburg as the romised land. Russian became the hall-mark of gentility. Jkrainian gentlemen began to distinguish themselves in Russian iterature, but the one outstanding Ukrainian writer of the period, Gregory Skovoroda (1722-94), though he used a Ukrainised Rusian in his writings, was still thoroughly Ukrainian. This wandering philosopher with his doctrine of Christ-Epicure and his Swedenborgian illuminism is one of the most striking figures in Jkrainian history.

The Ukrainian national revival began as a purely provincial novement with an ethnographical rather than a national consciusness. In the west it was encouraged by Polish squires; a whole "Ukrainian school" of Polish poetry grew up that idealised the Kozaks as the servants of the Polish king, ignoring that they were he enemies of the Polish *pans*. In Central and Eastern Ukraina, iterature in the vernacular was cultivated by some of the gentry s a dilettantesque *heimatkunst* that did not aspire to the higher orms of poetry.

In the following generation, the provincial and dilettantesque haracter of the Ukrainian revival was revolutionised mainly by he genius of Taras Shevshenko (1814-61), the greatest of Ukrainian oets and the real founder of the new national consciousness. A erf from West Ukraina, from the districts where the *haydamaks* had oeen the last to assert the tradition of Kozak and peasant indeoendence, Shevchenko was profoundly imbued with Kozak tradition and with the forms of folk poetry. He began as a romantic nationalist, but developed into a consciously democratic and internationalist revolutionary. His poetry has become the principal xpression of Ukrainian patriotism; it was also the favourite poetry f the first generation of Russian socialists.

In White Russia the social conditions were similar to those in Western Ukraina, except that the country was poorer, and the oeasants proportionately poorer too. The dark age which began or the White Russian people in the 17th century continued till fter the end of serfdom. The Poles and the Jews were the only

socially and culturally active elements at the time of the Partitions. North-Eastern White Russia, annexed under the first
Partition of Poland (1772), was exposed to the Russification and
assimilating policy of Catherine II, long enough to be substantially de-polonised. Large sections of the only recently polonised
lower and middle *szlachta* entered the services and became Russian
whilst numerous and large estates were given to Russian nobles
But in the West, Polish culture lost no ground till after 1831. Vilna
was one of its greatest centres; the greatest Polish poet, Mickie-
wicz, was a native of Nowogródek, and the Polish *szlachta* of White
Russia and Lithuania took a most active part in the rebellion of
1831. Under Nicholas I there came a wave of Russification, which
took the form of a campaign against the United Church. The
"Uniats" were forcibly re-united to the Orthodox Church, but
many White Russians remained Roman Catholics. All this hardly
affected the inner life of the White Russian people and did not
improve its position. It remained as oppressed, as poor and as
illiterate, as passive and as unresisting as ever. Only in the last
decades of the period was there a widespread movement of peasant
disturbances in the North-East. As for a national or literary revival the infinitesimal educated minority was not sufficient to
produce more than a very exiguous and provincial manuscript
literature of comic verse.

Though the Cossacks have no claims to be regarded on a footing
with the Ukrainian and White Russian peoples they have sufficient
originality to be treated apart from the main mass of the Great
Russian people. The autonomy of the old Cossack communities—
Don and Yaik—was successively curtailed by Peter and his successors. The *krug* ceased to be assembled. The *ataman* began to be
appointed by the government. The Cossacks did not give in without resistance. The revolt of the Don under Bulavin (1707) was
the most serious rising of Peter's reign. It was followed by the
migration of a number of Don Cossacks to Turkey, where they
still survive as an independent community in Asia Minor. Pugachev was a Don Cossack and the revolt of the Yaik Cossacks, to
which he gave his name, grew into a revolutionary movement
that menaced the very foundations of the state. But, prosperous

and essentially conservative, the Cossacks were not so difficult to deal with. Though deprived of their autonomy, they retained their lands and water rights and their legal usages, and remained completely distinct from the rest of the population. In return for the obligation of service—an obligation shared till 1762 with the gentry—they were given extensive privileges and permanent exemption from all taxation. The Cossacks were rich enough not to murmur at the obligation of presenting themselves with their own horse and arms, all the more as for a long time their service largely consisted in defending their own lands from the nomads and mountaineers, while in foreign wars they had ample opportunity for loot, and took care not to miss it. They formed units of their own under their own commanders, with a much looser and more democratic discipline than that of the regular army. They were a picturesque and exotic feature in the Russian army whenever it invaded Europe. In 1813-14 their presence in Germany and France was resented in much the same way as was that of French coloured troops in the occupied Rhine lands. Their fighting qualities in regular warfare were never very high, and their inveterate predatory habits made them rather inconvenient when looting ceased to be countenanced by international military opinion.

The Cossacks consolidated in the course of the 18th century into several different types of society. The Don Cossacks and the Cossacks of the Kuban (settled in 1791 and later) became mainly agricultural. For a long time gardening, grazing, and fishing remained more important than tillage, but the rise of the wheat trade made of the Don and Kuban Cossacks, whose lands lie in the best part of the wheat-belt, a typical class of wealthy farmers.

Similar communities, only less rich and more military, were the Cossacks of the Terek and the new Cossack forces settled by the government along the military frontier that lay in less favoured lands than the Don and Kuban wheat area. Such were the Orenburg and Siberian Cossacks, who guarded the line from Orenburg to Omsk and the Altai, and the Trans-Baykal Cossacks on the Mongolian frontier. They were originally recruited from very various sources, including a fair number of natives, and the infusion of Turkic and Mongol blood (especially among the Trans-Baykal Cossacks), was considerable.

The Ural Cossacks (re-named so after the Pugachev rebellion), formed a different type of community—a curious kind of *kulak* communism. Their territory formed one immense land commune, in which all Cossacks had their share. As tillage is unproductive in those parts, the community of land was not so important as the organisation of the fishing rights, which also belonged to the whole Cossack community: some types of fishing were organised on a communal basis, while in others all Cossacks were given a rigorously equal opportunity for individual fishing. It is needless to add that this communism was strictly exclusive; the Cossacks were a privileged aristocracy much richer per head than any of their neighbours. They were strongly conservative—Old Belief being dominant—and they rank next to the Northern peasants in the preservation of old Russian customs and songs.

II. THE NATIONAL MINORITIES.

WHILE the only more or less populous non-Russian district incorporated by Muscovy was the old Kingdom of Kazan, the Petersburg Empire proceeded from conquest to conquest of territories essentially alien in race, religion and culture, some of them more densely inhabited and more economically advanced than the Russian centre. For a long time the Imperial government made no attempt to assimilate the new acquisition, to the main mass of the Empire. They retained to a very large extent their inner autonomy, and the more European a national group was the more favourable was the treatment accorded to it. The gentry were given support, their privileges confirmed, and even restored or increased. Where there were no gentry the commercial class was chosen as the object of encouragement. Established religion was given full recognition and support. Old laws and institutions were as far as possible preserved, and the social order that prevailed at the moment of annexation continued and safeguarded.

The phileuropeanism of the Petersburg government manifested itself, among other things, in the encouragement of European immigration. The services were wide open to foreigners, the diplomatic service, especially, became in the 19th century predominantly foreign. German colonists were settled in the wheat belt, where they were given the best lands and considerable privileges. Even an essentially anarchistic sect like the Anabaptists (Mennonites) were accorded special favours and exempted for all time from military service. The Germans who settled on the Volga under Catherine II failed to make good, and the standard of living they set was not much superior to that of the Russian farmers. But those who settled in the Black Sea steppe became exceedingly prosperous.

The most characteristic illustration of the phileuropean, aristocratic and conservative policy of the Empire, is to be found in the Baltic provinces. Ever since the middle ages Baltic society consisted of an aristocracy of German barons who owned all the

237

land and ruled the country as unlimited masters; of a small class of German burgesses, and of *literati*, equally German, from whom the rural clergy were recruited; and of a mass of Letts and Estonians, the serfs of the German nobility. The political and manorial privileges of the barons had been considerably reduced by the Swedish kings, but Peter won the Barons to his side by promising them the complete restoration of their liberties. The *Ritterschaft* of Esthonia, Livonia and Oesel were given special charters under which the provinces were governed by the corporations of the nobility (*Landtag*). *The German squires were far more progressive landlords than the Russian, and produced more extensively for the world-market. As serfdom (which was of the European type—not a quasi-slavery, as in Russia), was a hindrance to the growth of capitalistic farming, it was abolished at the request of the barons in the beginning of the 19th century, but all the land was retained by them, the Letts and Estonians becoming a landless mass of labourers and cotters. As the Baltic gentry were numerous and inclined to multiply, even all the land in the country was not enough to support them and large numbers of them constantly entered the Russian service. In the army and in the civil service they were conspicuous for their loyalty to the dynasty and for their spirit of discipline. They were the principal moving force of the militaristic transformation of the army under Paul, Alexander I and Nicholas I. The Russian gentry regarded them with envy, but not without a certain degree of contempt, for their meticulous, frugal and economical ways.

Like Livonia, the main part of Finland† was annexed during a war with Sweden. To attract the population, Alexander I proclaimed Finland a separate Grand Duchy with an autonomy so extensive that most non-Russian students of the question maintain that it never formed part of the Russian Empire, but that the Emperor of Russia merely became the Grand Duke of Finland (what German jurists call "personal union"). The Russian Emperors loyally observed their obligation. The Finlanders remained loyal, but they kept much more aloof from Russia than the Germans did. Only in the navy was the number of Swedish officers at

---

*Courland, on its annexation in 1795, received similar treatment.

†South Eastern Finland had been annexed in 1721 and 1743.

ll considerable. Finland itself remained unaffected by Russian
influence.

The partitions of Poland were made at a time when a great
progressive movement of the lower *szlachta*, inspired by the
French Revolution, was sweeping the country. Kościuszko, the
commander of the anti-Russian army whose defeat marked the
end of Poland," became not only a national hero, but a hero of
European Liberalism. The most active elements of the lower
szlachta joined the French Revolutionary armies, but the aristocracy had no particular sympathies for democratic France. When
the anti-Polish policy of Catherine was superseded, under Paul
and Alexander I, by the restoration of Polish ascendancy in the
annexed provinces, there formed itself a pro-Russian party which
hoped that this was the first step towards the reconstruction of
Poland "in the boundaries of 1772." When, at the Congress of
Vienna, Alexander succeeded in annexing to Russia the greater
part of Poland proper ("Congress Poland"—*Kongresòwka*) the
Poles showed themselves fairly satisfied. Alexander was even ready
to restore a great Poland which would be distinct from Russia
and of which he would be king, but the Russian gentry were
unanimous in crying out against the project. Nevertheless, the
West Russian provinces remained virtually Polish, with Polish
the official language and the local administration in the hands
of Poles.

The Kongresòwka was given a liberal constitution and the first
years of its existence were a time of rapid industrial, agricultural
and commercial development. But the union of autocratic
Russia with constitutional and liberal Poland was incompatible.
The Polish *szlachta* would forget neither the great days of independence, nor the military tradition of Kościuszko and Napoleon.
The army became the centre of revolutionary activity, which
culminated in the Revolution of 1831. But the Poles were ultimately defeated, the Constitution abolished and Poland subjected
to military government. Theoretically she continued to be an
independent kingdom, and pro-Russian Poles were as much as
possible employed in the administration. But all liberty was done
away with, and all active patriots found themselves in Siberia, or
in exile. Hatred of Russia became the first duty of a good Pole,

and the intelligentsia lived in an unreal world of romantic dream
of sacrifice and revenge. Still the aristocracy continued to accep
honorary office at court, and large numbers of Poles, especial
from the Lithuanian and Ukrainian provinces, continued to serv
in the army and in the civil service. A policy of Russification bega
in these provinces, but the Polish gentry not only retained the
land and serfs (only the estates of open rebels were confiscated
but a dominating influence in the local administration; indee
the corporations of the gentry, in which the Poles formed an ove
whelming majority, retained all their rights till the second rebe
lion of 1863.

Polish influence, which had played so important a part in th
early stages of the europeanisation of Russia, ceased almost com
pletely after 1700, never to be revived. Neither could Russia
influence penetrate into Poland. The numerous Poles or quas
Poles in the Russian service were, of course, more or less Russia
ised in the long run. But political hatred was a safeguard again
Russian influence on the main body of the nation. The Pol
regarded the Russian conquerors as Asiatic barbarians and them
selves as the outpost of European civilisation in the East. Th
felt humiliated by being the subjects of an inferior nation, an
this "superiority complex" contributed powerfully to prevent a
possibility of a *rapprochement*.

If the aristocratic nations of the West were the "most favour
nations" of the Petersburg Empire, the Jews were undoubtedly t
least favoured. Old anti-Jewish prejudice, common to Muscovit
West Russians and Poles; the social contempt of a ruling nobili
for a people of plebeians; and the contempt of an enlighten
government for a people of bigoted fanatics combined to ma
the Jews the pariahs of the West. They were allowed to rema
where already domiciled, but not to settle on old Muscovite ter
tory*; this was the origin of the famous "Jewish Pale." They r
mained segregated, retaining much of their communal autonom
but were debarred from entering the crown service. Under Nichol
I, a prolonged attempt was made to break down their isolati
and to assimilate them to the Christian population. They we

*The Black Sea provinces, annexed under Catherine II were, howev
opened to the Jews.

rbidden to wear their traditional dress, and their characteristic
cks and beards. They were submitted to conscription, which
:came the occasion for horrible vexations and cruelty. Small
ys were taken away from their parents, forcibly baptized, and
ought up in regimental schools. The attempt failed and the Jews
mained intensely race-conscious. But the modernist movement,
e echo of German-Jewish "Enlightenment" which reached
ussian Jewry in the eighteen 'thirties was destined to succeed
here coercion had failed. At first, its language was German, but
the middle of the century a large section of the Jewish bour-
oisie was ready to cast off its isolation and to become part of
ucated Russian society.

Greeks and Armenians were treated on a level with Europeans
d encouraged to immigrate. Greeks from the Crimea were given
nd in the Azov steppe. Greek merchants formed powerful com-
unities at Nizhen (which, for a long time, almost monopolised
krainian commerce), Odessa and Taganrog; Armenian mer-
ants at Astrakhan, and Nakhichevan on the Don (now a suburb
Rostov). The Russian annexation of Georgia and Azerbaijan
nfirmed the Armenians as the dominating commercial element
ere. The conquest of Erivan gave Russia the monastery of
:hmiadzin, the residence of the Katholikos (Patriarch) of All the
rmenians. The consistently pro-Armenian policy of the Russian
vernment, the profits the Armenian bourgeoisie made out of
ussian territorial aggrandizement, the part played by Russia
the scourge of Turkey and Persia—the two arch-foes of Armenia
made Echmiadzin a powerful centre of Russian influence among
n-Russian Armenians. They became the most wholly and most
clusively pro-Russian of all subject nations. In commerce and
the Near East they played the same role as the Baltic Germans
d in the services and in the West.

Russia's prolonged efforts to annex Moldavia and Wallachia
d, in 1812, to the annexation of Bessarabia and in 1829 to a
rtual protectorate over both the principalities. Moldavia and
allachia were purely squire-ruled states. An aristocracy of
iars strongly hellenised by two centuries of Phanariote rule,
vned all the land, though the peasants were not serfs. At the
ne of the annexation of Bessarabia no section of Roumanian

society had attained to national consciousness. The newly annexe
province retained, for a short time, certain peculiarities, but tl
landlords were only too eager to become Russian nobles and ve
soon lost all consciousness of being anything else. The peasant
though they adhered very firmly to their speech, displayed x
desire whatever to unite with their compatriots over the Prut
But in the principalities the upper classes had discovered by 18
that they were the descendants of Romans and cousins of tl
French, and so came to resent the protectorate of barbarous Sla\
The growth of Latin national consciousness, which led to tl
Revolution of 1848 and its suppression by Russian troops, ma
the Roumanian upper classes and intelligentsia the bitter
enemies of Russia next to the Poles. Roumania was, in all respec
the greatest failure of Russian Imperialism.

The annexation of the Kingdom of Georgia, followed by th
of the Georgian principalities west of it, was an event of tl
greatest moment for the history of Russia, for of all the nation
minorities, the Georgians, excepting only the Jews, became mc
organically part of the Russian system and were destined
play the most active role. The Georgians are an ancient natio
The grafting of Byzantine and Iranian influence on the o
Caucasian stock resulted in a national type of its own, n
reducible to any other. Georgian civilisation had had a Gold
Age in the 12th century. In the 16th century Georgia became
Persian dependency which, however, played a considerable pa
in the life of the Empire. At the time of its annexation, Georg
like Persia, was in a state of decadence. Russian domination w
accepted almost without protest. As Georgia was not "europea
and the Georgians were commercially less important than tl
Greeks or Armenians, the newly annexed country received sca
recognition of its national entity. Russian was made the offici
language, and Russian bureaucratic government was introduce
However, the Georgian nobility received the rights of Russi
gentry with the consequent control of most local affairs.

Georgian society was purely feudal. The very numerous nobili
was economically stagnant and inefficient. The bourgeoisie w
Armenian; the peasants medieval serfs, patriarchally attach
to their lords. Socially and economically the Georgian nobles l

thing by the Russian conquest. The Russian services—especially
e army (where many of them proved first-rate soldiers)—absorbed
eat numbers of them, while others early discovered the way to
e Tsar's privy purse. All this contributed to make the Georgian
bility pro-Russian and politically harmless. Russian rule intro-
ced the germs of European civilisation into Georgia, and Georgi-
poets began to produce poetry that was no longer in the old
tional Persian tradition, but followed the models of Byron and
shkin. But, on the whole, the first half-century of Russian rule
d little to revive Georgia. Her nobility was hopelessly decadent.
he revival came in the second half of the century with the rise of
e Georgian bourgeoisie and farmer-class.

Islam was not at first viewed by the Petersburg Emperors with
uch favour, and under Elizabeth there was even a tendency
persecute it. But the enlightened despotism of Catherine II
alised its value as a force to keep the people quiet. The Muham-
adan clergy were given a regular organisation and an official
erarchy based on the Lutheran model. They were given every
pport in their relations with their co-religionists and encouraged
convert heathen and to make good Muhammadans of nominal
nverts.

The first new Muhammadan country annexed by the Peters-
rg Emperors was the Crimea. This took place at the height of
atherine's dreams of a great Russo-Greek Empire. As the Crimean
reeks had only recently migrated to better and larger lands in
e Azov steppe, Catherine's Hellenic sympathies could only take
e form of a wholesale conversion of Tartar place-names into
reek, and of extensive donations of land to Russian nobles. The
artars lost their dominating position, but the nobility obtained
e rights of Russian gentry. The proximity of Turkey kept alive
n-Islamic feelings, and after the Allied invasion of 1854-55, great
umbers of Tartars emigrated to Turkey.

In the Transcaucasian provinces annexed from Persia, Russian
nquest deprived the Muhammadans of their dominating posi-
on, and gave increased importance to the Armenian bourgeoisie.
t the Russian governors, themselves squires, could not fail to
cognise in the Muhammadan *beks* their social kin. Though under
lamic law the *beks* (like the Indian *zemindars*) were not the

243

owners of the land they held, it was recognised as their propert
the peasants that lived on it became, in fact if not in nam
their serfs. This attached the leading Moslems to Russian ru
and firmly established the landed interest in opposition to tl
commercial interest represented by the Armenians.

It was only in Caucasia (as distinguished from Transcaucasia
that the Russian Empire found in Islam a long irreducible enem·
The mountain land of the Caucasus falls into three main section
In the west, the well-watered and densely wooded highland
between the Kuban and the Black Sea were occupied by tl
Circassians. They lived divided into tribes, organised on strictl
aristocratic and feudal lines. They were excellent agriculturist
skilled in irrigation and gardening, and great warriors. As th
country was over-populated, and as the women of Circassia (lik
those of Western Georgia), are widely famed for their classic
beauty, one of their important sources of income was the sale c
their daughters to the Turkish harems. Turkish influence wa
strong and till 1828 the Circassians recognised the suzerainty c
the Sultan. They were Moslems, but recent converts; not so lon,
ago they had been Christians, and they retained many features c
a more ancient paganism.

Central Caucasia, the basin of the Terek, had a more mixec
population. The country was traversed by the main route t
Georgia and Persia, and had often been the theatre of wars anc
migrations. On both sides of the passes leading to Georgia livec
the Ossetes, who were the descendants of the Sarmatians, anc
were known to medieval history as the Alans; in the middle age·
they had been the paramount power in the country. North·
west of them were the Circassian Qabardis who in the 16th
century established their hegemony over all the neighbourhood
and were still regarded as the aristocrats of the Caucasus. Farther
east lived the Ingush and the Chechens, who had never played
any active part in general history. All these peoples except the
Ossetes were Moslems. The Russians occupied all the piedmont
region in the end of the 18th century, establishing Cossack
settlements on land taken from Qabardis and Chechens, and
proclaimed their sovereignty over all the Central Caucasian
nations. The first quarter of the 19th century was filled with risings

d punitive expeditions against the mountaineers. The Ossetes
one, many of whom were Christians, were the enemies of all
eir neighbours and consistently pro-Russian. The aristo-
atic Qabardis, once their aristocracy was won and controlled,
ased to be dangerous. But the Chechens who lived in democratic
llage communities and who suffered most from Cossack en-
oachment, remained defiant and permanently in arms.

Daghestan, the eastern section, consists of a flat piedmont
gion inhabited by peaceful Turki-speaking Kumyks, whose
iefs submitted themselves as soon as the Russians appeared,
d of Daghestan proper—"the land of the Mountains"—a verit-
le chaos of semi-arid massives and narrow ravines occupied by
numerous population speaking a bewildering number of related
t mutually unintelligible languages, and collectively known to
e Russians as Lezgians.* Part of the country was organised on
democratic basis into villages and federations of villages. Other
stricts were ruled by Khans. Inhabiting as they did an over-
pulated and naturally poor country, they had no other resource
an to loot their neighbours—they were the scourge of the low-
nd Georgians—or to have recourse to industry. Daghestan metal-
ork was famous as far as Persia, and Daghestan woollens found
market in all the Eastern Caucasus. The Lezgians were good
uhammadans well versed in Arabic and in the Shariat; it was,
nong them that the movement arose which organised the resist-
ce of the Caucasians to Russian aggression. It took the form—
miliar to the Iranian world and well known in N.W. India—of
uridism, that is to say, of a hierarchy of holy men reigning over
sciples pledged to absolute obedience. The Chechens joined the
ovement. Shamil, a man of great organising genius, made of the
astern Caucasus an impregnable fortress, garrisoned by fanatic
ldiers, which proved capable of resisting the besieging Russians
r a quarter of a century. The Qabardis, Ingush and Ossetes re-
ained loyal, and this enabled Russia to preserv her connections
th Georgia. But the Circassians, though they remained dis-
ited and outside the influence of Shamil and his *muridism*,
posed a no less fierce resistance to Russian advance. Shamil

*" Lezghi " is really the name of one of the Daghestan nations, and has
w ceased to be officially applied to the others.

was not finally defeated till 1859, the Circassians till 1864. Nin-
tenths of the latter refused to submit to Russian domination an
emigrated to Turkey, leaving their country a waste land to b
occupied by Russian Cossacks. The Caucasian war left a profoun
impression on the Russian imagination and is abundantly re
flected in literature. Not the least curious feature of the Russia
conquest of the Caucasus was that it led to the adoption of
number of Caucasian, mainly Qabardi, cultural traits—dress
arms, and dances—by the Russian Cossacks and Georgians.

The oldest Muhammadan subjects of Russia—the Kazan Tar
tars—profited most by the pro-Islamic policy of the Enlightene
Emperors. They supplied mullahs to all the imperfectly Islamise
pastoral nations. Their influence advanced with the advance c
Russian rule in the steppe. An essentially merchant nation, the
founded prosperous commercial colonies in Orenburg, Petro
pavlovsk and Semipalatinsk, whence they dominated the Qazac
steppe, acting as sole furnishers of Russian and European good
to the nomads. Though staunchly Muhammadan, the Tartar
adopted many Russian ways: a mosque imitating the classic
forms of contemporary Russian architecture is a prominent feature
in almost every town of eastern Russia.

The nomad Bashkirs and Buryats had begun to come under
Russian rule before the time of Peter, but the extensive inclusion
of nomadic territory is characteristic of the Petersburg period.

The Bashkirs suffered most in the process, for the land they
occupied, the Southern Urals and the parkland between these
and the Volga, was only too tempting a country for agricultural
and industrial colonisation alike. Turki-speaking Muhammadans,
they were strongly under the influence of Kazan, whence they
received their mullahs. But their society was of a nomadic type
headed by a pastoral aristocracy and included various incom-
pletely assimilated ethnic groups, whom the Bashkirs held in a
state of inferiority and whom the Russians used to break up Bashkir
resistance from within. Russian aggression provoked a succession of
rebellions (the most serious of which was that of 1736), and made
the Bashkirs take a prominent part in the Pugachov movement.
The suppression of the latter was followed by the pacification
of Bashkiria and a period of equipoise during which the spolia-

tion of native land was stopped, and the process of disintegration of tribal life accelerated. The Bashkirs were made to recruit special cavalry units. In 1813-14 their regiments, armed with bows and arrows, were one of the most picturesque—and most resented—features of the Russian invasion of Europe.

The nomads of Qazaqstan began to recognise Russian suzerainty as early as 1730. But it was only a century later that Cossack posts were established in the Qazaq steppe, and tribal organisation was placed under the control of the Russian administration. It was among the Qazaqs that the Kazan Tartars had most occasion to act as *Kulturträger* and pioneers of Islam.

Two other nomad nations, the Kalmuk and the Buryat, introduced a purely Mongol and Buddhist element into the Empire. The story of the greatness and decline of the Kalmuks and of their destruction on the tragic trek from the Volga to Dzungaria has been told in English by De Quincey and need not be repeated here. The remnants of the nation, which were prevented from trekking by the floods of the Volga, remained as Russian subjects between the Volga and the Don, under the rule of their aristocracy.

The Buryats of Trans-Baykalia began to be converted to Buddhism and to become spiritual subjects of the Dalai-Lama after they became Russian subjects. Buddhism was given the support of the government, for it was the kind of organised religion the government wanted above all to civilise and render harmless a "savage" nation.

The non-Muhammadan agricultural peoples of the Volga—Mordva, Chuvash, Mari and Votyak—took a prominent part in the movements of colonisation that carried agricultural occupation beyond the Volga and over the Urals. In many parts of the trans-Volga parkland they formed the majority of the new settlers. Even when isolated in the middle of a Russian population they showed a remarkable tenacity in preserving their speech and their ethnic distinctness. Only the Mordva adopted Russian ways on any extensive scale. But the missionary campaign which reached its highwater mark under Elizabeth resulted in the conversion to Christianity of the great majority of the other nations. Only among the Mari a substantial minority remained officially pagan. A large proportion of the Mordva were serfs; the others remained "free" in so far as "freedom" is a word that can be applied to crown peasants, who, owing to their ignorance of the official language, were even more exposed to arbitrary treatment by the administration than their Russian class-fellows. All four nations took a prominent part in the Pugachov rebellion, but subsided after that into the torpor common to the peasant class.

The forest peoples of Northern Siberia, on whom the fur-supply depended, largely preserved their tribal organisation, though most of them nominally accepted baptism. But the influence of the traders, who were completely free to fleece them as they liked—and to poison them with spirits and syphilis—led by degrees to degeneration and decrease. Only the Chukchi in the extreme North-East remained independent and vigorous. In the South of the forest-belt and in the island steppes of the Yenissey basin the natives came under more effective Russian influence, learned agriculture and were Russianised. Castrén, in the eighteen 'forties, in several cases met men who were the last to speak the tribal language. The fisher peoples of Kamchatka and the Aleutian islands, and even some of the Alaska Indians, were also rapidly detribalised and Russianised, in mode of life, if not in language. American tourists are still brought to see Russian samovars in the log-huts of the Tlinkit of Sitka. The only Siberian nation—except the nomadic Buryat—who neither declined in number nor lost its nationality were the Yakut, the Turki-speaking inhabitants of the Lena basin. Unlike the other peoples of the Siberian forest they were not hunters, but cattle grazers and their occupation of the land relatively intensive. They preserved their clan organisation and their language, which even became the *lingua franca* of the North-East in preference to Russian. The Russians of Yakutia were more strongly influenced by the Yakuts than *vice versa*. Together with the Zyryans, the Yakuts showed themselves the only nation of the *tayga* capable of making good in the conditions created by the Russian conquest.

Chapter VII

THE LATER PETERSBURG PERIOD

1. "THE GREAT REFORMS" AND THE INDUSTRIAL REVOLUTION.

THE abolition of serfdom in 1861 was followed by other reforms intended to liberalise and modernise the social fabric of Russia, to bring her into line with the bourgeois countries of the West, and to open the way for the growth of capitalism. The reform of 1864 substituted for the old bureaucratic and secret courts public trial by jury with the independence of judges and a corporation of the bar, completing, in theory, the transformation of the arbitrary monarchy of Peter the Great, into a legal absolutism of the European type. The *zemstvo* reform of 1865 instituted elective councils for the administration of local affairs, where the propertied classes were given preferential representation, but the peasants too were represented. The municipal councils were modernised; the taxes reformed; commercial legislation brought into line with capitalist requirements; corporal punishment abolished; conscription extended to all classes: the Jews given access to the schools and to the liberal professions; greater publicity introduced into official procedures; and a certain amount of liberty granted to the press. But the general character of the political institutions remained unchanged. The legislative power of the crown was not limited. The political police remained as arbitrary and ubiquitous as under Nicholas I. The bureaucracy retained the control of all affairs. Moreover, a series of "counter-reforms" under Alexander III, did much to undo all this work of modernisation.

The 'sixties and 'seventies were a time of speculation and adventurous enterprise. The export of grain grew; the population of the towns increased; the home market expanded; machine-made cottons and woollens replaced homespuns in the dress of the peasants; railways connected the main ports and the main producing districts, and steam-shipping developed on the Volga.

This was followed in the 'eighties by a depression, but the last decade of the century was again a period of intensive industrialisation, which is associated with the name of Witte, Minister of

Finance from 1892 to 1903. His policy was to industrialise the country at a forced rate, by direct governmental encouragement and by the extensive attraction of foreign capital. Heavy industry became the hero of the day; coal, iron, and oil, kings. The South (Donets coal and Krivoy-Rog iron)and the Baku oilfields became the vital centres of the new economic system. But this industrial progress, which did not go hand in hand with any general growth of the home market or of agricultural production, entailed the importation of foreign capital on a very extensive scale. From the outset the new industries were very largely foreign-owned. The alliance of the Russian monarchy with French finance laid the first stones towards the transformation of the Empire into a semi-colony of Western capitalism.

The building of railways and the opening up of new industrial areas radically changed the economic geography of Russia. Petersburg retained its importance as the seat of government and consequently of banking,and as a newly created centre of heavy industry; but Moscow, as the centre of the national railway system and the metropolis of the textile industry, began gradually to rival the northern capital in economic importance. It was surrounded by a number of active industrial centres, covering all the old Mesopotamia, of which the chief was the cottonopolis of Ivanovo-Voznesensk. But apart from this the new development favoured the periphery rather than the centre. The over-populated agricultural centre (the parkland south of Moscow), in particular, entered on a prolonged and hopeless crisis. The greatest urban development took place in the west and south. Warsaw and Lodz, after the abolition of the Polish customs frontier, became cities second only to the two capitals. Riga on the Baltic; Kiev as the sugar capital; Kharkov as the principal railway junction of the south and the financial metropolis of the Donets; Odessa and Rostov as the great grain-exporting ports; and Baku as the oil-capital, all came before any provincial city of Great Russia for their commercial and industrial importance.

Territorial expansion emphasised these centrifugal tendencies. The government of Alexander II, though it sold to the United States Russia's American colonies, annexed new territories that cannot be regarded otherwise than as colonial. The annexation from China of the Amur and Ussuri valleys with the port of Vladivostok in 1859, introduced a Russian wedge into the Chino-Japanese world. As long as there was no railway through Siberia, the new possession was "beyond the seas," for the best way of reaching it was *via* Suez and Singapore. The colonisation of Siberia by peasants fleeing land-hunger at home, and the hope of finding new markets for Russian industry on the Pacific, led to the construction of the Trans-Siberian trunk, started in 1891 and completed in 1904. This was a necessary stage in the development of the outlying territories, but the premature Imperialism of Petersburg, unjustified by any economic possibilities, and largely due to irresponsible and personal action on the part of the Tsar, provoked the Japanese war which played a part similar to that of the Crimean in showing up the inefficiency of the bureaucratic State.

Turkestan, conquered in 1864-73 (Transcaspia, followed in 1873-85) must also be regarded as a purely colonial acquisition, for it incorporated a land separated from the metropolis by sparsely inhabited deserts, and peopled by a purely Asiatic population of sedentary agriculturists. Turkestan was, however, a safer possession, for it was not exposed to the attack of any military power, nor to the competition of any foreign capitalism on its markets.

A further effort at expansion made in 1877 against Turkey, ended in very indifferent success, for the Dardanelles remained closed, and Bulgaria refused to be treated as a Russian colony. The acquisition of Batum was the only economically valuable outcome of the war.

2. THE PEASANTS AFTER THE EMANCIPATION.

THE Act of Emancipation made the peasant free to dispose of his labour, and, except for a short transitional period, severed every juridical tie between him and his master. He received an amount of land that was, nominally, calculated on the customary size of his holding under serfdom, but in practice considerably smaller. He had to pay an annual sum to the government as the price of the land obtained, while the treasury compensated the landlord. These payments were higher than the current price of land, and included, in a covered form, the price of the peasant's own liberty. All non-arable land, in the vast majority of cases, remained in the hands of the landlords.

But, though emancipated, the peasant did not become the equal of the other citizens. The newly freed serfs and the former crown and Imperial-family peasants formed a *sostoyanie* that was sharply marked off by law from the rest of the population. Their personal rights were restricted. Their village communities were placed under vigilant administrative control. Alone of all Russians they remained subject to corporal punishment. Their property relations were not regulated by the general law of the land, but by the un-codified customary law that had grown up in the course of the serfdom period. Most important of all, the egalitarian commune was preserved and enforced by law. This was done partly from fiscal considerations (communal responsibility for taxes was abolished only in 1903), and partly under the influence of the Slavophil promoters of the reform, who saw in the commune an instrument for the preservation of the conservative "Russian" virtues of the peasants, and a safeguard against their conversion into proletarians. To put it in plainer language: by tying the peasant to his holding the commune was intended to keep him at the disposal of the landlord as an agricultural labourer. The pressure of communal ownership was greatly increased by the communal land being made inalienable. The peasants thus remained what they had been under serfdom—"a nation within a nation," segregated from the other classes. Chained to a holding that was insufficient to support him, but for which he had to pay taxes, *zemstvo* rates, and compensation-annuities for the landlord, the peasant was forced to work as a labourer on the landlord's estate, or to look for work in the towns and industrial districts. The army of workmen from the emancipated villages thrown on the labour market was more than sufficient to satisfy the rapidly growing demand. Though very low by Western standards, industrial wages were higher than the peasant could hope to earn at home. The necessity of working for wages prevented the bulk of the peasants from acquiring the conservative "farmer" mentality, and made of them a potential revolutionary force that was very soon to become real.

As most of the landlords failed to invest the money they received in compensation for their serfs into agricultural improvement, large quantities of land were leased to the peasants. The demand being practically unlimited, rents were very high, and the additional acreage contributed little to increase the average peasant's well-being. As, moreover, the peasant population increased rapidly there developed a real "land-hunger." Emigration to Siberia, which was at first forbidden by the government so as not to drain the central districts of cheap labour, became a necessity. But it did little to still the land-hunger. By the end of the century the peasants, who had always viewed the squires' land as essentially theirs, began to grow increasingly impatient of the existing conditions and to hope more actively for agrarian reform and additional holdings.

Meanwhile the commune had not preserved the village community from increasingly rapid differentiation. The trader, the money-lender, the owner of several horses, the farmer of several dozen additional acres of squire's land, became more and more differentiated from the main mass of semi-proletarian peasants. The *kulak* class became a social reality, but the artificial trammels of legislation concealed to a certain extent the growing disunion of the village.

Culturally, the peasant still remained segregated and distinct from the upper classes, but his apartness was steadily giving way before new conditions. The workman became an increasingly important link between the urban and the rural world. At the same time primary education, which had been ignored by all previous regimes, was taken more or less seriously in hand by the *zemstvos*, and by degrees illiteracy was reduced. A new class of rural intelligentsia (or "semi-intelligentsia") of schoolmasters, accountants, clerks, medical assistants grew up, largely recruited from among the peasants, and became an immensely important "zone of contact" between urban and rural civilisation. Religious conservatism and attachment to the Church declined, while Protestant sects (Baptists and similar groups) found increasing favour. Old customs, rites and habits died out. A new type of song (*chastushka*) evolved by the urban masses, spirited, pointed and flippant, substituted itself for the old melancholy tunes. But while all that was old and conservative was gradually disappearing from the peasant's life, he retained his profound class-consciousness, his "racial" sense of distinctness from the *gospoda*, and a profound mistrust in them. It was this psychological and cultural gulf between people and gentry that made the propaganda of the agrarian socialists of the 'seventies so utterly abortive. It was not till after the turn of the century that the peasant opened his ears to intelligentsia radicalism and entered political life as an element in the revolutionary movement.

3. THE UPPER CLASSES.

THE social character of the monarchy was not much affected by the "great reforms," but culturally it degenerated with extraordinary rapidity. Catherine, Alexander I, even Nicholas I, had been in a sense intellectual and cultural leaders. Under their successors the taste and the intellectual level of the Russian court fell below that of the middle classes.

The great landlords all over the country, and the bulk of the squires in Ukraina and the adjoining districts, succeeded in transforming themselves, more or less, into a modernised class of agrarian capitalists. But even in the larger estates the level of agricultural methods was lower than the average farmer's in England or France. The majority of the Great Russian landlords were not successful in passing to capitalistic farming. Those that stuck to their estates clamoured for subsidies and preferential treatment. They formed the armies of extreme reaction and social and economic stagnation, and their interest was the paramount factor in the counter-reforms of Alexander III. 18

But another section of the middle gentry who ceased to rely mainly on their land, became an important ingredient in the formation of the liberal intelligentsia.

The representatives of the bourgeois interest fell socially into two distinct groups. On the one side were the bankers, the railway promoters and the heavy industrialists, who were closely associated with the ruling class and with the bureaucratic machine, had easy access to official support—guarantee and subsidy—were given "ranks" and orders and were consequently "gentlemen." The railway and other engineers, the most consciously bourgeois group of the intelligentsia, were socially closely connected with this section of the bourgeoisie. The political champion of this class was Witte and their most remarkable ideologist, the great chemist Mendeleyev.

The typical "merchant" was to be found among the wholesale dealers, the grain brokers and mill owners, the river steamship

owners, and the textile manufacturers. These were not "gentry."
They were very often of peasant and servile descent; equally often
they belonged to the Old Faith. They had great economic but
little social ambition. They did not believe in education. They
were frugal and pennywise, but at the same time capable of the
most adventurous daring and the most extravagant outlay. Gorky
in *Fragments from a Diary*, has given a remarkable portrait of one
of the most prominent of these pioneers of capitalistic accumulation—the Old Believer millionaire Bugrov, the ship and lumber
king of Nizhni. It was only towards the very end of the century
that the "merchants," especially those of Moscow, began to aspire
to culture and play a part in cultural life.

The most obvious change in the political consciousness of the
upper classes was the rise of nationalism, which had its roots in the
Slavophilism of the 'forties. It was originally the doctrine of that
section of the gentry who wished to rid themselves from the burden
of serfdom without unconditionally submitting to Western bourgeois civilisation. It united the moderately conservative middle
gentry with the growing forces of "merchant" industrialism. The
Emancipation of the serfs was carried out under their influence.
The Polish rebellion of 1863 made nationalism an almost official
creed. The merchants and the Slavophils enthusiastically supported the conquest of Turkestan, and inspired the Turkish war
of 1877. They formed what in foreign countries was considered
to be Russian public opinion. The principal inspirer of extreme
reactionary doctrines, which dominated the bureaucracy from
1881 to 1904, was Pobedonostsev, *ober-prokuror* of the Holy Synod,
whose tenure of office marks the lowest degradation of the Orthodox hierarchy. The essence of Pobedonostsev's conservatism was
an intense fear of change, and the conviction that if a stone was
touched the whole edifice would fall. It was thus one of the aspects
of the degeneracy of the monarchic power, and a sign of growing
impotence.

But the mainstay of reaction was the political inadequacy and
opportunism of the industrial bourgeoisie. They were quite satisfied
with the economic liberty established by the "Great Reforms" and
gave no support to constitutional liberalism. This made Russian
liberalism impotent and inactive. As it could do nothing better

han trade on the government's fear of revolutionary terror, its
ocal power rose and fell with the rise and fall of the revolutionary
vave. But the Liberals did much useful civilising and technical
vork, especially in connection with their two strongholds—the
emstvos and the law courts. The actual promoters of this work in
he *zemstvos* were their technical staffs—medical, agronomic,
tatistical—that went by the name of the "third element," the first
wo "elements" of rural society being the squires and peasants.

THE Socialist and Revolutionary wing of the intelligentsia in
cluded two main social types. The one, mainly of plebeian origin
represented the potential intellectual and political élite of the
"people" which, in a Russia that would be a free democracy o
peasants, would replace the old genteel educated classes. The
other, more largely composed of *déclassé* gentry, was the mor
distinctly rootless. Revolution for them was an emotional and
ethical reaction against a hated old order, rather than the con
struction of a new. They were "conscience-stricken nobles" con
scious of springing from a class that had oppressed the peopl
for centuries and obsessed by a "social-guilt complex." Thei
Socialism was purely altruistic and utopian. Their spiritual fathe
was Michael Bakunin, the rival of Karl Marx in the leadershi
of the First International, and the founder of European Anarchism

The democratic intelligentsia (as we may call the former sectio
to distinguish it from the spiritual children of Bakunin), was mor
realistic. Revolution for them was a means to an end. Socialism
for them, was not a "myth" but a possibility. Though their idealisn
might be as disinterested as that of the "conscience-stricken nobles,"
it was less self-consciously altruistic, for the cause of the peopl
was their own. There was among them a strong tendency toward
purely educational work, for it was incumbent on them to forr
an élite that might be able to lead the people.

The early Russian Socialists were "populists"—*narodniki*. The
believed that the Russian peasant was *naturaliter* a Communis
and that consequently Socialism could be attained in Russia with
out the country traversing the stage of Capitalism. Constitution
reform was undesirable; it would only strengthen the bourgeoisi
and this was not (as it is in Marxian theory) an inevitable stage o
the way to Socialism.

The first cells of the revolutionary movement were founde
abroad by Herzen and Bakurin, nobles of the "conscience-stricken

type. The democratic intelligentsia had its first citadels in the censored home press whence Chernyshevsky, Dobrolyubov and Pisarev carried on from 1856 to 1866 a most effective propaganda battering down all the old traditions connected with the gentry, and forming a "young generation" (the phrase was current) of scientific Radicals and agrarian Socialists. Actual revolutionary activity was for a long time sporadic and, though sometimes sensational, quite superficial. But in the early 'seventies there suddenly began an extensive movement of "conscience-stricken" young intellectuals "into the people." Enthusiastic young men and women went into the villages to preach Socialism to the peasants, or rather to bring the "innate Communism" of the people to clear consciousness. But the peasants remained unresponsive. The Emancipation had infused new life-blood into their Monarchism, and they had no wish to listen to propagandists coming from the gentry. The "educated" and the "people" spoke mutually unintelligible languages. The police was soon able to lay hands on the propagandists, and the "movement into the people" came to an end. The mammoth trials "of the Fifty" and "of the Hundred and Ninety-Three" revealed to the general public men and women who, whatever their political wisdom, were unquestionably the ethical pick of their generation. It became apparent at the same time that "peaceful propaganda" was an impossibility in police-ruled Russia and that before it could be resumed a political revolution was necessary. At a secret conference at Voronezh, in the summer of 1879, a group of *narodniki* formed the party of *Narodnaya Volya* (which means both People's Freedom and People's Will), that started a campaign of terror against the government, and more especially the person of Alexander II. It was led by Zhelyabov, the son of a serf and a man in advance of his generation in political understanding. The Liberals were at first sympathetic to the *Narodovoltsy* and the government ready to buy liberal support by pseudo-constitutional reform. But the death of the Tsar at the hands of the terrorists (1st March 1881), produced a reaction. The revolutionaries found themselves isolated, and though the revolutionary movement continued to recruit new forces from the young generation, so that the campaign of terror was prolonged till 1887, the police carried on the work of suppression with ruthless efficiency, filling the prisons and Siberia with revolutionaries. Though defeated, the campaign of 1879-81 was ultimately immensely profitable to the cause of Revolution in a variety of ways: the reactionary counter-reforms of the 'eighties, coming instead of the expected "Constitution" of 1881, increased the discrepancy between political form and social realities, thus giving greater strength to the contracted revolutionary spring; the Tsar was terrorized into becoming a prisoner in his own palace and lost personal touch with his subjects; the cruelty of the government in its work of suppression made Tsarism hated all over the world, and increased the "drawing power" of the revolutionary parties. Above all, a revolutionary tradition was created which organised the whole of the radical intelligentsia, especially the younger generation in the universities, into a camp permanently hostile to the monarchy.

"Professional revolutionaries"—one of the most characteristic products of modern Russian history, formed the staff of the revolutionary movement. "Professional revolutionism" was the only satisfactory outlet for those of the Socialist intelligentsia who aspired to action and to ethical integrity. Among the older generation there were men of wide cosmopolitan culture and great intellectual refinement, the successors of the cultured gentry. Such, for instance, were Kropotkin and Plekhanov. But the typical revolutionary was a man with a single purpose, whose knowledge of life might be extensive and profound, but was purely practical—like an intelligence officer's knowledge of the enemy. His natural element was the *podpolie*—the "underground" of illegal existence under the Damocles' sword of detection by the police. There was no revolutionary but passed a great part of his life in prison or in the wilderness of North Siberia. The headquarters were abroad—in London, in Paris, or in Switzerland, where large colonies of Russian émigrés grew up and survived till 1917. The active revolutionary nucleus of these colonies was surrounded by a less distinctly active outer circle of students and bohemians. The peculiar conditions of life of the Russian revolutionary could breed men of colossal will-power and ascetic discipline, which in combination with intellectual genius could produce such a figure as Lenin. But from less disciplined and more individualistic characters were produced neurotic adventurers of very inferior moral quality. The practice introduced by the police of using *agents provocateurs* to corrupt the revolutionary organisations did much to poison the *podpolie* by an atmosphere of mutual mistrust, so that if it was a school of character it was also a severe moral test.

Individual industrial workmen were drawn into the revolutionary movement as early as the 'seventies, but the proletariat as a whole did not begin to acquire class consciousness till the middle of the 'eighties, when the first great wave of economic strikes traversed the country. While the imperfect differentiation of the industrial workman from the peasants retarded the development of a proletarian consciousness, the great concentration of Russian industry was, on the contrary, a favourable factor: about one third of all the Russian workmen worked in enterprises of 500 hands and more. This facilitated organisation and helped to make the conception of class a concrete reality. The first strikes were spontaneous and purely economic and it was not till the end of the century that the workmen began to be politically organised. The *narodniki* regarded the workmen merely as peasants corrupted by urban civilisation, and only made use of them as propagandists. But soon after 1881 Plekhanov, a former *narodnik*, founded the first Marxian organisation. By 1890 Marxism commanded the allegiance of most of the younger generation of the radical intelligentsia. It had a right wing of "legal (i.e., non-revolutionary) Marxists," bourgeois radicals, who had discovered in it a philosophy that justified industrialisation against the *narodniki*. The left wing formed the Social Democratic ("S.-D.") Party, which became the revolutionary organisation of the industrial proletariat. Inside the party there were again two wings: the Mensheviks, led by Plekhanov, who believed in collaboration with bourgeois Liberalism and were sceptical about armed action; and the Bolsheviks*, led by Lenin. They insisted on an alliance with the peasants (whom the Mensheviks regarded as a purely reactionary element), and on armed rebellion as the most effective revolutionary means. They insisted, too, on strict party discipline. The two groups

*" Menshevik " and " bolshevik " mean " minority-man " and " majority-man." The names allude to the number of votes received by the two points of view at the party congress of 1903.

corresponded to two clearly distinct social and psychological types. The Bolsheviks gradually attracted all that was most active, determined and disciplined among the revolutionaries.

The government attempted to deflect the workmen from revolusionary consciousness by factory legislation of a very rudimentary kind, and by forming workmen's unions run by police agents, to counteract Social-Democratic influence. But this was playing with fire, for it was the head of one of these police-run unions, the priest Gapon, that led the workmen of Petersburg on 9th (22nd) January 1905 to the Winter Palace with a petition to the Tsar. Their massacre by the troops proved the signal for the first Revolution.

The advent of the industrial workmen as the principal revolutionary class transformed the whole character of the Russian revolutionary movement, and gave it those qualities of natural collectivism, realism, and spontaneous discipline that became so strikingly apparent in the course of the Bolshevik Revolution. For the first time the Russian people produced an organised body of politically conscious working-men who knew what they wanted and how to obtain it.

But while the proletariat was growing into the leading revolutionary force, the old tradition of the *Narodovoltsy* was given new life by the formation of the Socialist-Revolutionary ("S.-R.") Party, who revived the tradition of individual terror, and rejecting Marxism placed their revolutionary hopes in the peasants. More emotional and individualistic than the "S.-D.s," the "S.-R.s" easily prevailed among the masses of the radical intelligentsia and semi-intelligentsia. From 1902 to 1905 they successfully carried out a succession of assassinations that produced a stronger impression on the government and on the public imagination at home and abroad than any growth of the labour movement.

The revival of revolutionary interest in the peasant was due to a decided turn of political sentiment in the villages. Land-hunger, by the beginning of the century, had become conscious and vocal. In 1902 a wave of agrarian disturbances traversed the country which exceeded anything since the days of Pugachev, though it fell far short of that standard. The movement was particularly acute in Eastern Ukraina. It was already semi-organised, but still professed to place all its hopes in the Tsar.

The revolutionary tide was rising on all sides. The Japanese war precipitated events. As in 1854-5, in 1877-8 and again afterwards in 1915-17 a foreign war inevitably showed up the technical and administrative inefficiency of Tsarism, and by increasing its unpopularity among the propertied classes created favourable conditions for revolutionary activity.

The year 1905 saw "the Ninth of January," which started the Revolution going.* The terrorist acts of the "S.-R.'s," the strikes of the workmen, and the "agrarian disturbances" of the peasants which usually took the form of the destruction of the houses and buildings of the landlords, were the fighting front behind which the Liberals grew bold enough to demand constitutional reform with increasing insistence. Latvia, Estonia, Georgia and Armenia took an active part in the general movement, while Poland and Finland advanced their particular national policies. The Revolution reached its most victorious moment during October and November, as the result of a general strike which was passively supported by the professional classes and facilitated by the unreliable state of the army. It forced the Tsar to issue the Manifesto of 17th (30th) October, which gave legislative power to an elective Parliament (Duma) and promised all the usual constitutional liberties. The promises pacified the Liberals, who now abandoned the revolutionary cause, but the proletariat and the revolutionary parties continued the struggle, aiming at the conquest of power, and not at further concessions from the autocracy. This second phase of the Revolution, which culminated in the Moscow rising (December), ended in the victory of the Government. This was largely due to the disunion of the revolutionary forces, who had no one directing staff, but were split up between three parties—the S.-R.s, the Mensheviks and the Bolsheviks—of whom the last-named alone were seriously working for victory. At the critical moment the Government was able to send to the decisive point a small number of reliable troops of the Guards who won the campaign.

The Liberals concentrated on the Duma, and so did the peasants,

*The best history of the first Russian Revolution is the third volume of Pokrovsky's *Russian History in the briefest outline*, Moscow 1928 (in Russian). The account is not as brief as the title would imply.

who were convinced that as soon as the Tsar would hear from their deputies how real their need for land was, he would at once agree to the "compulsory alienation" of private estates to meet it. The elections were held under a law that had been framed under the delusion that the peasants were a more conservative element than the intelligentsia and consequently favoured the election of peasants as deputies. The Duma was divided between the Liberal "Cadets" and the peasant "Labour group." It at once demanded land reform, but the victorious Government refused to consider the demand, and the Duma was dissolved. The second Duma, elected in January 1907, proved to be more Radical than the first. The country was as hostile and as unreconciled as ever, but its revolutionary energy had been broken a year earlier. The dissolution of the first Duma had still been able to provoke disturbances, though on a much smaller scale than those of 1905. But when in 1907 the Government dissolved the second Duma, and changed the electoral law so as to give a clear majority to the landlords, the country remained quiet. The armed struggle had decided the issue in favour of the Government, and no amount of speaking in the Duma or elsewhere could affect the course of reaction.

But though the Revolution had been defeated it had not been in vain. The struggle and the defeat had hammered the workmen into a homogeneous and conscious proletariat, ready to resume the fight immediately after recovery. The peasants had at last cast off their passive conservatism and their belief in the Tsar. For the first time in Russian history the masses were an active force, conscious of their own interests and prepared to fight for them. The reaction that followed the first Revolution was but the trough before a bigger wave. Already by 1912 its first approaches were beginning to be felt. It was again a mass-massacre that became a turning-point: the shooting of the workmen of the Lena Goldfields Company at Bodaibo marks the end of the post-revolutionary torpor of the Russan proletariat. When, in 1917, the strategical moment came, both the workmen and their leaders were better prepared for the coming battle than they had been in 1905.

5. THE INTER-REVOLUTIONARY PERIOD (1906-17).

THE Constitution of 1906, amended by the electoral law of 1907, was a product of the reaction that followed the Revolution. It gave the landowners of Russian origin a clear majority in the Duma over the other propertied classes, the peasants and work-men retaining only nominal representation. The administration was not affected by the constitutional reform, and except for a slightly greater freedom of the press and in religious matters, re-mained what it had been before 1905. The police continued to be as arbitrary and as omnipotent as ever; the courts absolutely depended on the Minister of Justice. The gentry retained all their privileges and the Church continued to be an instrument in the hand of the Government. As for the national minorities, the policy of Russification and suppression was carried to lengths hardly dreamt of by Alexander III, or Pobedonostsev.

But Stolypin, Prime Minister from 1906-11, realised that measures of suppression were not enough to avert a new Revolu-tion. The disagreeable discovery made in 1905-6 that segregation, illiteracy and the commune had not sufficed to keep the peasants in their place as the passively conservative foundation of society, made it imperative that they should be transformed into something more nearly approaching the European farmer class. It was conse-quently decided to quicken the social differentiation of the peasant class by "backing the strong man," that is to say, helping the rich peasant to grow richer, and the poor peasant to get rid of his land. The law of 1906 authorised the breaking up of the communes by encouraging the private ownership and free sale of peasant hold-ings. It remained in force till 1917, and succeeded in breaking up a large proportion of the rural communes.

But its anti-revolutionary influence could not become effective at once. More immediate measures had to be taken to still the acute land-hunger of the peasants. As the victory of the gentry made the transfer of private land to the peasants by legislation out of the question, other means had to be tried. Emigration to *land hunger made available*

Siberia and Qazaqstan was organized on a hitherto unprecedented scale. The purchase of private land by the peasants was encouraged by extensive credit facilities. The more adequate squires, capable of capitalistic regeneration, retained their land, but the less fit were helped to get rid of theirs at comfortable prices, and it went to strengthen the "strong peasant."

The political reaction of 1906-14 was accompanied by an economic boom that was more general and organic than the "Witte boom" of the eighteen 'nineties. While the former was mainly limited to the heavy industries, the "Stolypin boom" was a direct effect of the growing capacity of the home market and affected agriculture as much, and even more, than industry. Agricultural development meant the strengthening of the South and East at the expense of the centre. Ukraina, Ciscaucasia and Western Siberia were the sections that profited most by the boom. Turkestan, too, developed into a great cotton-producing area.

The great boom did much to conciliate the propertied classes and their intelligentsia with a monarchy that proved itself so profitable. The Liberals, who had always piqued themselves on being liberally cosmopolitan, began to assume definitely imperialistic hues. But while Socialist ideas were on the wane, the plebeian bourgeoisie, including the textile manufacturers, and especially the bourgeoisie of such new provinces as Ciscaucasia and Western Siberia, though economically highly satisfied, felt itself politically slighted. They were not members of the ruling class, but the inferior allies of the ruling coalition of the agrarian capitalists with the heavy industries and the banks. So the plebeian bourgeoisie was ready to flirt with democracy and radicalism, supremely indifferent to the person of the Tsar, and by no means averse to an agrarian reform that would deprive the nobles of their estates.

But the real danger to the régime lay in its imperialistic appetites and in its growing dependence on foreign capital. The government had the full backing of the propertied classes in its policy of militarism and expansion. Leaders of the plebeian bourgeoisie in the Duma were even constantly denouncing it for supineness in the matter of armaments. The advance into Persia and Mongolia was mainly the affair of the plebeian bourgeoisie, and there was no serious opposition outside the Socialist parties to the policy that aimed at winning Constantinople. But the growth of imperialistic aggressiveness proceeded parallel to the loss of national independence.

Foreign capital began to invade Russia on an extensive scale under Witte. The ties with France became particularly strong. The Paris Bourse helped the Monarchy to defeat the Revolution in 1905-6. The banks, after that date, came under predominantly foreign control. The heavy industries were likewise mainly owned by foreign shareholders.* By 1914 Russia had gone a good part of the way towards becoming a semi-colonial possession of European capital. The prevalence of French, Belgian and English over German capital in Russian investments was such† that quite apart from the imperialistic appetites of her bourgeoisie, Russia had no choice but to fight on the side of the Entente.

When the war came the bourgeoisie, which had desired it, did all it could to keep away from the front. The fighting was done by the mobilised peasants and by the professional soldier. The incompetency of the military and general bureaucracy was exceeded by the irresponsible wastefulness of the non-official organisations of the *zemstvos* and municipalities that had been summoned to help the State in munition work. The people, gradually but irrevocably, realised that the war was a class-war waged in the interests of land-owners, industrialists and foreign shareholders, in which the peasant had to do the fighting and dying while the upper classes profiteered and drew mammoth salaries as munition or red-cross workers. The officers, of course, shared the dangers of the mobilised men, but the deep class-distinction inherited from the times of serfdom placed them in socially so different a position, that the resentment of the mobilised peasant against the officer's corps was even more acute and immediate than against the less conspicuous bourgeois.

The Revolution came as the result of the growth of the class-consciousness of the workmen and peasants provoked by war-time conditions. It was only hastened by the scandalous conduct of the

*Of the capital invested in mining 90 per cent. was foreign-owned.
†Of the total foreign capital invested in Russia, 70 per cent. was Anglo-Franco-Belgian, 20 per cent. German and Austrian, 5 per cent. American and 5 per cent. neutral.

Imperial family, of which sufficient has been written and which was merely the last phase of a long process of degeneration of the old ruling classes. The Rasputin affair weakened the governing classes by sowing disunion among them. The more vital elements of the gentry and capitalist class represented by the Duma, and supported by "public opinion," found themselves in a tragic dilemma. To submit to the mad policies of the Court meant certain and rapid ruin; to revolt against them meant letting loose the formidable forces of a revolutionary people, whom the war had at last cleansed of all traditional conservatism. The best solution would have been a quiet little "palace revolution" in which the people would not have been allowed to play a part. But it was too late. Before the Duma men had made up their minds, the workmen and garrison of Petrograd* began the Revolution which from that moment it was in no one's power to stay.

---

*St. Petersburg was thus renamed in August 1914 as an " anti-German " gesture.

6. INTELLECTUAL AND ÆSTHETIC CULTURE.

THE generation of writers that came of age between 1835 and 1850 produced the realistic novel that gave Russian literature universal recognition. The work of Turgenev, Dostoyevsky and Tolstoy has come to be regarded as the fullest expression of the "Russian soul" and synonymous with Russia's message to the world. In reality, however, the realistic novel is only the expression of a single phase in the development of the intellectual élite of the Russian educated classes. Its specific qualities and its philosophy were conditioned by the nature of the social groups that produced it—the middle gentry faced with the disintegration of all the social system to which it belonged, and the mixed intelligentsia that had no satisfactory place in existing society and was by definition maladjusted and "rootless." The comprehensive humanity of the work of "the Russians" was natural in an élite essentially unattached to any definite social forms. Their realism, on the other hand, had its source in an intense desire to see transformed the reality they were familiar with, and was closely linked with current political and social problems. Many of its masterpieces, including all Turgenev's novels and Dostoyevsky's *The Possessed*, are immediate echoes of transitory phases of social life. One of the great lessons of Russian realism is that no amount of "actuality" detracts from the "permanent" value of a literary work.

If the *déclassé* squire, and unadjusted *raznochinets* gave the dominant tone to the Russian realistic novel, less "rootless" and "unattached" groups had a no less important part in its achievements. Tolstoy—more especially in *War and Peace*—represents the more stable elements of the gentry that had successfully turned the danger point of emancipation; Ostrovsky and Leskov, on the other hand represent the more distinctly bourgeois type of *raznochinets* unaffected by the idealisms of the dissatisfied gentry and intellectuals, and more closely acquainted with the social strata in which the new bourgeoisie was beginning to grow.

The generation born between 1830 and 1850 takes as excep-

271

tional a place in the history of Russian music as the preceding generation in that of literature. The latter is represented in music only by Dargomyzhsky, the pioneer of musical realism, whose *recitativo* operas had a powerful influence on the formation of the nationalist and realistic group of "the Five" (or the *Kuchka*). Their most representative figure was Rimsky-Korsakov, whose deliberate "Russianism" was often distinctly operatic. But by their side there lived a greater and stranger man—Musorgsky. The music of his "popular dramas" has only recently been uncovered from the plaster overlaid on it by Rimsky-Korsakov. He is one of the greatest expressions of the creative unrest of the intelligentsia—akin on the one side to Dostoyevsky, on the other to the revolutionaries of the 'seventies. Quite apart from the main nationalist current stands Tchaikovsky, one of the most mysterious figures of Russian history, the last—and next to Pushkin the greatest—manifestation of the humanistic civilisation of europeanised Russian society.

The Radicalism—"nihilism"—of the 'sixties was closely connected with the abandonment of the historical and æsthetic idealism of the 'thirties and 'forties for scientific materialism and positivism. From the 'fifties to the end of the century scientific atheism dominated the intelligentsia. Science, however, was little affected by current radicalism. The learned profession remained non-political. Even history became a closed speciality practised by pure technicians, deeply versed in their sources but unguided by general ideas, like Klyuchevsky and Platonov. In the sciences our contemporary, the great physiologist Pavlov, may be taken as the type of the detached and secluded specialist. But science had its points of contact with life, and economic development. Mendeleyev, the greatest of all Russian scientists, did much for the applied sciences and was passionately interested in the capitalistic development of Russia. His name is closely connected with the "Witte era" of industrialisation, but it is still greater in the history of chemistry; and his periodic system of elements is Russia's greatest contribution to pure science.

The main current of Russian civilisation remained irreligious. The official Church continued till 1917 in "the state of paralysis" denounced by Khomyakov. The few intellectual leaders who came in touch with its more vital ascetic undercurrent were unable to dissociate religion from nationalism. By the middle of the 19th century Orthodoxy became a badge of the conservatives and Slavophils, and an abomination to the Westernisers and Radicals. In the 'eighties Vladimir Soloviev tried to break this alliance. His religious philosophy was free from nationalism, but was tainted instead by Romanism and Gnosticism. Irresponsible religious speculation, often with an obviously sexual foundation, and not based on any real religious experience, became, under the influence of Soloviev, one of the characteristic features of early 20th century Russian culture.

At the same time as Soloviev, Tolstoy began to preach his ethical Christianity, which became the first point of contact between the religious rationalism of the intelligentsia and the rationalist dissent of the people. But on the whole Tolstoy's religious influence was stronger abroad than in Russia.

The 'eighties, though a period of general gloom and disillusion that reflected the economic depression and political reaction of the time, produced a beautiful Indian summer of realistic fiction in the work of Anton Chekhov, an intellectual of plebeian birth, and an artist of unsurpassed ethical delicacy. The 'eighties were followed by the livelier pre-revolutionary 'nineties. In literature they produced Maxim Gorky, the last great realist of pre-Soviet Russia, and the only big writer produced by the genuinely revolutionary intelligentsia.

Already, before 1905, the leadership in all cultural things began to pass from the old civic Liberal and Radical intelligentsia to a new semi-bourgeois and semi-bohemian élite, aggressively individualistic and "highbrow," art-loving and anti-social. The influence of Nietzsche and of French and English æstheticism amalgamated with that of Dostoyevsky and Soloviev. It represented on the one hand the advent of a new bourgeoisie which, being free from a "social-guilt complex," considered itself equally free from "civic" obligations and was bent on "making life beautiful." But it also reflected the profound uneasiness of a class and a civilisation that was approaching an inevitable doom, before having really enjoyed social ascendancy. This gives the work of the Russian Symbolists—the principal expression of this uneasiness—a strangely prophetic appearance, which is particularly apparent in the poetry of the greatest of them, Alexander Blok.

On the eve of the Revolution a second generation of "modernists" was growing, more bohemian than bourgeois, less sophisticated and freer from the influence of Dostoyevsky, free also from all *fin-de-siécle* æstheticism, and, for the most part, from all ideas and philosophies. This younger generation was only to come to maturity after 1917.

All the arts were powerfully affected by the modernist and æsthetic revival. In music they first produced the gushing expressionism of Skryabin, but afterwards the severe constructive formalism of Stravinsky, one of the Russians who has had the greatest influence on European art. In painting and in the decorative arts Russian modernism did not show itself to be very creative, and Russian painting remained provincial and second-rate. But the level of artistic culture rose; art became a vital element in the cultural make-up of the intelligentsia, and the understanding of native and foreign beauty the duty of every educated citizen.

The art that is perhaps most characteristic of the period is the theatre. At every time of its history the Russian stage produced actors of great talent. The age of realism in literature was parallelled by a brilliant galaxy of realistic actors who were brought up on the plays of Ostrovsky and concentrated on the representation of manners and of social types. But the modern Russian theatre is dominated by great producers. The first of them was Stanislavsky, the creator of the Moscow Art Theatre. His great achievement was the subjugation of his cast (which was a regular "all-star cast") to the rigid discipline of team work. His extreme documentary and psychological realism achieved its greatest triumphs in the early years of the century in staging the plays of Chekhov. He was followed by younger producers who introduced more conventional and anti-literary styles of staging which attained their greatest exuberance after the Revolution. One of the results of the æsthetic movement was the brilliant revival of the ballet. The classical ballet, managed mainly by Frenchmen, had been a feature of the Russian Imperial theatres ever since the age of Alexander I and Didelot. About 1907 it began to be modernised, and in the able hands of Serge Diaghilev (who had previously organised the rather abortive revival of Russian painting), a new Russian ballet was formed which in the decade of the great war conquered all the stages of Europe, North and South America. The best composers (including Stravinsky) worked for Diaghilev, and he was able to discover and produce a whole galaxy of dancers who surpassed anything ever seen on a European stage. Next to the Russian novel Diaghilev's ballet was the most spectacular success of Russian culture in the West. The exotic and highly sophisticated æstheticism of the "Russian ballet" is the most characteristic cultural achievement of the Russian bourgeoisie, a class decadent and condemned before it was mature.

UKRAINA, as has already been said, played a leading part in the capitalistic development of the Empire. Her heavy industry was the most important in the whole country; her towns, Kiev, Kharkov and Odessa, were second only to the two capitals. Farming on the big Ukrainian estates was far ahead of the Great Russian provinces. But this capitalistic development was not in the hands of Ukrainians. In the large towns they were a minority. The working class in the mines and foundries was predominantly Great Russian, the native minority easily amalgamating with the rest. The landlords who were the pioneers of agrarian capitalism were Russians (sometimes of Ukrainian origin) or Poles, and the industrialists, mine-owners and managing engineers were very largely foreigners. Still, the consciousness that their country was the most progressive and potentially the most prosperous part of the Empire could not fail to stimulate the national feeling of the Ukrainians, which throughout the period made steady, if not always apparent, headway.

The peasants, however, remained little affected by it, and the Ukrainian movement remained mainly a movement of the intelligentsia. At first it had no particularly marked class-character, and, in spite of Shevchenko, bourgeois and even landlord elements dominated it till about 1880. Its centre at this stage was the University of Kiev and its principal expression the study of Ukrainian history and folklore. Politically and socially it was moderate. Most of the numerous socialists and revolutionaries produced in the 'seventies by the Ukrainian intelligentsia had no particular national tendencies. The rising wave of Russian nationalism and general reaction induced the government to strike at the Ukrainian movement and in 1876 a *ukaz* was published which put such restrictions on Ukrainian publications as practically amounted to a prohibition of Ukrainian printing.

This drove the Ukrainian leaders to Galicia, where, under the Austrian constitution of 1866, the "Ruthenians" were relatively free to develop a national culture. Emigrés from Russian Ukraina had an enormous influence on Galician cultural and political life and Lvov became the cultural centre of Ukrainian literature and nationalism. The latter was supported by the Austrian Government, partly as part of its policy of playing off one nationality against another, partly as an eventual Piedmont for action in Russian Ukraina. Ukrainian became one of the officially recognized *Landessprachen* of Austria and the Ukrainian nationalists of Galicia and Bukovina devoted patriots of the Hapsburg monarchy. As the sting of Ukrainian nationalism was directed against Russia, the literary language (which in the work of Shevchenko and his followers was still very close to Russian in its vocabulary) began to be studiously weeded of all traces of the hated Muscovite tongue. The learned and abstract vocabulary was permeated with Polish influence, so that the literary Ukrainian of to-day is deliberately unlike literary Russian. The leader of the movement during this Galician period was Professor Hrushevskyĭ, a Russian Ukrainian settled at Lvov, and an historian whose works form a veritable encyclopædia of Ukraina's past.

In the meantime, in "Ukraina Major," though everything Ukrainian was forbidden, the social development was creating an increasingly favourable soil for the national movement by the growth of the rural intelligentsia and "semi-intelligentsia." These groups were almost entirely Ukrainian in their consciousness, and when the revolution of 1905 came the movement was in their hands. It was now more pronouncedly democratic than ever and overwhelmingly socialist. The peasants played no active part in it, but as the Ukrainian intellectuals and "semi-intellectuals" were very largely of peasant origin the movement assumed an increasingly definite peasant class-colouring. An Ukrainian press was reconstituted; Ukrainian literature rapidly grew in quantity, and gained a more capacious market. It produced a galaxy of significant writers, among whom the novelist Kotsyubinsky, and the poetess Lesya Ukrainka were the more important.

After 1907, and especially during the war, the national movement again became the object of persecution and suppression. But by that time it was irrepressible. When the pressure of Tsarism was lifted it became apparent that practically all the democratic intelligentsia and "semi-intelligentsia" of South-Western Russia was conscious of itself as Ukrainian, that the peasants were on the verge of becoming conscious of the same, and that Ukraina was going to be an independent nation.

In White Russia the development was quite different. Ground down by landlords, as capitalistic and as ambitious as in Ukraina, the White Russian peasant showed comparatively little initiative even in 1905-6, and at the elections allowed himself to be led by the Polish squires or by the Orthodox priests. A small nucleus of a national intelligentsia was, however, in existence by that time. A literature in the vernacular was beginning to grow, and produced in Michael Bahdanovich and Yanko Kupala poets of no mean talent. After the Revolution the political development, which led to the creation of a White Russian republic, was ahead of national consciousness. Hence, the difference between Russo-Ukrainian and Russo-White Russian relations; for while the former are still coloured by the memory of long years when the Ukrainians demanded, and the Russians refused them, recognition as a nation, to the White Russians nationhood came as an almost unsolicited gift of the Russian Revolution.

By the side of Ukrainian and White Russian nationalism certain sections of the Great Russian people aspired, more or less actively, to regional or sectional autonomy. The Cossacks, whose past would best justify such velleities, had been finally deprived of all administrative autonomy under Nicholas I. They remained, however, a privileged class, much richer on an average than their neighbours, and exempt from taxes, though submitted to manhood conscription. The isolation of the Cossacks from the rest of the population enabled the government to make extensive use of them in the suppression of revolutionary movements, and round about 1900 the name of Cossack was almost as hated as that of gendarme. But many Cossacks resented this and the growth of a Cossack intelligentsia on the one hand, and of internal class differentiation on the other, made them less and less reliable as bull-dogs of the Monarchy. In the Duma most of the Cossack deputies belonged to the Liberal opposition. The Cossacks always clung very decidedly to their privileges and their particular status, but it was only after the Revolution that their particularism assumed the form of separatism—especially active among the Kuban and (to a lesser extent) the Don Cossacks. They proved the principal fighting force of the counter-revolution, and the victory of the Soviet dealt a decisive blow to their privileges.

Only the Siberian Cossacks of North-Eastern Qazaqstan proved more actively separatist. It was among their intelligentsia that Siberian particularism (*oblastnichestvo*) first became vocal in the 'sixties. But it never became a really popular movement; the Siberian peasant and merchant, for all their dislike of the new-comers that were pouring into the country, were profoundly indifferent to all so-called abstract and not immediately practical problems. Like Cossack particularism, Siberian autonomy became a practical issue only after the October Revolution; like the former it showed very little vitality and died a rather inglorious death crushed between the military counter-revolution and the victorious Soviets.

8. THE NATIONAL MINORITIES.

As the supra-national monarchism of the earlier Empire was transformed into the new nationalism of the "post-reform" monarchy, the old phileuropean and aristocratic attitude to the national minorities was superseded by a policy of assimilation. The Polish rebellion of 1863 proved a crucial landmark in the adoption of the doctrines of nationalism by the Russian State and propertied classes. Its suppression was followed, in Poland, by a period of ferocious Russification, when the very name of Poland was changed to that of "provinces by the Vistula." But it was accompanied by reforms that raised the status of the Polish peasant who, unlike his class-fellow in Russia, was made a full member of the civil community, so that for a time he was rendered almost immune to anti-Russian feeling. Polish industry, which had profitted immensely by the abolition of the customs frontier between Poland and Russia (1850), and was largely in the hands of Germans and Jews, was likewise pro-Russian, and its rapid growth had a powerful effect on the decline of Polish nationalism. The aristocracy—as is the nature of aristocracies—tried to conciliate itself with the government. Polish opposition was reduced to purely sentimental forms, and the nation, as a whole, did not even oppose Russification by non-co-operation. At the same time the influx of Poles into Russia was immense. The bourgeoisie, the liberal professions, the "semi-intelligentsia," the industrial proletariat, even the army, were strongly polonised. By the end of the period very slight concessions to the Poles—such as administrative autonomy within ethnical boundaries—would have completely conciliated both the upper classes and the peasants. But these concessions were never made.

In the meantime a revolutionary movement, with roots in the democratic intelligentsia and in the industrial proletariat, raised its head, opposing a revolutionary patriotism to the conciliatory policy of the propertied classes and to the passivity of the peasants. The Polish Socialist Party ("P.P.S.") one of whose leaders was

Pilsudzki, became the most active enemies of Tsarism and, ultimately, the political nucleus of the new Poland. By their side there also grew up in Poland a less influential, but highly developed, internationalist Social-Democracy, which, among others, gave Russian Bolshevism such a prominent leader as Felix Dzierżyński.

The conflict with Finland began later and gave Tsarism probably a worse reputation in the world at large than any other single policy except the persecution of the Jews. In Poland, if the policy of Russification was a complete failure from the cultural and national point of view, it was to a certain extent successful politically and economically. In Finland there was no social fact to justify it and the success of the Finnish nation in resisting it was complete. It never became anything more than a superficial and ineffective tyranny imposed *manu militari*, and produced an estrangement between the two nations, which made the Finlanders more absolutely free from Russian cultural influence than any European nation except perhaps Spain and Portugal.

The third of the dominant nationalities of the West, the Germans, suffered less from the policy of Russification. The Baltic barons were considerably curtailed in their administrative autonomy; and German lost its position as the official language. But they retained their economic and social predominance in the Baltic provinces, as well as their prominent place at court and in all the services. When in 1905-6 their existence was threatened by the agrarian Revolution of the Lettish labourers, the government sent the best troops it had at its disposal to save its loyal subjects, and the rising was suppressed with more than ordinary cruelty. Outside the Baltic provinces the Germans were exposed to no manner of persecution. In the West they were encouraged as an anti-Polish element; in the South as a farmer-class whose interests were at one with those of the squires and opposed to agrarian unrest. Though the University of Dorpat was Russianised, numerous secondary schools remained German—the last survivals of the cultural policy of the phileuropean Emperors. It was only after the outbreak of the Great War that the Germans of Russia were to feel the full weight of a savage nationalism aggravated by wartime hysteria.

A fact of primary importance in the history of Russia was the integration of the Jews in the general life of the nation. The reign of Alexander II was for them a period of emancipation. They did not obtain equal rights with the other citizens, but they were given free access to the schools and professions, and numbers of them were allowed to settle in the inner provinces, outside the Pale. Very rapidly there grew up a new Jewish bourgeoisie, and a Jewish intelligentsia that spoke Russian, neglected Jewish obser-vances, and invaded the liberal professions, especially the bar, the medical profession and the press. The reaction of Alexander III put an end to this semi-liberal policy, and the rights of the Jews were again curtailed. Percentage quota were introduced in the schools, and they were excluded from the technical colleges. Their rights of residence were again reduced. Thousands of Jews were deported from Moscow into the Pale, and even there they were for-bidden to live in the rural districts. The first pogroms took place in the late 'seventies and were at first spontaneous manifestations of the lower bourgeoisie against Jewish competition. But very soon they began to be encouraged by the police, as a safety-valve for the anti-bourgeois feeling of the lower classes of the towns. Pogroms were, however, a secondary cause in the growing emigration of Russian Jews to America; the main cause was the over-population of the Jewish towns of the West where they were penned up. It made New York the capital of Jewry, and created in America and in Europe an influential body of Jewish opinion bitterly hostile to Tsarism. Meanwhile, the social composition of Russian Jewry was changing and by the side of a Russianised intelligentsia a working class grew up. This did much to shatter the old frames of ghetto conservatism, but the main mass of Russian Jews remained a wretchedly poor crowd of tradesmen, middlemen and artisans, intensely conservative and religious, segregated and ignorant, speaking Yiddish and writing Hebrew, dominated by the old forces of rabbinism and hasidism, or by the new nationalist movement of Zionism. The social leaders of the Jewish masses were the rich bourgeoisie of the Pale, relatively unaffected by Russian culture, national and conservative, indifferent to Russian politics, but often enthusiastically Zionist. They had their in-telligentsia, and produced an interesting literature in Hebrew whose principal figure was the poet Bialik. The Jewish proletariat of the Pale retained its national consciousness, but were opposed to segregation as they were to religion, advocating the creation of a modern Jewish national culture, that would use Yiddish as the national language. Yiddish literature was generated by this movement, which produced some writers of importance. But a large part of the Jewish intelligentsia, both in and outside the Pale, was opposed to national segregation and free from anti-Russian feeling. In Poland, where they were less limited in their rights, the Jews even became the principal agents of natural, as opposed to official, Russification. To-day, in Poland and in Bessarabia, the Jews are the principal pro-Russian element. The wealth of the Jewish bourgeoisie grew apace; by 1914 they were prominent in practically all branches of commerce and industry. As Jewish "merchants" had now the right to settle outside the Pale, Jewish capital became active all over the Empire. Those Jews who were connected with the banks and other forms of semi-official capital were closely linked with the bureaucracy, but all others were naturally more or less Radical and anti-Monarchist. The Liberal opposition, as well as the revolutionary parties, all contained a high proportion of Jews (especially high among the Mensheviks). The cultural role of Jews increased very rapidly and in the creation of the modernist civilisation of the pre-revolutionary decades their part was very prominent.

The rise of Estonian, Lettish and Lithuanian national consciousness was a necessary outcome of the development of these economically progressive districts. The new nations, composed as they were of peasants and self-made bourgeois, were essentially democratic. Their nationalism was mainly directed against their alien landlords and did not assume any pronounced anti-Russian colouring, nor did the demands of the national leaders ever go beyond cultural and administrative autonomy.

The Lithuanians were a rural nation of fairly well-to-do peasants, strongly under the influence of their Roman clergy; their ties with the Russian economic system were loose, and more Lithuanians emigrated to America than sought work in Russia. This made them more segregated and potentially more inclined to separatism.* The Letts and the Estonians, on the contrary, had

---

*The " Russian orientation" of Lithuania to-day is due to purely political causes and has no solid cultural background.

their face turned to the interior of Russia; they were two landless nations of bourgeois, tenants, agricultural labourers and industrial workmen. Capitalistic development in their country was ahead of the rest of Russia. More European, and much more highly developed than the Russian peasant, the Lettish and Estonian democracy could aspire to a very prominent role in the economic and cultural life of the Empire. Their interests were opposed to those of the Russian Monarchy in so far as the latter was the ally of the German barons, but they were closely linked with all the progressive forces of Russia. The growth of Estonian, and especially of Lettish, nationalism was counteracted by intense class-differentiation. The Lettish proletariat, urban and rural, developed a very high degree of class-consciousness. Their rising against the German squires in 1905-6 was the most fierce and ruthless episode of the first Revolution, and the role of the Letts in the building of the Bolshevik power is universally known. But from the outset, all the three democratic nations of the West were free from the Russian, serfdom-inherited, opposition between "educated" and people.

A somewhat similar democratic movement transformed Georgia. The feudal nobility, impoverished and incapable of economic revival, lost its cultural leadership of the nation. Instead, especially in the Western lands of the Black Sea slope, a sturdy plebeian bourgeoisie, based on a solid bedrock of poor but progressive peasantry, made of Georgia, by the end of the 19th century, one of the culturally most advanced countries in the Empire. The feudal nobility, dependent mainly on crown service, and on subsidies from the Privy Purse, was politically negligible. Those of the Georgian nobles who could not have their finger in the pie formed a party of romantic nationalists, that dreamt of restoring the ancient independence of the country. But the movement found no favour among the Georgian democracy. It was in the interest of Georgia, as of Estonia and Latvia, to preserve the unity of the Russian system, for only a free access to the wide possibilities offered by the Empire as a whole, could give a sufficient outlet to the energies of this highly gifted race. As early as the 'seventies the Georgian democracy began to play a considerable role in the Russian Socialist and Radical movement. In 1905 the peasantry of Guria (Western Georgia), organised by the Social-Democratic party, showed a remarkable spirit of revolutionary discipline and self-help. Georgians played a very prominent role in the Russian Social-Democratic movement, their leaders remaining definitely hostile to any form of autonomy for Georgia. In cultural matters, however, they supported the great national-democratic revival which led to the re-establishment of Georgian as a language of civilisation. By the beginning of the century Georgian cultural life was substantially democratised, and the firm foundations were laid for a new Georgian culture which began to bear fruit in the Soviet Georgia of to-day.

The Armenian bourgeoisie remained moderately progressive and highly prosperous, while the urban and rural Armenian democracy of Transcaucasia produced an intelligentsia which, without ceasing to be on the whole pro-Russian, took an active part in the revolutionary work against Tsarism. But the government's policy of curtailing the privileges of the Armenian Church made even the big bourgeoisie restless and impatient. In 1905-6 the Armenian nation as a whole were definitely on the side of revolution; anti-Armenian pogroms were then organised throughout Transcaucasia by the Moslem beks, which were viewed not without satisfaction by the government. But at the time of the Great War the Armenian revolutionaries took their stand whole-heartedly on the side of Tsarism against Turkey—a circumstance that bore tragic fruit for the Armenian nation. The cultural development of the Russian Armenians partly drifted into the common Russian channel, but there was also a considerable national revival which produced a literature, strongly influenced by Russian models, that is not inferior in achievement to the Francophil literature of the Turkish Armenians.

Of the other Christian nations the Moldavians of Bessarabia hardly disassociated themselves from the Russians. Their entirely Russianised gentry and bourgeoisie formed a mainstay of extreme conservatism and anti-semitism; some of the most notorious reactionaries of the inter-revolutionary period were Moldavians of Bessarabia. The peasants, though they preserved their Moldavian speech, remained equally free from Roumanian sympathies. Neither did they take any part in the agrarian movement of 1905-6.

At the Ministry of Interior Bessarabia was classified as the least troublesome province of the whole Empire.

The minor peasant nations of Eastern Cisuralia shared on the whole the destinies of the Russian peasants. Strangely enough, they were given schools with instruction in their native languages, and this gave rise to a native rural intelligentsia, which, in the case of the Chuvash, Votyaks and especially Zyryans reached by degrees a high level of culture. The policy of forceful Christianisation was only sporadically continued, though in Siberia it took particularly odious forms in regard to the Altai Turks. The minor nations of the Siberian tayga and tundra continued to diminish in numbers, poisoned by alcohol and syphilis, and mercilessly exploited by traders, among whom Zyryans were quite as prominent as Russians. Only the two major Siberian nations—the Yakuts and Buryats—held out. The latter, a gifted and active people, gave rise to a native intelligentsia, educated in the Russian Universities, national in feelings but by no means anti-Russian. Educated Buryats were freely made use of as emissaries of Russian Imperialism in Mongolia and Tibet. On the other hand, the advanced Buryat intelligentsia is playing to-day a leading part in the political education of the Republic of Mongolia.

The Moslems, in spite of a great variety of local conditions remained, on the whole, the most stagnant and conservative section of the population.

Pan-Islamic and Pan-Turkish feelings of a modern kind were strong only among the urban Tartars and Turks of the Volga, Crimea and Transcaucasia. On the Volga the general conditions affecting the peasants did much to counterbalance the nationalism of the Tartar merchants and Bashkir squires, but in Azarbaijan the Moslem peasants remained particularly dominated by the local Muhammadan gentry, whose serfs they had been practically made by Russian legislation. The Turks here were an essentially reactionary element which the Tsarist government could play off against the revolutionary Armenians. Many of the beks and khans served in the army: in Guria, the revolutionary movement was suppressed by a Muhammadan general. The growth of Baku as a great industrial centre was the first modernising factor on the conservative milieu of Azerbaijan, but the influence of the oil city on the rural districts was very limited. The growth of cotton plantations on the eve of the war was becoming a more powerful solvent, but its full effect was anticipated by the outbreak of the Revolution.

The mountaineers of Chechnia and Daghestan, conquered in 1859, were not at once reconciled to their Russian conquerors. During the Turkish war of 1877 they attempted to rise, and bandittism survived throughout the period as a protest against foreign rule. In the years before the Great War the bandit, Zelim-Khan, was regarded as a sort of national hero, and carefully concealed from the Russian police. On the other hand, Muhammadan mountaineers—especially recruited from among the cut-throat and thievish Ingush—were extensively employed in 1905 and after by Russian landlords and industrialists to defend them from Russian peasants and workmen. Islam remained stronger in Daghestan than anywhere else in the Empire. But modernising forces were active more or less everywhere, the greatest single influence in this direction being the opening up of the Grozny oilfields, in Chechnia.

The Ossetes, non-Muhammadan, and traditionally hostile to their Moslem neighbours, easily adopted Russian ways. Many of them studied in Russian schools and Universities and an Ossete intelligentsia was formed who, though devoted to their nationality, played proportionally almost as active a part in all-Russian life as the Georgians and Armenians.

In Turkestan the Russian Government adopted a policy imitating that of the French in Algeria. The native population was kept, legally and topographically, segregated from the invaders and allowed to retain its old Muhammadan forms of life. It remained, on the whole, unaffected by Russian influence, culturally stagnant and politically passive. Only at rare intervals was some group or other roused to frantic rebellion (as in 1898 and 1916) immediately followed by savage repression. Some native groups, like the aristocratic Tekke Turkomans—though they had been the only natives to offer serious resistance to the Russians—received preferential treatment and became strongly attached to Russian rule. In the native Khanates of Khiva and Bokhara the Russian authorities abstained from all intervention, thus consecrating a degenerate and corrupt despotism, which survived till the Great Revolution. The capitalistic boom of the first decade of the 20th century introduced important changes into Turkestan. A few natives, mostly Bokharan Jews, made large fortunes, and a native proletariat began to be formed. The majority of the population remained wretchedly poor and progressively pauperised peasants (*dehkan*), ground down by an army of native money-lenders, who acted as middlemen between the *dehkan* and the cotton industrialists. The native proletariat had no time to develop a class consciousness before 1917, but a modernist and progressive ("jaddist") movement among the native bourgeoisie was already on the way by that time, and played an important part in the Sovietisation of Turkestan.

The nomad Qazaqs and Qirghiz of the steppes and mountains between Turkestan and Siberia had never been good Muhammadans, but their clan constitution gave them a no less effective backbone to fall back on in their resistance to Russian advance. The Russian administration had set about breaking up the clans of the Northern Qazaqs as early as the eighteen 'twenties. The Southern Qazaqs of the Sir and Ili basins, and the Qirghiz of the Tien-Shan came in contact with the Russians only in the third quarter of the 19th century. The Qirghiz, one of the most archaic of the Turkish nations, retained their clan organisation in considerable purity and remained almost unaffected by Russian cultural influence. Both the Qazaqs and Qirghiz had to give up much of their best land in the Northern black-earth belt and in the fertile piedmont and mountain steppes of the South to Russian colonists, at first to Cossacks, afterwards to peasants, more than a million of whom settled there in the decades before the Revolution. This led to intense national tension between the nomads and the new-comers, which culminated in the rebellion of 1916. The reprisals that followed it were the last and one of the worst atrocities of Tsarism. All the country round Lake Issyk-kul was laid waste, and hundreds of thousands of Qirghiz and Qazaqs trekked away into China, to return only after the establishment of Soviet Rule.

*In pre-Revolutionary Russian publications the Qazaqs are usually called Qirghiz, the Qirghiz Qara-Qirghiz.

860   Russians (*hoi Rhos*) attack Constantinople.

882   Oleg, King of Novgorod, conquers Kiev ⎤ Dates according
882– 915   Oleg, King of Russia (Kiev).   ⎟ to Russian
915– 945   Igor,   ,,   ,,   ⎰ Chronicle of c. ⎱ 1100

945– 972   Svyatoslav.
957   Olga, Queen of Kiev, receives baptism.
967– 971   Svyatoslav's campaigns in Bulgaria.
980–1015   Vladimir, King of Russia.
988   Christianity received from the Greeks.
1019–1054   Yaroslav, " the Wise."
1054–1093   Sons of Yaroslav.
1068   Battle of Alta, Russian Kings defeated by Cumans.
1068–1100   Wars between the Kings.
1093–1113   Vladimir Manomakh, King of Pereyaslavl.
1113–1125   ,,   King of Kiev.
1125–1132   Mstislav, King of Kiev; after his death wars between the
           Kings recommence.
1157–1175   Andrew of Bogolyuby, King of Suzdal and Vladimir.
1169   Andrew's army sacks Kiev.
1176–1212   Vsevolod, "Big-Nest," King of Vladimir and Suzdal.
1185   Campaign against Cumans, described in the *Campaign of
           Igor.*
1199–1205   Roman, King of Galicia and Volynia.
1223   Battle of the Kalka, first appearance of the Tartars.
1237–1240   Conquest of Russia by Batu.

GREAT RUSSIA.	WHITE RUSSIA and UKRAINA.
1240–42 Victories of Novgorodians under St. Alexander Nevsky over Swedes and German Knights.	1235–1266 Daniel, King of Galicia and Volynia.
1246–1263 St. Alexander Nevsky, Great Prince of Vladimir.	1248–1263 Mindowh, Duke of Lithuania.
1305–1326 St. Peter, Metropolitan of Russia (the first to reside in Moscow).	

GREAT RUSSIA.

1313–1341 Uzbek, Khan of the Golden Horde, acme of Tartar power.

1327–1341 Ivan Kalita, Prince of Moscow, Great Prince of Vladimir.

1353–1378 St. Alexis, Metropolitan of Russia.

1359 Decline of Golden Horde begins.

1362–1389 Dimitri, "of the Don," Great Prince of Vladimir and Moscow.

1380 Battle of Kulikovo.

1382 Tokhtamysh, a lieutenant of Tamerlane, invades Russia and sacks Moscow.

1389–1425 Vasili I, Great Prince of Vladimir and Moscow.

1395 Tamerlane invades Russia.

1425–1462 Vasili, "the Dark," Great Prince of Moscow and Vladimir.

1439 Union of Florence.

1446 Church of Russia declared autocephalous.

1453 Fall of Constantinople.

— Vasili, "the Dark," triumphs over the last of his enemies.

1462–1505 Ivan III, *Cosudar* and Autocrator of All Russia.

1472 Ivan III marries Zoe Paloaeologue.

UKRAINA.

1316–1341 Hedymin, Duke of Lithuania.

1386 Yahaylo (Jagiello) Duke of Lithuania, becomes King of Poland.

1392–1430 Vitowt (Witold), Duke of Lithuania.

GREAT RUSSIA.   UKRAINA.

1478 Novgorod annexed.

1480 Tartar suzerainty discarded.

1482 Tver annexed.

1500 Battle of Vedrosha, followed by annexation of South-West Great Russia from Lithuania to Muscovy.

505–1533 Vasili III, *Cosudar* and Autocrator.

1511 Pskov annexed.

1517 Ryazan annexed.

533–1584 Ivan, "the Terrible."

533–1547 Ivan's minority.

1547 Ivan crowned Tsar.

1552 Conquest of Kazan.

1553 White Sea Route to Russia discovered by the English.

1556 Conquest of Astrakhan.

1558–1582 Livonian War (Muscovy against German Knights, Lithuania and Poland).

1564–1571 The *Oprishnina*.   1569 Union of Lithuania and Poland ("Union of Lublin.")

1571 Krim Tartars burn Moscow.

1582 Conquest of Siberia begins.

84–1598 Theodore Tsar, Boris Godunov, "Lord-Protector."   1592 First Kozak rebellion.

1589 See of Moscow raised to Patriarchal rank.   1596 West Russian clergy accepts Roman supremacy ("Union of Brest.")

98–1605 Boris Godunov Tsar.

GREAT RUSSIA.	UKRAINA.

1604–1613 "Time of Troubles."

1605–1606 "False Demetrius" Tsar.

1606–1610 Vasili Shuysky Tsar.

1606 Bolotnikov Rebellion.

1610–1612 Polish occupation of Moscow.

1612–1649 Parliaments (*Zemsky Sobor*), convened regularly.

1613–1645 Michael Romanov, Tsar.

1633–1647 Peter Mohila, Metropolitan of Kiev.

1638 Kozak rebellio suppressed by Poles.

1645–1676 Alexis, Tsar.

1648 Victorious rebel lion of Kozas under Bohdan Khmelnytskyĭ.

1648 Revolutionary movement in Moscow and other towns.

1649 Code of Laws of Tsar Alexis—legislative crystalisation of serfdom.

1652–1658 Nikon, Patriarch.

1654 Ukrainian Kozaks recognise Muscovite suzeraint

1654–1667 Schism of the Old Believers.

1654–1681 Wars in Ukraina b tween Muscovy, Poland an Turkey (*Ruyina*).

1667 Eastern Ukraina ceded by Poland to Muscov (Treaty of Andrusovo).

1669 Artamon Matveyev starts first pro-"German" administration.

1670–1671 Revolt of Razin.

1676–1682 Theodore III.

1682–1689 Ivan V, and Peter, nominal Tsars, their sister Sophia, Regent.

1688–1708 Ivan Mazeppa, He man of Ukraina.

GREAT RUSSIA.   UKRAINA.

1689–1725 Peter the Great.

  1689–1698   Administration of his mother's friends.

  1697–1698   Peter in West Europe.

  1698–1725   Peter's personal administration.

  1700–1721   War with Sweden.

  1703   St. Petersburg founded.

  1709   Battle of Poltava.

                        1722   Autonomy of Ukraina abolished (afterwards temporarily restored).

1725–1727 Catherine I. ⎰ Administration of Supreme
1727–1730 Peter II.   ⎱ Privy Council.

1730–1740 Anne.

1740–1741 Ivan VI, Anne of Brunswick, Regent.

1741–1761 Elizabeth.

1761–1762 Peter III.

  1762   "Liberty of the Nobility" Manifesto.

1762–1796 Catherine II.

  1764   Autonomy of Ukraina finally abolished.

  1772   First partition of Poland; North-East White Russia annexed.

1773–1774 Revolt of Pugachov.

1774–1791 Black Sea Steppe and Crimea annexed.

1793–1795 Second and Third partitions: West Ukraina, West White Russia and Lithuania annexed.

1796–1801 Paul.

  1799   First French War; Suvorov's campaign in Italy.

  1800   Georgia annexed.

1801–1825 Alexander I.

  1804–1813   Conquest of Transcaucasia.

  1805–1807   Second French War.

  1807–1811   Speransky, Secretary of State.

  1809   Finland annexed as autonomous Duchy.

GREAT RUSSIA.   UKRAINA.

1812–1814   Third French War.

1815   Poland annexed as autonomous Kingdom.

1825   Revolutionary attempt of Decembrists.

1825–1855   Nicholas I.

1830–1831   First Polish Revolution and War.

1832   Holy War against Russia proclaimed in Daghestan.

1853–1856   Crimean War.

1855–1881   Alexander II.

1859   Conquest of Daghestan completed.

1861   Emancipation of the Serfs.

1862–1863   Second Polish Revolution suppressed.

1864   Conquest of Circassia completed.

1864–1873   Conquest of Turkestan.

1877–1878   War with Turkey.

1879   *Narodnaya Volya* party formed.

1881   Tekke oasis (Transcaspia) conquered.

1881   March. Alexander II killed by the *Narodnaya Volya*.

1881–1894   Alexander III.

1885   First important strike.

1892–1903   Witte, Minister of Finance.

1893   Franco-Russian Alliance.

1894–1917   Nicholas II.

1896   Great wave of strikes.

1897   Port Arthur occupied.

1898   Social-Democratic Party formed.

1903   Social-Democratic Congress in London, scission of party into Bolshevik and Menshevik groups.

1904–1905   Japanese War.

1905   First Revolution.

—   22nd January, "Red Sunday."

—   October, General Strike.

—   30th October, Constitution granted.

—   December, Armed Rising in Moscow defeated.

GREAT RUSSIA.   UKRAINA.

1906   Suppression of Revolutionary movement; First Duma convened and dissolved.

1906–1911   Stolypin, Prime Minister.

1907   Second Duma dissolved.

1912   Lena Goldfields massacre.

1914   Great War begins.

1917   12th–15th March, Revolution begins : Fall of the Monarchy.

—   March-November, "Kerensky régime."

—   7th November, Soviet Republic established: Lenin, President of Council of the People's Commissars.

1917   November—November 1920, Civil War.

1922   Formation of the Union of Socialist Soviet Republics.

1924   Death of Lenin.

1929   Five-year Plan for the Development of Industry adopted.

APPENDICES

1. DISTRIBUTION OF SOME PHYSICAL FEATURES IN RUSSIA AND ADJOINING COUNTRIES.

2. SYNOPTIC TABLE OF PEOPLES OF U S S R AND SOME ADJOINING COUNTRIES.

THE Slavs, being a linguistic and not a racial unit, there can, of course
be no question of a Slavonic race. One feature, however, is common
to most Slavs—they are for the most part broad-headed, cephalic
indices of over 82 predominating over the whole area and indices under
80 occurring only on the extreme periphery of Slavonic expansion.
The broad-headed type, however, presents considerable variety. The
Yugoslavs, like their neighbours the Albanians, are tall (over 1.70 m.)
dark and pronouncedly broad-headed (C.I. 85 and more). This type
has been given the name of Adriatic (Deniker) or Dinaric (Guenther)
race. A similar type, but less tall (1.65-1.67), and less dark, is pre
dominant among the Ukrainians, both in the plain and in the Car
pathians. The extreme Alpine type (dark, very broad-headed and
short) is strongly represented only among the Poles and Slovaks of th
Carpathians. The Poles, the White Russians and the Great Russian
present a fairer type, which shades down to real blondness in the Nortl
of Poland, in many parts of White Russia and in North Great Russia
The White Russian and North Russian blond type is also dominan
among the Suomi (Finns), especially among their Karelian branc
(in Finland as in Soviet Karelia), and among the Zyryans. It is no
infrequently associated with a fairly tall stature (up to 1.66) and ver
generally with straight and coarse hair. Chepurkovsky has establishe
the fact that in Great Russia and White Russia, typical broad-headed
ness (C.I. 84) is located in the more "backwood" districts (such as i
the Pinsk marshes of Southern White Russia), while the river valleys ar
occupied by a more nearly mesocephalic type (C.I. 80-83).

The fair Finno-Russo-Polish type, which was called "Vistulan c
Eastern" by Deniker, has recently been given the name of "East
Baltic" by Guenther, who regards it as one of the five main races a
Europe (the others being Nordic, Alpine, Mediterranean and Dinaric
It is obvious, however, that it occupies a strikingly transitional positio
between the Nordic type (blond, wavy or straight-haired, tall, meso
cephalic), and the Arctic type represented by the Lapps and Samoyec
(dark, coarse-haired, short and broad-headed). The snub-nose whic

is a predominant racial feature of the Lapps is fairly frequent in the North of Russia. Towards the South, in Poland as in Russia, the proportion of blondness diminishes and the "East-Baltic" type (or whatever we call it) approximates to the Alpine.

The relatively long-headed type (C.I. 79) of Great Russia is concentrated south-east of Moscow, in sixteen contiguous districts of the former provinces of Ryazan, Tambov and Penza, that is to say, in the extreme south-east of the original Great Russian territory. It is relatively dark and short. Chepurkovsky who was the first to describe it and christened it the "Ryazan type," regards it as descended from the long-headed people who inhabited the steppe in the neolithic, bronze and early iron age ("ochre-grave" and Scytho-Siberian culture). A very similar type, however, is prevalent further north-east among the Chuvash and the Mari, while long-headedness associated with brunette-ness and small stature extends without a break still further east through part of Bashkiria to the Voguls of N.W. Siberia, the latter having already a definitely Mongoloid facies. On the other hand, the Mordva, who are the nearest geographical neighbours of the Great Russian long-heads, are distinctly broad-headed (C.I. 83), presenting features scarcely different from the dominant sub-brachicephalic type of Great Russia.

The "steppe long-heads" are usually regarded as standing in some kind of relation to the Nordic race and are supposed to be a clue to the prevalence of quasi-Nordic ("proto-Nordic") elements (i.e., of long-headedness associated with increased stature and relative blondness) South of the steppe belt, among the Circassians and Ossetes, in West Georgia and even among the Turcomans of Transcaspia, whom some anthropologists (Bunak) regard as the direct physical descendants of the Scytho-Sarmatians.* Separated from these "Proto-Nordics" by all the breadth of Russia are the typically Nordic Lithuanians, Letts and Estonians. They are marked off from the Russians by a fairly sharp dividing line. Among the Russians typically Nordic features are rare; only one district in the Dvina basin (round Solvychegodsk) stands out in this respect.

Another area of long-headedness adjoining Russia is the North-West Coast of the Black Sea, where both the Roumanians and Bulgarians present a northward extension of the Mediterranean type, possibly mixed with the "steppe long-heads." This type is by no means a national characteristic of either of these peoples, for in the east of both Bulgaria

*The relation between the Proto-Nordics and the real Nordics has been much ventilated in connection with the problem of Indo-European origins.

and Roumania the Alpine and Dinaric types are very definitely dominant. In Bulgaria the contrast is particularly striking, the cephalic index rising from 78 on the coast to 85 in the neighbourhood of Sofia.

The Mongoloid type is present in countries adjoining Russia, chiefly in the form of the Turanian variety, which presents a transition from the real Mongolian† to the Adriatic-Alpine type. In its purity, it is presented by the Qazaqs and Qirghiz (C.I. 89, very tall stature, white skin, dark-haired, but with a minority of relatively fair individuals, attenuated Mongolian facies). Adulterated in various proportions with other blood it is found among the piedmont and mountain population of Ciscaucasia, among the Tartars of North Crimea (those of the South Coast are typical Dinarics), the Bashkirs and Volga Tartars. Distinctly Turanian faces not infrequently occur among the Great Russians, especially on the Volga.

†The real Mongolian is not met with West of the Altai ; the Kalmuks who are recent (17th century) immigrants being the only exception.

APPENDIX II

Synoptic table of Peoples of U S S R and some adjoining countries, showing classification of languages, territorial distribution, religion and cultural type.

The first column of the following table gives the language, the linguistic classification being taken as the guiding thread. In cases where the same language is spoken by different nations or ethnic groups this is also indicated in the first column. Square brackets [ ] denote dead languages ; round brackets ( ) languages whose principal territory lies outside the U S S R and the former Russian Empire.

The second column indicates the territorial distribution of the languages and peoples in the first column ; in the case of those contained in round brackets ( ) only the territory of the U S S R and former Russian Empire is taken into consideration.

The third column indicates the religion ; the fourth the material culture (e.g. agricultural, pastoral, &c.) of the given ethnical group ; and the fifth its cultural affinities. In the latter case recent (19th-20th century) Russian and European influences have not been taken into account.

The figures in the second column, except where explicitly stated, refer to the U S S R only, and are based on the census of 1926.

Some of the terms used call for an explanation. In the case of "Caucasian" all the associations with the Anglo-Saxon use of the term in the sense of "European," "White," "non-coloured," must be dismissed. It is used here in the purely geographical meaning of "relating to the Caucasus." As a linguistic term "Caucasian" covers those languages of the Caucasus (tabulated below) that are unrelated to either the Indo-European, the Semitic, or the Turkic family. The term "Japhetic" was introduced by Professor Marr of the Soviet Academy of Science with the same meaning and has won general acceptance in the U S S R.

In the fifth column "Caucasian culture" is used to denote the primitive agricultural and pastoral culture of the mountaineers of the Caucasus. Geographically, "Caucasian culture" and the "Caucasian languages" are not co-extensive, for while the majority of the people of Caucasian culture speak Caucasian languages the Caucasian-speaking Georgians have developed a more complex culture in which Byzantine and Iranian elements play a considerable part and which is here referred to as "Georgian." On the other hand, the Iranian-speaking ("Scythian") Ossetes and several Turki-speaking peoples belong to the cultural group designated as Caucasian.

Of the other terms in column five, "Neo-Siberian" covers those peoples of the Siberian forest and tundra who have been more or less strongly influenced by the pastoral culture of the Steppe; while Palaeo-Siberian is reserved to those who remained unaffected by Steppe influence and is synonymous with the perhaps more familiar term "Palaeasiatic." For Bulgar culture, see page 21 of the text.

I.	II.	III.	IV.	V.
A. INDO-EUROPEAN FAMILY.				
1. *Slavonic Branch.*				
a. E. Slavonic, or Russian group.				
Russian (Great Russian).	77,750,000 { White Russia, 4,740,000; Poland, 2,500,000; Ukraina and various parts of USSR 31,200,000; E. Galicia, 3,000,000; Bukovina & N. Bessarabia 600,000	Orthodox; dissenters small minority	Agricult. & urb.	Russian culture.
White Russian		do. R.C.	Agricultural	do. } Strong Polish influence.
Ukrainian		do. Uniats (United Greeks). Orthodox	Agricult. & urb. do. do.	do. do. do. Balkanic influence.
	Carpathian Russia, 500,000	Uniats (United Greeks)	do.	do. Hungarian do.
b. Bulgarian group [Church-Slavonic, survives as liturgic language.] (Bulgarian, belongs to "Balkanic community of languages".)	Colonies in Ukraina, Crimea, &c 110,000 Bessarabia			
(*c.* Yugoslav group.)				
(*d.* Czechoslovak group.)				
e. Polish	Poland, upper and middle class in Lithuania, White Russia, W. Ukraina & E. Galicia; 780,000 in USSR	R.C.	Agricult. & urb.	Polish Culture.
2. *Baltic Branch* (vocabulary closely related to Slavonic branch).				
a. Lithuanian	Lithuania (Small groups in various parts of USSR). 41,000	R.C.; Lutherans (Memel)	do.	Polish Culture.
b. Lettish group	Latvia 141,000	Lutherans	do.	German Culture.
Latgalian	Latgalia (E.Latvia) 10,000	R.C.	do.	Polish Culture.

303

I.	II.	III.	IV.	V.
3. *Latin Branch.* (*a.* Western group.) *b.* Roumanian, or Vlakh, group (belongs to "Balkanic community of languages"; vocabulary 45 p.c. Slavonic).				
Spoken by Moldavians	Bessarabia, and Soviet Moldavia 280,000	Orthodox	Agricult. & urb.	Balkanic Culture.
Roumanians	Roumania	do.	do. do.	do.
4. *Germanic Branch.* (*a.* Scandinavian group.) (*b.* Anglo-Saxon group.) *c.* Continental group (German)	Estonia, Latvia, Colonies in various parts of USSR; 1,240,000 Poland, Lithuania, W. Russia, Ukraina, Bessarabia, Roumania; 2,600,000 (including Russian speaking Jews)	Protestant; R.C.	Agricult. & urb.	
Yiddish (slight admixture of Hebrew elements)	(Colonies in Ukraina and Bessarabia).	Jews	Urban	
(**5.** *Albanian Branch* (belongs to "Balkanic community of languages").)			Agricultural	
6. *Hellenic Branch.* (Modern Greek (influenced by "Balkanic community of languages").)	Ukraina, Crimea, Caucasus; c. 180,000	Orthodox	Urb. & agricult.	
7. *Iranian Branch.* (Closely related to Indo-Aryan) *a.* Northern (*Scythian*) *Sub-branch.* i. Ossete : Digor dialect Iron dialect	N. Ossetia (C.Ciscaucasia); 8,000 N. Ossetia (C. Ciscaucasia); 205,000 S. Ossetia (N.Georgia) : 50,000	Sunni Mosl. Orthodox { on substratum of Caucasian paganism	Agricult. & past do.	Caucasian Culture. do.
Tval dialect		do	do do	Georgian Culture.

304

I.	II.	III.	IV.	V.
ii. [Old Soghdian, medieval texts.] Yaghnobi	Upper Zeravshan basin (Tajikistan) ; 1,800	Sunni Moslems	Agricultural	Persian Culture.
b. Southern Sub-branch. i. Western group (Kurdish, several dialects) { Spoken by Kurds / Yezidi	Small groups in Transcaucasia ; 55,000 Small groups in Transcaucasia ; 15,000	Moslems Dualistic religion of Avestic or Manichean origin	Agricultural do.	Primitive Iranian Culture with Syrian affinities.
Persian	Small groups in Caucasus and Turkestan ; 55,000	Shiya Moslems	Urb. & agricult.	Persian Culture.
Tajik (literary language Persian)	Tajikistan ; 960,000	Sunni Moslems	Agricult. & urb.	do.
ii. Eastern group Pushtoo & Balooch iii. Galcha group Several dialects (lit. language Persian)	Small groups in Turkestan; 8,000 Pamir & Hindu-Kush ; 19,000	Ismailiya Moslems (spiritual subjects of the Aga-Khan)	Agricultural	Persian Culture.
iv. Caspian group Several dialects in N. Persia Talysh Tat (also spoken by Daghestan Jews)	Lenkoran district ; 77,000 North of Baku ; 29,000 Derbend & environs ; 26,000	Shiya Moslems Shiya & Sunni	do. do.	do. do.
8. *Indo-Aryan Branch.* Gypsy dialects.	Dispersed over all USSR ; 61,000	Nominally Orthodox, Armeno-Gregorian, or Moslem	Parasitic Nomads	
Abis. INDO-EUROPEAN ON CAUCASIAN (JAPHETIC) SUBSTRATUM. *Armenian group.* [a. Classical Armenian, survives as liturgic language.]				

305

x

I.	II.	III.	IV.	V.
b. Modern Armenian (not direct descendant of former), with two literary dialects: Eastern Western	Armenia and various parts of Transcaucasia, N. Caucasus, &c.; 1,470,000 Turkey, &c.	Armeno-Gregorian; United Armenian (small minority)	Urb. & Agricul.	
B. CAUCASIAN OR JAPHETIC FAMILY. The genetic relationship of the two sub-families is not recognised by all authorities. 1. *North-Caucasian Sub-Family.* *a. North-Western Branch.* i. Circassian.	Western Ciscaucasia, great majority migrated in 1864 to Turkey; 65,000 Qabarda (C. Ciscaucasia); 140,000	Sunni Moslems	Agricult. & past.	Caucasian Culture
Qabardi		do.	do. do.	do.
ii. Beskesek-Abaza	W. Ciscaucasia; 14,000	do.	do. do.	do.
Abkhazian	Abkhazia; 57,000	Orthodox, & Sunni Moslems } On substratum of native paganism	Agricultural	do. (Georgian and Turkish influence)
b. North-Eastern Branch. i. Chechen group, including Ingush	C. & E. Ciscaucasia; 320,000 75,000	Sunni Moslems	Agricult. & past.	Caucasian Culture
ii. Twenty-nine "Lezgian" languages classified under six or seven groups (principal languages: Avar, Dargi, Lak, Tabasaran, Lezgi proper or Kuri, &c.) Udi	Daghestan and North Azerbaijan; 500,000	Sunni Moslems	Agricultural, pastoral & home industries	Caucasian Culture (strong Arabic influence)
	North Azerbaijan; 2,500	Armeno-Gregorian	Agricult.	Armenian Culture

I.	II.	III.	IV.	V.
2. *South-Caucasian, or Kartli Sub-Family.* Georgian, spoken by—				
Georgians	Georgia; 1,500,000	Orthodox	Agricult. & urb	Georgian Culture
Ajars	Ajaria (Batum); 72,000	Sunni Moslems	do. do.	Turkish Culture
Khevsur, Pshav and Tush	High Valleys of N.E. Georgia	Orthodox, on substratum of native paganism	Agricult. & past.	Georgian Culture, with numerous Primitive Caucasian survivals
(Also by Georgian Jews)				
Mingrelian (lit. lang. Georgian)	21,000 W. Georgia; 240,000	Orthodox	Agricult. & urb.	Georgian Culture
(Laz)	Turkey	Sunni Moslems	do. do.	Turkish Culture
Svan	High Valley of Ingur (S. side of W.C. Caucasus); 13,000	Orthodox on substratum of native paganism	Agricul. & past.	Georgian Culture on Caucasian substratum
C. SEMITIC FAMILY.				
[1. Hebrew, survives as liturgic & literary language]				
(2. Arabic, liturgic language of all Moslems; literary & cultural language of Daghestan)				
(3. Modern Syrian, spoken by Aisors)	Small groups in Transcaucasia; 10,000	Nestorian	Agricultural	
D. FINNO-SAMOYED FAMILY. (Not genetically related to Altai family)				
1. *Finno-Ugrian Sub-Family.*				
a. *Western Branch.*				
Finnish, spoken by (Fins or Suomi, including W. Karelians)	Finland	Lutheran	Agricult. & urb.	Scandinavian Culture
Karelians	Soviet Karelia & upper Volga basin; 250,000	Orthodox	Agricultural	Russian Culture
Leningrad Fins	Leningrad district; 115,000	Lutheran	do.	Scandinavian Culture
Estonian	Estonia; in U S S R; 155,000	Lutheran	Agricult. & urb.	German Culture

307

I.	II.	III.	IV.	V.
Vodi, Veps & Izhora (Livonians)	Leningrad region; 50,000	Orthodox	Agricultural	Russian Culture (strongly Russianized)
	Latvia	Lutheran	do.	German Culture
b. Lappish Branch.	Murman district; 1,700 Finland, Sweden, Norway	Orthodox Lutheran } on substratum of native paganism	Reindeer rearing	Western branch of Arctic Culture
c. Permian Branch. i. Komi group Zyryan Permyak	Pechora, Mezen, Vychegda basins; 220,000 Upper Kama; 150,000	Orthodox (convert. 15th c.) do. (convert. 16th c.)	Agricult. & commercial trap'g Agricultural	Russian Culture do.
ii. Votyak	Between Vyatka & Kama, 505,000	Orthodox on substratum of Bulgar paganism; pagan	Agricultural	Russian on substratum of Bulgar Culture
d. Volga Branch. i. Mari (Cheremis)	Between Volga, Vyatka & Vetluga; numerous colonies further East; 430,000	do.	do.	do.
ii. Mordva (two dialectical and ethnical groups)	Between lower Oka and Middle Volga; numerous colonies further East; 1,349,000	Orthodox on substratum of Bulgar paganism	do.	do.
e. Ugrian Branch. (i. Hungarian; vocabulary largely Bulgar-Chazar and Slavonic) ii. Vogul Ostyak	East side of Middle Urals; 5,000 Lower Irtysh & Ob; 13,000	Orthodox on substratum of Shamanism	Hunting do.	} Western variety of Neo-Siberian Culture.
2. Samoyed Sub-Family. a. Samoyed (five languages)	Tundra from White Sea to Taimyr peninsula; Tayga between Ob and Yenisei; 9,000	Shamanists; nominally Orthodox	Reindeer rearing	
b. Soyot; Kamasi; Karagas, &c., replaced by Turki in course of 18th—19th cent.	Upper Yenisei basin	(v. infra.)	(v. infra)	

I.	II.	III.	IV.	V.
E. ALTAI OR TURANIAN FAMILY. (relationship between three sub-families remote and partly doubtful)				
1. *Turkic Sub-Family.*				
a. Chazar-Bulgar Branch.				
[Chazar & Bulgar; Turkic element in Hungarian] Chuvash (Caucasian affinities in vocabulary)	Between Sura and M.Volga; colonies further East; 1,120,000	Orthodox on substratum of Bulgar paganism; pagans	Agricultural	Russian on substratum of Bulgar Culture
b. Turki Branch.				
i. North-Western or Kip-shak group. closely related dialects spoken by:				
Volga Tartars and Mishar	M. Volga basin; Astrakhan; smaller groups all over U S S R 3,000,000	Sunni; small minority (115,000) Orthodox	Agricult. & urb.	Muhammadan Culture
Siberian Tartars	Tobolsk district and other parts of W. Siberia	Sunni Moslems	do. do.	do.
Bashkir and Tepter	Bashkiria; 740,000	do.	Past. & agricult.	Steppe Culture
Qazaq	Qazaqstan (and W. China); 3,960,000	do. (superficially)	Pastoral	do.
Karakalpak	Amu delta; 145,000	Sunni Moslems	Agricult. & past.	do.
Qirghiz	Tien Shan; Qirghizia (and W. China); 770,000	do. (superficially)	Pastoral	do. { Tribal organisation well preserved
Altai Turks (" Oyrats ")	W. Altai; 45,000	Shamanists	do.	do.
Nogai Tartars	Between Lower Volga and Caucasus; 36,000	Sunni Moslems	do.	Steppe Culture
Kumyk	N. Daghestan; 50,000	Sunni Moslems	Agricultural	Caucasian Culture
Balkar	Qabarda; 33,000	Sunni on substratum of Caucasian paganism	Agricult. & past.	do.
Karachai	Upper Kuban valley; 55,000	} Sunni Moslems	do.	do.
Tartars of N. Crimea (locally known as Nogai)	N. & C. Crimea; 115,000	Sunni Moslems	Agric., past & urb.	Muhammadan Cult. strong Turkish influence
Karaites	Crimea; 8,000	Karaite Jews	Urban	} Strong Turco-Tartar influence; Chazar survivals
Crimean Jews (Krymchak)	Crimea; 6,500	Jews	do.	

I.	II.	III.	IV.	V.
ii. *South-Western group.* (Turkish (Osmanli)) Azeri (Azerbaijan Turki)	Turkey (N.W. Persia) Soviet Azerbaijan; (*lingua franca* from Teheran to Tiflis and Daghestan); 1,700,000	Sunni Moslems Shiya (&Sunni) Moslems	Agric.,urb.,past. do.	Turkish Culture Persian Culture
closely related dialects of: Turcomans Tartars of S. Crimea (locally known as Tat) Crimean Greeks Gagauz	Transcaspia (and Persia); 675,000 S. Coast of Crimea; 60,000 S.E. Ukraina (Mariupol) c.40,000 Bessarabia and Dobruja	Sunni Moslems do. Orthodox do.	Pastoral Agric. (Mediterranian type) Agricultural do.	Turanian Culture Turkish Culture Balkanic Culture do.
iii. *South-Eastern group.* [Chagatai literary language, strongly Persianized and Arabized, used 13th-19th cent.] Uzbeg, spoken by: Tribal Uzbegs non-tribal Uzbegs ("Sart")	Uzbekstan; 4,000,000	Sunni Moslems	Agr. & urb. with strong surv. of pastoral	Persian Culture on Steppe substratum
Kashgari & related dialects	(E. Turkestan) smaller groups in S.E. Qazaqstan, &c.; 110,000	do.	Agricult. & urb. do. do.	Persian Culture do.
iv. *North-Eastern Group.* [Old Turki of runic inscriptions, 6th cent.; Uighur, 11th-14th cent.] Tuva (Soyot, Uryankhai)	Republic of Tannu-Tuva (Upper Yenisei Valley); 50,000	Lamaists (Buddhists)	Pastoral	Steppe Culture (Tibetan Influence)
Shor, &c. Khakas, &c. Karagas Yakut	Upper Tom basin .: 15,000 Upper Yenisei basin; 50,000 E. Sayan Mountains; 500 N.E. Siberia (basins of Lena and Yana); 215,000	Shamanists do. do. Orthodox on Shamanist subst.	Pastoral & hunt. do. do. Hunters Pastoral	Steppe Culture do. Neo-Siberian Culture Strongly specialised branch of Steppe Culture

I.	II.	III.	IV.	V.
2. *Mongol Sub-Family.* *a.* Northern group. Buryat	Irkutsk district } 240,000	Shamanists & Orthodox	Past. & hunters, passing to Agric.	Steppe Culture
	Transbaikalia }	Lamaists (Buddhists)	Pastoral	Steppe Culture (Tibetan Influence)
b. East Central group Khalkha	Outer Mongolia ; *c.* 700,000	do.	do.	do.
c. Southern group	"Inner" Mongolia	do.	do.	do.
d. Western group. Dzungars, &c. Kalmuk	Kobdo district (W. Mongolia) Steppe between Volga, Don, & Caucasus ; 130,000	do. do.	do. do.	do. do.
Sart-Kalmuk	Tien-Shan ; 2,800	Sunni Moslems	do.	Steppe Culture
3. *Tunguz Sub-Family.* *a.* Tunguz	E. Siberia ; backwood districts from Yenisei to Sea of Okhotsk ; 20,000	Shamanists & Orthodox	Hunters & reind. rearers	Tunguz variety of Neo-Siberian Culture
	Transbaikalia ; *c.*39,000	Lamaists & Orthodox	Pastoral	do., strongly Russianized or Buryatized
b. Oroch, Olcha, &c.	Lower Amur & Saghalin ; 3,000	Shamanists	Hunt. fish, partly reind. rearing	Tunguz variety of Neo-Siberian Culture
c. Gold (*d.* Manchu)	Between Ussuri & Pacific ; 7,000	do.	Hunting & fish.	do., Chinese influence
F. PALAEO-ARCTIC LANGUAGES. (Families not demonstrably related) 1. *North-Eastern Family.* Chukchi	Extr. N.E. of Eurasian Continent ; 11,000	Shamanists	Reindeer & fish.	} Palaeo-Siberian Culture
Koryak	South of the former ; 7,500	do.	do. do.	
Kamchadal (Itelmen)	Kamchatka ; 4,200	Orthodox on Shamanist substratum	Fishing	Amerindian affinities ; strongly Russianized

I.	II.	III.	IV.	V.
2. *Yukaghir Family* (two languages)	700	Orthodox on substratum Shamanists / Shamanist	Reinder rearing	Palaeo-Siberian Culture
3. *Ghilak*	Lower Amur & Saghalien; 4,000	Shamanists	Fishing	do.
(4. *Ainu*)				
5. *Yenisei Ostyak* (possibly related to Tibeto-Burman)	Middle Yenisei Valley; 750	Shamanists	do.	do.
6. *Eskimo Family* (a. Eskimo ; three dialects) (b. Aleut)	Coast of Behring Straits ; 1,300 Commanders Islands (off Kamchatka), 350	Native religion / Orthodox	do. / do.	Eskimo Culture / do., Russianized / Strongly
G. INDO-CHINESE FAMILY. 1. *Chinese Sub-Family.* Chinese, spoken by : (Chinese) (Dungan) 2. *Tibeto-Burman Sub-Family.* (a. Tibetan (used as liturgic language by all Lamaists)) b. Yenisei Ostyak (?) (H. KOREAN) (I. JAPANESE)	(Far East and gold-mining districts of East Siberia) Tien Shan Region;14,500 *v. supra* Vladivostok district; 90,000	Sunni Moslems	Agricultural	Chinese Culture

INDEX

A

INDEX

INDEX

INDEX

Kingdom of, 35-56; — Academy, 83, 177; — University, 276

Kimry, 197

King, use of word to render *knyaz'*, 35 note, 96 note; Kings, Old Russian, 35-41, 48, 54; of Galicia, 65-6

Kiprensky, painter, 217

Kipchak, meaning of term, 93-94 note (and see *Golden Orda*) — dialect, 98, 129, 155

Kirghiz, (see *Qirghiz* and *Qazaq*)

Kirilitsa, 51, 184

Kirilov monastery, 109

Kishinev, 6

Kizhi, 223 note

Klyuchevsky, historian, 272

Knyaz', title, 35 note, 96 note

Kobza, 83

Kolenda, 26

Kolmogory, 126, 160 note, 222, 223

Kolomenskoye, 207 note

Komi, 20 (see also *Permyaks* and *Zyryans*)

Kondakov, 115 note

Kongresowka, 239

Korets, Princes of, 73

Korol, title, 65

Kosciuszko, 239

Kostroma, 98, 127

Kotsyubinskyi, Ukrainian writer, 277

Kozaks (Ukrainian), 73-4, 76-9, 80, 81, 83, 84, 159, 177, 231 235, 279

Krasnodar (Ekaterinodar), 63

Krasnoyarsk, 131

Kremlin, 127, 132, 168

Krim Tartars, 73, 77, 131, 132, 155 (see also *Crimea*)

Krivichi, 26, 62

Krivoy Rog, 252

Kropotkin, Peter, 262

Krug, 153, 234

Krylov, fabulist, 226

Kuban, River, 16, 37, 193, 244; — Cossacks, 231, 235, 279

Kuchka, 272

Kulak, 219, 236, 255

Kulikovo, battle of, 99, 111

Kumyks, 245

Kuptsy, 215

Kurbsky, Prince Andrew, 75, 159

Kurile Islands, 189

Kursk, 191

Kuskovo, 229

Kuznetsk, 131

Kyakhta, 188, 189

Kylymy, 75

L

Ladoga, Lake, 7

Land, ownership and tenure of, 40, 49, 70, 74, 76, 78, 81, 103, 105-6, 143-4, 145-6, 149, 186, 195-6, 205, 218-219, 236 (of Ural Cossacks), 238, 243-4 (Azerbaijan), 254-5, 257, 267 (see also *Monastic landowning*); — donations of, to members of the gentry, 186, 206, 234, 243; — hunger of peasants, 255, 264, 266, 267

Landlords (after abolition of serfdom) 254, 255, 257, 266, 273 ; in White Russia, 278 (see also *Gentry*)

Language, and linguistic evidence, 25, 27, 81, 114, 121, 122, 171, 172 (see also under *Russian, Turkic, Ukrainian, Finno-Ugrian*, etc.)

Lapland, 8

Latin language, 23, 26, 67, 225

Latins (Western Europeans), 20, 25, 35 note, 37, 43, 65, 75, 80, 83, 96, 114, 158, 159-60, 177

Latvia, and Letts, 10, 21, 47, 238, 265, 283-4

Law, 35, 41-2, 71, 89, 103, 147, 166, 201, 222, 254

Law courts (see *Justice*)

Legislation, 147, 201 (see also *Code, Digest, Reforms, Lithuanian Statute*)

INDEX